Inside the Common Core Classroom

Inside the Common Core Classroom

Practical ELA Strategies for Grades 9–12

Katherine S. McKnight

National Louis University

PEARSON

Boston • Columbus • Indianapolis • New York • San Francisco • Upper Saddle River
Amsterdam • Cape Town • Dubai • London • Madrid • Milan • Munich • Paris • Montréal • Toronto
Delhi • Mexico City • São Paulo • Sydney • Hong Kong • Seoul • Singapore • Taipei • Tokyo

Vice President and Editorial Director: Jeffery Johnston
Acquisitions Editor: Kathryn Boice
Editorial Assistant: Carolyn Schweitzer
Executive Field Marketing Manager: Krista Clark
Senior Product Marketing Manger: Christopher Barry
Program Manager: Karen Mason
Project Manager: Barbara Strickland
Editorial Production Service: Electronic Publishing Services Inc., NYC
Manufacturing Buyer: Linda Sager
Electronic Composition: Jouve
Interior Design: Electronic Publishing Services Inc., NYC
Photo Researcher: Jorgensen Fernandez
Cover Designer: Central Covers

Credits and acknowledgments borrowed from other sources and reproduced, with permission, in this textbook appear on the appropriate page within text or on page 205.

Cover Image Credit: © Michael Jung / Shutterstock

Note: Every effort has been made to provide accurate and current Internet information in this book. However, the Internet and information on it are constantly changing, so it is inevitable that some of the Internet addresses listed in this textbook will change.

Library of Congress Cataloging-in-Publication data was unavailable at press time.

10   9   8   7   6   5   4   3   2   1

ISBN 10: 0-13-336296-5
ISBN 13: 978-0-13-336296-1

Dedication

For Jim, Ellie, and Colin, who bring joy to my life

About the Author

Katherine McKnight is an author, educator, and consultant. Her career in education began as a high school English teacher in the Chicago Public School system more than 20 years ago. She received her B.A. degree from George Washington University, her M.Ed. from Northeastern Illinois University, and her Ph.D. from the University of Illinois at Chicago. Today, she serves as a professor of secondary education at National Louis University. She is passionate about creating curricula that engage all students in the regular education classroom. And she is completely committed to the development, sharing, and promotion of ideas and strategies that develop literacy skills in adolescent students so that they can grow to be active, creative adults.

Dr. McKnight visits schools all over the world, where she teaches administrators, teachers, and parents about the power of literacy and differentiated instruction—and provides strategies and hands-on support so they can implement them in their very own classrooms.

She regularly publishes in professional journals and is the author of many books including *The Common Sense Guide to the Common Core* and *The Teacher's Big Book of Graphic Organizers, Grades 5–12* (recipient of the 2013 Teachers' Choice Award).

Contents

Preface

WELCOME TO THE AGE OF THE COMMON CORE! Thank you for joining us in our quest to teach students to meet the Common Core English Language Arts (ELA) Standards.

This volume, *Inside the Common Core Classroom: Practical ELA Strategies for Grades 9–12*, is part of Pearson's *College and Career Readiness Series*. The books in this series have been written for in-service teachers to support their implementation of the Common Core State Standards for English language arts in K–12 classrooms. The four volumes in the series address the standards in grades K–2, 3–5, 6–8, and 9–12, respectively.

The purpose of the series is to help teachers create connections between the Common Core and their school curriculums. Each book provides in-depth information about the standards at a particular grade-level band and offers examples of a variety of teaching ideas to support students' meeting the expectations of the ELA Standards.

About This Book

"GOOD GRIEF, ANOTHER INITIATIVE!" THAT'S A COMMON response of English language arts teachers to hearing about the Common Core State Standards (CCSS). Whether they're delighted that the CCSS will put control back in their hands, reduce the endless hours of test prep, and eliminate the setting of unattainable goals or questioning the prospect of adapting well-established lesson plans to yet another set of standards, teachers everywhere are wondering, "How will this time be different?"

Good question! So how *are* the CCSS different?

- The CCSS are a national initiative. The developers of the standards took the best from each of the individual states' standards and crafted a national set that will unify the country's educational goals. At the time of this writing, 45 states, the District of Columbia, 4 territories, and the Department of Defense Education Activity have all adopted the CCSS.

- The CCSS were developed by educators, not bureaucrats or politicians, who risk being heavily influenced by external forces.

- The CCSS are written from a student's perspective, stating expectations for learning knowledge and mastering skills. Consequently, these standards promote a different level of understanding—one in which students learn to synthesize, analyze, apply, and articulate new understandings.

- The CCSS have a "We're all in this together" approach to education that fosters cooperation among students, teachers, and parents; between English language arts and content area teachers; and between experienced and novice teachers.

As you'll learn in reading this book, the CCSS were designed to create clarity and coherence in curricula and instruction by articulating a single set of rigorous skills that will prepare students for college and career. When the goals of a student's education are clear, parents, teachers, and the community can best determine how to support him or her. And when goals and terminology are consistent across the English language arts and content area classes, students can spend more time focusing on subject matter than on deciphering various sets of educational requirements.

Over the years, teachers have been faced with many initiatives and significant amounts of contradictory information. Clarity and focus have been hard to come by. I travel all over the United States and visit many different types of high schools: public, private, parochial and rural, urban, suburban. The one thing that all of these schools have in common is that the vast majority of teachers and administrators are dedicated and engaged. They want to do what's right for their students. They're passionate about preparing all of their students not only for college and career but also citizenship.

Yet the typical teacher's day is filled with lesson planning, classroom time, parent–student–teacher consultations, department meetings, and assessments. As the hurried transition to CCSS commences, overworked teachers risk misunderstanding its purpose. The tangle of bureaucracy and schedules means that, more often than not, in-service teachers will manage to acquire little more than a passing understanding of the new CCSS.

The goal of this book is to provide these teachers with the necessary clarity and support. Having a full understanding of the CCSS will enable all teachers to work together in syncing the U.S. educational system with the demands of the twenty-first century. This is particularly important for high school teachers, whose students are about to enter that world. For these students, being college and career ready is an imminent need.

Acknowledgments

I'VE HAD A LOT OF HELP DURING MY CAREER as an educator—most notably, as I examined the CCSS, considered the larger implications of this new paradigm, and wrote this book.

First, I am most grateful to Donna Ogle—mentor, colleague, and friend—who generously gave me the opportunity to write this book. Her keen observations, advice, and insights have made this book a valuable tool for teachers in grades 9–12.

I would also like to thank Alison Hilsabeck, my dean at National Louis University. Without her professional support, writing this book would not have been possible. And I would like to express appreciation to my friend, Elaine Carlson, who provided valuable wordsmithing advice, pointed questions, and laughter.

In addition, I thank the many teachers who read drafts and made comments as I worked through the subject matter. I am particularly grateful to Warren Thomas Rocco and Deanna Gallagher. They participated in many curriculum "jams," helping me formulate and tackle questions and develop examples to demonstrate the impact and power of the CCSS. I write for my teacher colleagues, and they are the muses that matter most to me.

I would like to thank the reviewers for this first edition: Prudence Crewdson, Walt Whitman High School (Maryland); Heather Lombardo, Reading Memorial High School (Massachusetts); Gabrielle Paradise, Leesville Road High School (North Carolina); Kathryn E. Pokalo (Contestoga High School (Pennsylvania).

Finally, I thank Jim, Ellie, and Colin, my dear family, whose love and support I deeply cherish—especially at those times I needed to go to the "tower" to write.

Katherine S. McKnight

Inside the Common Core Classroom

Introduction

Donna Ogle

THE COMMON CORE STATE STANDARDS (CCSS) are a challenging set of expectations that students must meet to be college and career ready. According to the Common Core, all educators are responsible for teaching literacy. To support this thinking, the CCSS English Language Arts (ELA) Standards include literacy in science, social studies, and technical subjects. These standards support the importance of integrating reading, writing, and speaking and listening in the disciplines. The ELA Common Core State Standards invite teachers to work together within and across grade levels and content areas to ensure that students will meet the expectations delineated in the standards.

Michaeljung/Fotolia

Across the United States, the national, state, and local organizations that have taken this challenge seriously are in the process of analyzing current curricula and adjusting the focus of instruction and expected student outcomes according to these new needs and demands. The two national assessment consortia—the Partnership for Assessment of Readiness for College and Career (PARCC, n.d.) and SMARTER Balance (n.d.)—are in the process of designing new assessment systems, which will be administered for the first time during the 2014–2015 school year. These consortia have suggested how school curricula should be organized to encompass the broad-reaching outcomes elaborated in the CCSS. Taking the CCSS seriously means making some significant adjustments in how our schools have focused on literacy and the kinds of literacy-related opportunities they have provided. Our students deserve this support. They want to be successful both within and beyond schooling, and we want them to have this success.

Defining the Need for the Change

THE CCSS DESCRIBE IN GRADE-BY-GRADE DETAIL the wide range of competencies that literacy entails and that teachers need to develop in their students. The starting point for this effort is central to the standards' importance: What is required of students to be college and career ready?

Several research reports over the last decade have alerted interested educators to the decline in difficulty of many school texts and to the challenge faced by students with low reading proficiency when they take college-level tests. In fact, Appendix A of the CCSS cites a 2006 ACT report, *Reading Between the Lines,* to illustrate this two-part problem (NGA & CCSSO, 2010b, Appendix A, p. 2). Recognizing this problem led the developers of the CCSS to collect texts being used by students in freshmen-level college/university courses and by individuals entering the workforce after high school. These texts were compared with high school texts and the types and difficulty levels of assigned student work.

In this analysis, the CCSS developers identified a significant gap between the work required of upper-level high school students and the expectations for success in college and career. (See Appendix A of the CCSS for elaboration on this issue [NGA & CCSSO, 2010b].) The CCSS were then developed with this end point in mind: to determine the level of language arts development needed at each grade level for students to be prepared for these greater literacy demands and thus ready for college and career.

After the CCSS had been written, they were reviewed by college faculty who teach freshman- and sophomore-level courses, who gave the standards high marks. Interestingly, in addition to the need for students to read informational texts critically and to write effective analytical essays (not personal reflection pieces), these faculty rated the oral communication skills identified in the CCSS as particularly important.

The fact that perspectives from higher education and the workforce were included in developing the CCSS is important. The standards make this connection very clear: Students need to be college and career ready.

The CCSS are significant in another way, also. Since the first round of standards was developed in the late 1990s, individual states have crafted their own standards and measured achievement with their own state-specific assessments. The only comparison of achievement across states has been made by the National Assessment of Educational Progress (NAEP), and these evaluations have regularly revealed huge state-by-state differences in literacy achievement. Now, with the CCSS, we have, for the first time, a set of standards that has been adopted by most states across the country.

This high level of adoption will help all educators evaluate their success and feel confident that their students are receiving a high-quality education that will serve them beyond public school. Both the standards and the assessments being developed can help all educators engage in a shared conversation and commitment to excellence. Rather than relying on the current patchwork of state standards, the CCSS bring together a common set of standards and permit the development of more common assessments.

Expectations for Literacy Achievement

AS THE UNITED STATES MOVES FORWARD with the new standards, all educators need to be involved and take seriously new expectations for the future. The CCSS raise the bar for student literacy achievement in several ways:

- To be college and career ready, students must understand challenging texts and attend to authors' ideas and ways of presenting information. In the CCSS Reading standards, three clusters identify these foci: Key Ideas and Details, Craft and Structure, and Integration of Knowledge and Ideas. For both literature and informational texts, readers are expected to engage in careful reading of the ideas presented, to recall main ideas and details, to recognize the organization of information and author's craft, and to synthesize and critically respond to what they have read.

- This expectation for greater understanding is heightened by the expectation that students will read texts at a more accelerated level of difficulty than currently designated for grade levels by readability formulas and reading anthologies. For twelfth-grade texts, the expected level will be about 200 Lexile points higher than the current level.

- The CCSS also devote greater attention to reading informational text, so it receives the same instructional attention as literature. Most elementary programs and secondary language arts courses have been developed primarily around fictional/narrative literature. The CCSS create a broader framework for literacy development that includes the content areas, especially social studies, science, and technical subjects. With two sets of standards for reading—one for literature and one for informational text—this shift in foci to informational texts and to the importance of using reading to build knowledge is clear. At the secondary level, the CCSS differentiate expectations for literacy development in social studies, science, and technical subjects. The curriculum design from PARCC (n.d.), which establishes four basic modules, includes a balance of informational and literary texts across the modules.

- The CCSS emphasize not only the understanding of individual texts but also the importance of reading across texts to look for different authors' purposes and the evidence authors provide to support their ideas. Students who read only one text on a topic or theme have little opportunity to learn about how authors can vary in terms of purpose and presentation of ideas. The CCSS clearly advocate that students should read several texts on the same topic or theme. In addition, completing quarterly research projects provides individuals with opportunities to search for information across multiple texts and media sources and to use that information in their projects and performances.

- The shift in how information is communicated in the twenty-first century is also recognized in the CCSS. We live in a visual society: All sorts of images try to inform us and persuade us. The ability to use visual and graphic information thoughtfully is expected of students. In fact, visual images can be powerful motivators to engage students in thoughtful analyses of how ideas are communicated to us and influence us. Across the content areas, readers are also expected to use electronic sources in building their knowledge in presenting information and completing research projects.

- There is also a shift in focus in the writing standards from writing personal narratives to writing expository and argumentative texts. Students need to be able to use evidence to support their arguments, as well as to recognize possible alternative points of view. In addition, writing is now being used as a way of measuring students' reading comprehension. Students need to think about the meanings of the texts they read, how authors present and support ideas, and what counter-arguments and evidence are provided.

- Although speaking and listening have always been part of the language arts, the CCSS recognize the importance of these communication tools. This priority is evident in the Speaking and Listening Standards and also embedded in the expectations that students discuss what they read at every grade level and learn to report to classmates what they learn from individual research projects. The preliminary assessment design from PARCC (n.d.) includes a school-based assessment of oral skills midway through the year. Even though these skills are difficult to measure using large-scale assessments, they are important. The value of speaking and listening skills has been well established by the university and workplace communities.

- The CCSS also include expectations for vocabulary. Specifically, students should learn and use standard forms of English and appropriate general academic and domain-specific vocabulary in both writing and oral language. Vocabulary and word-learning strategies need to be developed concurrently with the knowledge and content literacy standards, especially as related to the domain-specific terms students need to know to understand the content of science, social studies, and technical subjects.

Implementing the CCSS

IMPLEMENTING THE CCSS REPRESENTS A SIGNIFICANT CHALLENGE to teachers and schools. To address the difficulty of this task, many states have put together teams to guide their thinking about what is already being done and what needs to be adjusted in the current curriculum to meet expectations for literacy in the twenty-first century. Other educational organizations have also made significant efforts to help in the development of curriculum and instructional frameworks—for example, the Lucas Foundation, Annenberg Foundation, Alliance for Effective Education, AchieveNY, Gates Foundation, International Reading Association, and National Council of Teachers of English.

Publishers have responded, as well, by reorienting materials to reflect the broader expectation for responding to texts and by including more academic writing and attention to content. An interesting publisher's initiative has brought together teacher teams from school districts and used their materials to reorganize the content and rewrite the questions in the published programs to align more closely with the CCSS.

The major goal of all of these efforts is to better prepare students for college and careers. Doing so requires addressing the range of texts students read, the depth of thinking they do, and the styles of writing they perform. Given these new and challenging expectations, professionals across the educational system need to collaborate in helping students from preschool through grade 12 develop the competencies, commitment, and confidence needed for life beyond high school.

Rethinking the Complexity of the Texts Students Read

The issue of text complexity is central to the CCSS and one that deserves study by teacher and school teams. Students need to engage in more challenging texts at each grade level, at least beyond the primary grades, and they need to read more informational texts, which are rich in content.

The authors of the CCSS have tried to move away from a single, numerically derived formula for determining the appropriate reading levels of texts of all kinds. According to the CCSS, three criteria should be considered when determining the level of any text:

1. **Qualitative evaluation of the text:** levels of meaning, structure, language conventionality and clarity, and knowledge demands
2. **Quantitative evaluation of the text:** readability measures and other scores of text complexity
3. **Matching the reader to the text and the task:** reader variables (e.g., motivation, knowledge, and experiences) and task variables (e.g., the purpose and complexity of the task assigned and the questions posed) (NGA & CCSSO, 2010b, p. 4)

Appendix B of the CCSS (NGA & CCSSO, 2010c) provides lists of illustrative books that have been "leveled." The purpose of these lists is not to imply that these books should be used in the schools but rather to identify books that are familiar to the educational community. However, teachers who want simply to select books from these lists need to remember the third criterion: matching the reader to the text and the task.

Given the variety of interests, experiences, and needs of students across the United States, many teachers will want to use contemporary, high-interest materials to motivate students to think and reflect deeply about important issues. Moreover, instead of permitting students to read only books at their designated levels (based on Lexiles or Fountas & Pinnell scores), teachers will ask students in the intermediate grades and higher to read several books or articles on the same topic, beginning with a comfortable-level book/article and then using the knowledge they have developed to read more difficult texts on the same topic.

Using this strategy is certainly one way to help students increase their reading power. The CCSS guidelines also provide models of how teachers can engage groups of students in close readings of anchor texts or targeted short texts. When teachers regularly model an analytical and questioning approach to reading, students will likely follow the same approach. It is also important that students engage with a large quantity of texts, finding their own favorite authors and experiencing the joy of being real readers.

Organizing Instruction into Content-Rich Units

The range and complexity of literacy standards included in the CCSS has prompted many organizations (e.g., PARCC and SMARTER Balance), as well as school districts and state education departments (e.g., Wisconsin Department of Public Instruction), to reorganize their literacy priorities to align with the CCSS by designing units with content-related themes and topics. Using this approach, instruction in literacy is combined with instruction in social studies and science. Many school districts have asked teams of teachers to develop one unit as a starting point with plans to expand this effort over time.

A clear message from the developers of the CCSS is that students need to be engaged in learning content in social studies, science, and technical subjects at a deeper level than is now often the case. In the CCSS guidelines, the final section about the elementary standards is entitled "Staying on Topic Within a Grade and Across Grades: How to Build Knowledge Systematically in English Language Arts K–5" (NGA & CCSSO, 2010a, p. 33). Included in this section is a matrix illustrating how students should encounter the same topic (in this example, the human body) at increasingly deeper levels across all of the grades. This shift in combining attention to content knowledge with literacy development is one of the hallmarks of the CCSS.

While combining these purposes makes good sense, it means that schools must expand efforts at integrating reading and writing with content area instruction. Classroom and school libraries should contain ample amounts of informational books and magazines at a variety of levels of complexity so that all students have access to the materials needed to develop deep knowledge. As the CCSS authors explain in the section "Staying on Topic Within a Grade and Across Grades":

> Building knowledge systematically in English language arts is like giving children various pieces of a puzzle in each grade that, over time, will form one big picture. At a curricular or instructional level, texts—within and across grade levels—need to be selected around topics or themes that systematically develop the knowledge base of students. Within a grade level, there should be an adequate number of titles on a single topic that would allow children to study that topic for a sustained period. The knowledge children have learned about particular topics in early grade levels should then be expanded and developed in subsequent grade levels to ensure an increasingly deeper understanding of these topics. Children in the upper elementary grades will generally be expected to read these texts independently and reflect on them in writing. However, children in the early grades (particularly K–2) should participate in rich, structured conversations with an adult in response to the written texts that are read aloud, orally comparing and contrasting as well as analyzing and synthesizing, in the manner called for by the *Standards*. (NGA & CCSSO, 2010a, p. 33)

At the secondary level, there is an even greater expectation for students to develop the strategies necessary for reading the varied texts and materials that contain the key content of disciplinary study. Reading primary source documents in history and science is a central part of students' literacy engagement. Also, the texts used in math and science require students to analyze a variety of visual displays, including equations, tables, diagrams, and graphs. As noted in the Carnegie Report *Writing to Read* (Graham & Hebert, 2010), for students to comprehend and produce these types of texts, they must be immersed in the language and thinking processes of these disciplines and they must be supported by an expert guide: their teacher.

Given the expectation for students to develop the competence needed to comprehend the wide variety of texts that is required for success in and beyond schooling, it is clear that the responsibility for literacy development cannot reside solely with English language arts teachers. Meeting this expectation requires both the development of foundational knowledge that makes deep learning possible and the skills needed to read a wide variety of text types and formats across the disciplines. The CCSS challenge all content area teachers to accept their part in developing the literacy skills, dispositions, discipline-specific discourse, and academic vocabulary requisite for students to become independent learners. The more often that elementary and secondary reading/literacy coaches team up with their content area colleagues, the more likely that CCSS goals will be met by providing interesting and positive instructional experiences for students.

The thematic-unit framework provides students with the opportunity to read several texts on the same theme or topic and build their background knowledge of a specific topic. Spending more time on a specific topic also helps students to deepen their knowledge of the content and become familiar with the academic and domain-specific vocabulary central to that learning. In addition, by reading across several texts, students can develop their understanding of the ways different authors select materials to include in particular texts and then organize that information, as well as the value of reading deeply to build clear understanding of complex ideas.

Having these commitments to reading makes students' written and oral communications much stronger. Students know what they are explaining and have options to represent their ideas, including visual, graphic, and oral formats. This ability to develop one's own understanding based on research and then to present one's ideas is woven into the four research projects students are expected to do each year In addition, the CCSS directive to engage in a deeper study of topics encourages teachers to vary the kinds of learning experiences they provide for their students—differentiating texts/materials, activities, products, and assessments (Tomlinson's framework).

Engaging in Schoolwide Collaboration for Change

The challenges and cross-content literacy expectations of the CCSS can be achieved within a long-range timeframe and with the understanding that they will develop over the course of students' schooling. Realizing these requisites for achievement can unite teachers. The CCSS underscore the importance of involving teams of educators representing all grade levels, special services (e.g., English language learning, special education, library and media), and content areas in studying the CCSS, analyzing their implications, and designing ways to implement them over time.

Discussing the CCSS across grade levels is a good way to start. Providing visual displays that trace the same standard across different grades will help teachers to understand the structure and rationale that underlie the CCSS. An example follows using Standard 3 of the grades 6–12 Anchor Standards for Reading, which appears in the category Key Ideas and Ideas:

Standard 3: Analyze how and why individuals, events, and ideas develop and interact over the course of a text.

Table I.1 shows the grade-level expectations for Standard 3 for reading literature and informational text across grades 6–12. The table also shows expectations at grades 6–8, 9–10, and 11–12 for the same standard for literacy in history/social studies and in science and technical subjects. Creating and reviewing a chart of this nature allows examination of the expectations across grades.

Clearly, within Standard 3, there is a gradual progression of difficulty from sixth through twelfth grade—both within the same standard and across its application in different contexts.

TABLE I.1 ● *CCSS Reading Standard 3, Key Ideas and Details: Grades 6–12*

Reading Standards for Literature

Grade 6 students:	Grade 7 students:	Grade 8 students:
3. Describe how a particular story's or drama's plot unfolds in a series of episodes as well as how the characters respond or change as the plot moves toward a resolution.	3. Analyze how particular elements of a story or drama interact (e.g., how setting shapes the characters or plot).	3. Analyze how particular lines of dialogue or incidents in a story or drama propel the action, reveal aspects of a character, or provoke a decision.

Grades 9–10 students:	Grades 11–12 students:
3. Analyze how complex characters (e.g., those with multiple or conflicting motivations) develop over the course of a text, interact with other characters, and advance the plot or develop the theme.	3. Analyze the impact of the author's choices regarding how to develop and relate elements of a story or drama (e.g., where a story is set, how the action is ordered, how the characters are introduced and developed).

Reading Standards for Informational Text

Grade 6 students:	Grade 7 students:	Grade 8 students:
3. Analyze in detail how a key individual, event, or idea is introduced, illustrated, and elaborated in a text (e.g., through examples or anecdotes).	3. Analyze the interactions between individuals, events, and ideas in a text (e.g., how ideas influence individuals or events, or how individuals influence ideas or events).	3. Analyze how a text makes connections among and distinctions between individuals, ideas, or events (e.g., through comparisons, analogies, or categories).

Grades 9–10 students:	Grades 11–12 students:
3. Analyze how the author unfolds an analysis or series of ideas or events, including the order in which the points are made, how they are introduced and developed, and the connections that are drawn between them.	3. Analyze a complex set of ideas or sequence of events and explain how specific individuals, ideas, or events interact and develop over the course of the text.

(continued)

TABLE I.1 ● *(continued)*

Reading Standards for Literacy in History/Social Studies

Grades 6–8 students:	Grades 9–10 students:	Grades 11–12 students:
3. Identify key steps in a text's description of a process related to history/social studies (e.g., how a bill becomes law, how interest rates are raised or lowered).	3. Analyze in detail a series of events described in a text; determine whether earlier events caused later ones or simply preceded them.	3. Evaluate various explanations for actions or events and determine which explanation best accords with textual evidence, acknowledging where the text leaves matters uncertain.

Reading Standards for Literacy in Science and Technical Subjects

Grades 6–8 students:	Grades 9–10 students:	Grades 11–12 students:
3. Follow precisely a multistep procedure when carrying out experiments, taking measurements, or performing technical tasks.	3. Follow precisely a complex multistep procedure when carrying out experiments, taking measurements, or performing technical tasks, attending to special cases or exceptions defined in the text.	3. Follow precisely a complex multistep procedure when carrying out experiments, taking measurements, or performing technical tasks; analyze the specific results based on explanations in the text.

Source: NGA & CCSSO (2010).

At first, differences in expectations may seem somewhat arbitrary, but looking across grade levels and text types reveals increasingly more complex expectations for students' ability to use the ideas and information that authors develop.

Sharing an analysis and discussion of instructional expectations can build a common language and focus among teachers. Moreover, it can provide a good starting point for conversations about the evidence that demonstrates what skills and knowledge students already have and what areas need to be developed to ensure ongoing progress in the important area of reading comprehension. Teachers at no one grade level are responsible for the mastery of any standard, but across the grades and content areas, teachers should guide students in applying reading skills to increasingly challenging and varied materials and contexts. By looking across grade levels and disciplines, teachers can work together to identify ways to help students develop their abilities to think broadly about how authors develop and connect ideas in the varied types of texts they read during their secondary school years.

Just as it is important for teams of teachers to look at the standards' expectations for skill development across the grades, it is important for them to read across the areas within the CCSS. In contrast to the orientation in some districts and schools, in which teaching focuses on one standard at a time, the areas within the CCSS are interrelated and build on each other. Not only are standards provided for both literature and informational text, but in addition, many key expectations are scattered across the reading, writing, and language standards and the literacy standards for history/social studies and science and technical subjects. For example, a category called Integration of Knowledge and Ideas is included in the standards for Reading Literature and Reading Informational Text, as well as in the Reading Standards for Literacy in History/Social Studies and the Reading Standards for Literacy in Science and Technical Subjects. Similar connections pertain to skills in reading texts of various types and complexities, conducting research and applying its findings, and writing for a variety of tasks, purposes, and audiences.

The Speaking and Listening Standards address the importance of students creating visual and media displays. In the past, visual and media literacy seem to have been the purview of secondary instruction, but in the CCSS, they are introduced in the early elementary grades. Providing this early start allows greater development of speaking and listening skills. In grades 6–12, the focus of the Speaking and Listening standards is on preparing students to be college and career ready.

Some important instructional areas that teachers are accustomed to seeing as parts of reading development are embedded elsewhere in the CCSS. Vocabulary, for example, does not have a separate set of standards, as do reading literature and writing, yet developing vocabulary skills is very important and is addressed in several sections of the CCSS. Teacher teams might begin by studying the Language Standards section Vocabulary Acquisition and Use, with its focus on learning academic and domain-specific vocabulary, and then locate other places in the standards where vocabulary skills are addressed. Once again, for grades 6–12, the standards focus on preparing students to be college and career ready.

In addition, teacher teams need to consider carefully the expectation to include science, history/social studies, and technical subjects that is part of their responsibility in implementing these new more content-focused standards. Some states, such as Wisconsin, have developed their own extensions of the CCSS (Wisconsin Department of Public Instruction, n.d.), and these models can provide valuable resources as school teams examine their curriculum options and make decisions about how to move forward. Moreover, the CCSS for grades 6–12 include sets of standards for reading and writing in history/social studies and in science and technical subjects. The reading standards, in particular, are intended to complement the content standards of these specific disciplines, not to replace them (NGA & CCSSO, 2010a, p. 60).

Figure I.1 provides several illustrations of how the standards in various sections and categories are connected. In each example, the Anchor Standard is provided first, followed by the grade-level expectations for one or more grades (as noted in parentheses at the end of each description).

Assessment in the CCSS

IN RECOGNIZING THE DEPTH OF THE CCSS and the high level of expectations for students' literacy development, teachers need to monitor the pace of their instruction carefully, challenging students on a regular basis but not overwhelming them. Similarly, assessment must be ongoing without overwhelming instruction.

Assessment should be formative, thus helping teachers modify their instruction. The best formative assessment is rooted in instruction and depends on teachers being adept at gathering information from students' classroom engagement and work. Throughout this series of books, the authors provide examples of ways to assess students' readiness and learning of key content and strategies. Assessment is an area in which teacher/administrative discussions and decisions are critically important.

FIGURE 1.1 ● Examples of Connections Across the CCSS

Anchor Standards for Reading

Integration of Knowledge and Ideas

Standard 7: Integrate and evaluate content presented in diverse formats and media, including visually and quantitatively, as well as in words.

- *Literature:* Compare and contrast a written story, drama, or poem to its audio, filmed, staged, or multimedia version, analyzing the effects of techniques unique to each medium (e.g., lighting, sound, color, or camera focus and angles in a film) (grade 7).
- *Informational text:* Integrate and evaluate multiple sources of information presented in different media or formats (e.g., visually, quantitatively) as well as in words in order to address a question or solve a problem (grades 11–12).

Anchor Standards for Writing

Research to Build and Present Knowledge

Standard 8: Gather relevant information from multiple print and digital sources, assess the credibility and accuracy of each source, and integrate the information while avoiding plagiarism.

- Gather relevant information from multiple print and digital sources, using search terms effectively; assess the credibility and accuracy of each source; and quote or paraphrase the data and conclusions of others while avoiding plagiarism and following a standard format for citation (grade 8).

Anchor Standards for Speaking and Listening

Presentation of Knowledge and Ideas

Standard 5: Make strategic use of digital media and visual displays of data to express information and enhance understanding of presentations.

- Make strategic use of digital media (e.g., textual, graphical, audio, visual, and interactive elements) in presentations to enhance understanding of findings, reasoning, and evidence and to add interest (grades 9–10).

In addition, the requirements of the CCSS include large-scale comparative assessments to ensure that schools across the country have the same expectations of students. These assessments involve students in responding to a variety of texts and in formulating some of their responses in writing. In fact, one of the most important changes in assessment prompted by the CCSS is the use of students' written responses to measure their reading comprehension. Achieving this deeper look at students' comprehension is complicated by several pragmatic issues, such as the time and cost involved in scoring students' writing. Regardless, this approach is certainly a major part of the assessment systems being designed. Assessment systems for research (using technology) and speaking and listening are also still being developed, so these are other areas in which teachers and informal classroom assessments will continue to be important.

Using These Books to Enhance Study of the CCSS

THIS SERIES OF TEACHER RESOURCE BOOKS is intended to support teachers, teacher teams, and administrators as they look across grade levels in building CCSS-responsive instruction. As noted earlier, the CCSS expect teachers to think broadly about the impact of their instruction and the foundations they lay for students' future literacy development. For many teachers, meeting this expectation will be a challenge, and these books can provide guidance in several areas: adjusting instruction, adding reading and writing of informational text, creating content-rich instructional units, and assessing students in different ways.

In writing the four books in this series, the authors have been conscious of the importance of helping teachers scaffold students' learning across grade levels. The authors hope that engaging in collaborative discussions will help teachers to learn from colleagues at other levels and to think through how to create the most supportive instructional sequence and organization using content-based themes and units.

These books are not intended to be used alone; rather, teachers should read them while studying the CCSS. To begin, all teachers should download the CCSS and appendices so they are accessible and can be referred to regularly (see URLs for these materials in the References). In addition, the standards and related tools are available on several useful apps from organizations such as Mastery Connect and Learning Unlimited (again, see the References). It is also helpful to bookmark the websites for PARCC (n.d.) and SMARTER Balanced (n.d.) and then check with them periodically. In fact, so many resource sites are coming online that it is worth checking from time to time to see what might be worth reviewing. School districts, educational organizations, and state departments of education are developing instructional units and often make them available (or at least provide some of the structural components).

Much within the CCSS themselves also deserves careful analysis, study, and discussion among teachers of all grades. These efforts should lead to an identification of what is already in the curriculum and where instruction is currently aligned versus misaligned with the CCSS. Teachers must bear in mind that with the central focus on understanding texts, assessments need to be refocused, too. Specifically, schools should ask students to respond in writing to the content of the stories and articles they read so that a baseline can be developed to guide instructional decisions and the time allotted to each aspect of engagement with texts. Many states and districts have developed pilot assessments to ascertain how well their students do on tasks similar to those proposed by the two large consortia: PARCC and SMARTER Balanced. All teachers will find it useful to review the development of the assessments periodically and to compare them to the tools they use to assess their own students.

In designing this series of books, we have attempted to focus on the most important aspects of the CCSS and to provide a set of instructional strategies and tools that will help teachers adjust their instruction as needed to address these standards. Most of these strategies and tools have been tested by teachers and research studies and can therefore be used reliably, and others are variations of good instructional practices that reflect particular emphases of the CCSS. Some of these strategies and tools may seem familiar to teachers and have perhaps already been incorporated into their instructional routines. Regardless, these measures now take on added importance, because they can help align instruction with the expectations of the CCSS and the requirements of the assessments currently being developed.

It is important for teachers to develop a few strong instructional routines that allow them to observe and monitor students' growth over time. These routines should underscore the components of good reading comprehension, thereby helping students adopt them as regular reading practices. It is also important for teachers to keep students central in planning. Students should be able to see the purpose in whatever they are asked to do, and they should be involved in the assessment of their learning needs and achievements. Moreover, students' particular interests and experiences should be honored in classroom activities and other forms of engagement.

The CCSS provide an opportunity for teachers and districts to rethink the priorities, emphases, and assessments that are currently in place and to review how students are already engaged. The CCSS also challenge schools to look at the materials being used and the collaboration taking place across disciplines in the development of students' literacy. As stated in the beginning of this Introduction, the CCSS present both an opportunity and a challenge. By responding to these tasks together, we can explore new territory and find solutions to make twenty-first century learning a reality for all of our students.

REFERENCES

American College Testing (ACT). (2006). *Reading between the lines: What the ACT reveals about college readiness in reading.* Iowa City, IA: Author.

Graham, S., & Hebert, M. (2010). *Writing to read: Evidence for how writing can improve reading. A Carnegie Corporation Time to Act Report.* Washington, DC: Alliance for Excellent Education. Retrieved from http://carnegie.org/fileadmin/Media/Publications/WritingToRead_01.pdf.

Learning Unlimited. (n.d.). Learning Unlimited Common Core resources. *Learning Unlimited.* Retrieved from www.learningunlimitedllc.com/common-core.

Mastery Connect. (n.d.). Goodies. *Mastery Connect.* Retrieved from www.masteryconnect.com/learn-more/goodies.html.

National Assessment Governing Board. (2008). Reading framework for the 2009 National Assessment of Educational Progress. Washington, DC: U.S. Government Printing Office.

National Governors Association Center for Best Practices & Council of Chief State School Officers (NGA & CCSSO). (2010a). *Common Core State Standards.* Washington, DC: Authors. Retrieved from www.corestandards.org/assets/CCSSI_ELA%20Standards.pdf.

National Governors Association Center for Best Practices & Council of Chief State School Officers (NGA & CCSSO). (2010b). Appendix A, *Common Core State Standards.* Washington, DC: Authors. Retrieved from www.corestandards.org/assets/Appendix_A.pdf.

National Governors Association Center for Best Practices & Council of Chief State School Officers (NGA & CCSSO). (2010c). Appendix B, *Common Core State Standards.* Washington, DC: Authors. Retrieved from www.corestandards.org/assets/Appendix_B.pdf.

Partnership for Assessment of Readiness for College and Careers (PARCC). (n.d.). *PARCC.* Retrieved from www.parcconline.org.

SMARTER Balanced Assessment Consortium. (n.d.). Common Core State Standards Tools & Resources. *SMARTER Balanced.* Retrieved from www.smarterbalanced.org/k-12-education/common-core-state-standards-tools-resources.

Wisconsin Department of Public Instruction. (n.d.) Common Core State Standards. *Wisconsin Department of Public Instruction.* Retrieved from http://standards.dpi.wi.gov/stn_ccss.

chapter 1

The English Language Arts for Grades 9–12

HIGH SCHOOL STUDENTS ARE DIFFERENT from their younger adolescent counterparts in many ways. Also, preparing secondary-level students to be college and career ready requires creating activities at a different level of rigor. This chapter will examine the unique developmental and social needs of high school students and suggest how to optimize their learning in the English language arts (ELA).

Michaeljung/Fotolia

Understanding Adolescents

ADOLESCENCE IS AN EXCITING TIME FOR STUDENTS, as they focus on preparing for their lives as adults in a democratic society. During this time in high school, students should have multiple opportunities to develop their reading and writing skills and to articulate their knowledge, beliefs, and opinions to the world. The Common Core State Standards (CCSS) recognize that during high school, adolescent students must continue to hone their literacy skills to become college and career ready.

Adolescent Traits

There are developmental differences between high school students and middle school students. The Common Core State Standards use a framework that is consistent throughout the grades, promoting a similar writing process and close reading activities throughout the literacy model. However, there are significant differences at each grade level. The significant developmental and maturation differences in middle school and high students require sophisticated differences in academic processes and in teacher expectations.

The increased maturity in high school students does not necessarily mean that students at this level can sit still longer than younger students. (This is a common misconception.) Students of all ages learn best when they interact with classmates and work collaboratively.

We often associate physical changes with adolescents, but there are also significant psychological changes in our adolescent students. These changes begin in middle school and continue through high school (Jensen, 2008; Pruitt, 2007). Adolescents at all ages demonstrate the need for peer support and peer social groups who possess common interests. As adolescents journey through the psychological changes that this developmental period presents, they may sometimes feel alienated or question authority. Pruitt (2007) indicates that adolescents often seek roles that resemble adult ones that provide opportunities to express their own opinions and ideas. The Common Core State Standards often echo these student needs. Within the standards, there are expectations for students to be able to assert an opinion (referred to as *claims* in the CCSS) and provide evidence. Students are also expected to apply their literacy skills through varied contexts and for different purposes. This echoes the assertion of Jensen (2008) and Pruitt (2007) that adolescents seek greater independence. The Common Core State Standards consider the developmental needs of adolescent students as complementary to the development of sophisticated literacy skills.

The High School Student Brain–Body Connection

We know more about adolescent brain development today than ever before. Primarily due to technological advances like magnetic resonance imaging (MRI), we can actually watch the brain as it processes information. We can witness a teenager's brain shift from the Piagetian concrete operational stage of childhood to the more abstract and metaphorical processing of the adolescent. At the onset of puberty, which can occur anywhere from early middle school to early high school, the brain changes. It is during this time that new neurological connections are established, allowing adolescents to engage in more advanced level and complicated thinking (Jensen, 2008).

However, students need to be active in order to develop these new neurological changes. This need for movement is often overlooked by high school teachers. In high school, we tend to put students in orderly rows of desks and "teach to their heads" (Gurian, 2008). As Gurian explains, when the body is active and moving, it stimulates the cells and chemicals that are critical to learning. When our students move and their bodies are involved in learning, it is less likely that their brains will forget the new information or experience. By learning and moving at the same time, the student is learning through procedural memory. The Common Core State Standards are conducive to active and engaged learning.

Literacy strategies and methods like writer's workshop, Literature Circles, learning centers, inquiry learning, and debating (which are all discussed in this text) are learning contexts that are conducive to movement and peer interaction. This leads to effective learning. In my work in classrooms, teachers often indicate to me that they are concerned that the students will lack focus and control if they are allowed to move around the classroom. In my experience, the opposite is true. As soon as movement is included with classroom instruction, there are changes. Students become more focused and engaged and actually express more enjoyment in their learning (Gurian et al., 2008, p. 24). Even the sounds in the classroom change as student chatter is about the exciting classroom tasks. Once we dispel the notion that sedentary is better at the high school level, more engaged and active learning becomes a reality.

Optimizing Adolescent Learning

Learning Styles

In addition to understanding adolescent brain development, utilization of a variety of learning styles is another key factor to high school student learning. Learning styles are the ways in which we process, internalize, and remember new and difficult information.

Everyone has a preferred learning style. I am a highly visual learner and also respond well to kinesthetic learning contexts. Auditory instruction is my least preferred and I experience great difficulty in remembering and retaining information through this kind of instruction. Teachers are usually well versed in learning styles and the effects for individuals. The Common Core State Standards acknowledge the importance of learning styles. The standards include statements such as the following, which represents auditory, visual, kinesthetic, and interpersonal learning styles:

> the Speaking and Listening standards require students to develop a range of broadly useful oral communication and interpersonal skills. Students must learn to work together, express and listen carefully to ideas, integrate information from oral, visual, quantitative, and media sources, evaluate what they hear, use media and visual displays strategically to help achieve communicative purposes, and adapt speech to context and task. (NGA & CCSSO, 2010, p. 8)

The standards for grades 9–12 indicate a variety of ways students can demonstrate their increasing sophisticated development of literacy skills. Students are not limited to one type of writing or text. Instead, students are expected to apply their literacy skills through a wide variety of contexts and opportunities. The CCSS authors incorporate what we know about learning styles to provide students with different contexts and learning opportunities to develop speaking and listening skills.

Multiple Intelligences

Providing different ways of learning is also important due to students' varying cultural backgrounds and differing dimensions of intelligence. Most educators are familiar with Howard Gardner's theory of multiple intelligences (2006). Introduced in the 1980s and revised in *Frames of Mind* (Gardner, 2011), Gardner posits that intelligence is multidimensional. According to Gardner, intelligence occurs at several levels: mind, body, and brain. As such, we have numerous ways in which we process information, learn information, and critically think. One is not better than the other; it's just different.

Gardner (2006) identifies the following intelligences:

1. Verbal–linguistic intelligence—"word smart"
2. Logical–mathematical intelligence—"number/reasoning smart"
3. Visual–spatial intelligence—"picture smart"
4. Bodily–kinesthetic intelligence—"body smart"
5. Musical–rhythmic intelligence—"music smart"
6. Interpersonal intelligence—"people smart"
7. Intrapersonal intelligence—"self smart"
8. Naturalist intelligence—"nature smart"

We all possess these eight intelligences to some degree, and most of us have strengths in one or more types. As Gardner (2006) reminds us, a strength in one or two areas doesn't mean that the student can't learn through different intelligences or that he or she can't develop the other intelligences.

As we consider the implications of the CCSS, we need to remember that students "learn, remember, perform, and understand in different ways" (Gardner, 1991, p. 11). As such, we need to "provide different ways for students to learn, that is various approaches and opportunities, students are more able to expand the intelligences they use" (Gardner, 2006, p. 17).

As we consider our classrooms, curriculum, instruction, and most importantly our students, there are five instructional approaches that Gardner (1991, pp. 245–246) recommends for connecting with the multiple intelligences to help students learn a concept:

1. Narrational—explaining a concept
2. Logical–quantitative—applying deductive reasoning
3. Foundational—providing a philosophical background
4. Aesthetic—relating to music and art
5. Experiential—providing hands-on experiences

Taking different approaches to instruction does not mean having to teach eight variations of each lesson. What it does mean is that we need to provide a wide variety of learning experiences for our students.

Classroom Environment

What does this knowledge about adolescent development and learning mean for teaching the English language arts in the classroom? The introduction to the CCSS echoes the qualities of independence and active inquiry. The increasing maturity and growing independence that students develop during their high school years are reflected in the standards under "Students Who Are College and Career Ready in Reading, Writing, Speaking, Listening, and Language":

> Students can, without significant scaffolding, comprehend and evaluate complex texts across a range of types and disciplines, and they can construct effective arguments and convey intricate or multifaceted information. Likewise, students are able independently to discern a speaker's key points, request clarification, and ask relevant questions. They build on others' ideas, articulate their own ideas, and confirm they have been understood. Without prompting, they demonstrate command of standard English and acquire and use a wide-ranging vocabulary. More broadly, they become self-directed learners, effectively seeking out and using resources to assist them, including teachers, peers, and print and digital reference materials. (NGA & CCSSO, 2010, p. 7).

The Common Core State Standards call for students to develop their literacy skills to greater depth with increasing independence. As students develop increasing independence in the development of their literacy, they also become more skilled in knowing *when* and *how* to use their skills to express what they know and understand. This is critical for college and career readiness according to the CCSS.

Teaching the English Language Arts

AN INTEGRATED MODEL FOR LITERACY HAS BEEN RESEARCHED in the last two decades and is well established as the preferred model for developing skills in reading, writing, speaking and listening, and language. Integrated literacy is addressed in the introduction of the CCSS as well as in Appendix A. Although the CCSS do not identify specific curriculum and instructional approaches, an integrated approach to balanced literacy is advocated:

> Although the Standards are divided into Reading, Writing, Speaking and Listening, and Language strands for conceptual clarity, the processes of communication are closely connected, as reflected throughout this document. For example, Writing standard 9 requires that students be able to write about what they read. Likewise, Speaking and Listening standard 4 sets the expectation that students will share findings from their research. (Council of Chief State School Officers, 2010, p. 4)

What does this integrated model look like in a high school ELA classroom? Students should engage in units and lessons that provide a careful balance of listening, speaking, reading, and writing activities. In developing units and lessons, teachers can emphasize specific language arts, but students should actively engage in all of the language arts on a continual basis. Students quickly tire of a curriculum that compartmentalizes the language arts—for instance, two weeks of giving speeches, followed by three weeks of writing essays or four weeks of reading literature. Obviously, people do not use oral and written language in such artificial, isolated constructs in the real world—and students know this.

In any form of communication—listening, speaking, reading, or writing—students' choices of language and style should be guided by the purpose, audience, and context of the setting. This principle of language use must permeate curricular and instructional design. Students' motivation comes from having a purpose—from having something to say and wanting to say it. This need is clearly articulated in the CCSS.

When we use any form of language, we engage in an active, ongoing cognitive process. Because we tend to view the language arts as an academic subject, we sometimes forget that reading, writing, speaking, and listening are active processes. As teachers, we should plan and implement language arts lessons with this principle in mind. In addition, we should recognize that students need sufficient time and experience to become competent or proficient in each language art. This need is also clearly outlined in the CCSS.

Another key principle underlying the language arts is that language processes develop holistically; that is, we do not master one skill and then move on to another. When we speak, listen, read, or write, we use various skills, all at the same time. However, we become competent or proficient in different skills at different times. In the classroom, teachers should provide choices of materials and methods that suit students' range of cognitive development. In addition, teachers should accept that making errors is normal and even necessary to students' growth.

When students listen, speak, read, and write, they do so at their own levels of physical, cognitive, and linguistic development. Certain tasks are too difficult for some students at the time they are introduced, and other tasks are too easy. Within a given classroom, students may be similar in age yet different in maturation and thus have different abilities to complete certain assignments.

Students may also display considerable differences in ability across the language arts, performing well in some areas but not in others. Similarly, student performance may vary from task to task, even within the same language art—say, writing. This variation confounds and frustrates teachers who forget that adolescent development is ongoing and ever changing. Remembering the fluid nature of adolescence is particularly important in the area of assessment. Teachers who assess students on the basis of absolute standards and expectations may push them away or convince them that they cannot learn. All of these concepts and principles are part of a philosophy of teaching and learning: knowledge about how students learn most effectively. As teachers, we should rely on this philosophy to guide our choices of materials, activities, and assessments.

Curriculum Development

Teachers sometimes think in terms of "What can I teach?" rather than "How can I best help my students best learn?" In planning an effective ELA curriculum, we should take the latter perspective.

We can best help our students learn by providing them with experiences that will help them grow in all domains: affective, behavioral, and cognitive. As stated by Maxwell and Meiser (1993), "Curriculum and instruction, then, should acknowledge and prepare for the inevitable changes that our students will undergo as they mature" (p. 33). For example, knowing that the needs and abilities of a 13-year-old differ from those of a 15-year-old is not enough. We must act on that knowledge. Intervening in our students' lives demands that we act on the best knowledge our profession has to offer.

Once we focus on our students, questions will follow about students' ability levels, learning styles, and interests. Student-centered learning is nothing new. Most famously, John Dewey argued for the value of this approach at the beginning of the twentieth century. Today, the CCSS recognize the critical need for students to be independent learners and thinkers for the twenty-first century. When students feel a sense of purpose, they discover the power of their own voices.

Textbooks and Other Resources

The days of solely relying on one textbook and a short list of novels in an ELA classroom are long gone. In order to be college and career ready in the twenty-first century, students must be able to use a wide variety of resources with competence. Students are expected to use print sources as well as digital media. Teachers can no longer depend on a series of textbooks as the scope and sequence for ELA instruction across multiple grade levels. (Just a reminder: *Scope* refers to the content, and *sequence* is the order in which the content is taught.) Instead of an overreliance on textbooks, it is time to shift to ELA units that incorporate each of the language arts (reading, writing, speaking and listening, and language) through focused theme-based units.

When teachers are given the professional time and support to develop the curriculum for their students, there are opportunities to create more contextually based instruction. If teachers are not restricted to a single textbook, it becomes easier to provide students with a wider range of reading materials that can include more culturally diverse works. When teachers are not restricted to a textbook or a single title or type of text, they are able to differentiate text types to meet the needs of diverse learners and provide a variety of research and writing experiences. According to the CCSS, teachers and curriculum specialists are the ones who are most skilled to develop the literacy skills and content knowledge for their students (NGA & CCSSO, 2010, p. 6.)

Tracking versus Balanced Literacy

Tracking, which is sometimes referred to as *ability grouping,* is a curricular issue that has a significant effect on students. The nature of this effect continues to be debated, despite the fact that several decades of research have suggested the impact is largely negative, especially on students who are already marginalized by the educational system. Noted ELA educator Nancie Atwell (1998) has suggested that "tracking allows us to blame students for our failure to teach them well—all those low-tracked adolescents of whom we ask and expect less and less" (p. 40). This statement represents the crux of the academic effect of tracking: low expectations of students, combined with assigning work that is largely rote and unimaginative.

The CCSS do not make any recommendations regarding issues such as tracking. However, they do emphasize the need for differentiated instruction to provide students with a wide range of accessible reading materials. Differentiating instruction in this way is necessary to help students meet the expectations of the standards.

Although tracking seems to be a poor instructional approach for students who are already struggling or alienated in some way, the option at the other end of the continuum— the so-called *feel-good curriculum*—is equally problematic. To base instruction primarily on whether students will feel good about themselves while they are learning is dangerous. Such a curriculum is purely affective and fails to provide students with the content knowledge, skills, and experience that are critical to their academic development.

Both intuition and common sense tell us that students need to develop healthy self-esteem to succeed in school and life. We must acknowledge that healthy self-esteem comes from authentic learning and achievement—both of which are by-products of a stimulating and developmentally appropriate curriculum.

The Common Core State Standards present a context in which students can develop greater independence and engagement in their learning, which stimulates student motivation. We can facilitate engaged learning through the "three C's of motivation: collaboration, choice, and content" (Kohn, 1994, p. 281). Educator Alfie Kohn writes that "Students do not come to believe they are important, valued, and capable just because they are told this is so"; rather, they "acquire a sense of significance from doing significant things, from being active participants in their own education" (p. 282). Curriculum and instruction must be contextualized and be meaningful for students, as articulated in the CCSS, in order to develop students' motivation and self-worth.

The CCSS do not dictate specific instructional practices, but the standards are rooted in educational theory, research, and data. In analyzing the CCSS and the associated theory, research, and data, most literacy educators will likely conclude that the *balanced literacy framework* is well suited to meeting the rigorous expectations of the standards.

The integrated literacy framework is an effective approach to teaching readers and writers, and it is commonly used in today's schools. The framework is grounded in the idea that all students can read and write well. In a balanced literacy classroom, students engage in a collaborative environment and participate in a variety of literacy activities, such as read-alouds, guided reading, Literature Circles, and vocabulary lessons (Fountas & Pinnell, 2008). In a balanced literacy activity, the goal is to develop language arts skills while successfully creating a shared authentic experience. In addition, the balanced literacy approach allows students to work at their own levels by providing differentiated instruction.

Students' Needs and Interests

Students' needs and interests are a curricular issue that teachers should address. Teachers understand many student needs from their education and understanding of developmental stages, the process of learning, and so on. However, they should find out some things directly from their students, whose needs and interests change rapidly in the course of an academic year. This kind of information can be easily gathered through quick writes, surveys, class discussions, peer discussions, and teacher-student conferences.

Considering students' interests is a recurring element in the CCSS. Students should have access to a wide variety of literature and informational texts as they develop reading, writing, speaking and listening, and language skills. Young adult novels, classic literature, graphic novels, and technology-based texts such as blogs are all critical components of the modern ELA curriculum.

The Joy of Learning

AS HIGH SCHOOL ELA TEACHERS, we want our students to develop powerful voices in a democratic society. We recognize that having literacy skills is vital for students to learn content and to understand and participate in the world around them. Nothing is more powerful than working with students to hone their reading, writing, speaking, listening, and language skills for college and career readiness and for their futures as young women and men.

REFERENCES

Atwell, N. (1998). *In the middle: New understandings about reading, writing, and learning.* Portsmouth, NH: Heinemann.

Fountas, I., & Pinnell, G. S. (2008). *Guiding readers and writers: Teaching comprehension, genre, and content literacy.* Portsmouth, NH: Heinemann.

Gardner, H. (1991). *The unschooled mind.* New York, NY: Basic Books.

Gardner, H. (2006). *Multiple intelligences: New horizons in theory and practice.* New York, NY: Basic Books.

Gardner, H. (2011). *Frames of mind: The theory of multiple intelligences* (3rd ed.). New York, NY: Basic Books.

Gurian, M., Stevens, K., & King, K. (2008). *Strategies for teaching boys and girls—A workbook for educators.* San Francisco, CA: Jossey-Bass.

Jensen, E. (2008). *Enriching the brain: How to maximize every learner's potential.* San Francisco, CA: Jossey-Bass.

Kohn, A. (1994). *What does it mean to be well educated? And other essays on standards, grading, and other follies.* Boston, MA: Beacon Press.

Maxwell, R. J., & Meiser, M. J. (1993). *Teaching English in middle and secondary schools.* New York, NY: Macmillan.

National Governors Association Center for Best Practices & Council of Chief State School Officers (NGA & CCSSO). (2010). *Common Core State Standards: English language arts and literacy in history/social studies, science, and technical subjects.* Washington, DC: Authors. Retrieved from www.corestandards.org/assets/CCSSI_ELA%20Standards.pdf.

Pruitt, D. (2007). *Your adolescent.* New York, NY: HarperCollins.

The Common Core State Standards for Grades 9–12

AS HIGH SCHOOL TEACHERS, WE SOMETIMES HAVE DIFFICULTY remembering that education is a quest for joy. The wide eyes and open arms of kindergartners are nowhere to be found in our high school classrooms. Instead, we often find ourselves facing the blank stares of teenagers and having our questions be met with shrugs.

Yet those of us who work with adolescents know that there is a lot happening beneath this façade of indifference. The joy that appears in a high school student's face when he recognizes himself in a 200-year-old fictional character he has read about is completely genuine. Likewise, the joy expressed by a high school student who wins an argument with her peers by stating evidence she found in primary source material is unmistakable. These are the joys of adolescents who are preparing to accept their roles as mature, thinking adults. And they share that joy with us, their teachers.

Monkey Business/Fotolia

The Common Core State Standards and Adolescent Literacy

IN CHAPTER 1, WE REVIEWED SOME OF THE KEY CONCEPTS that underlie adolescent students' learning, such as learning styles and multiple intelligences. We also discussed how we, as teachers, can optimize that learning in the English language arts by incorporating concepts such as balanced literacy and students' interests in our planning and instruction. In this chapter, we will revisit these concepts in the context of the Common Core State Standards (CCSS) for grades 9–12.

Learning Styles

Everyone has a learning style—a preferred way to study, process, internalize, and remember new and difficult information and skills. An individual's learning style affects not only how he or she learns and remembers but also he or she responds to an environment.

When planning lessons for students with various learning styles, we should keep in mind the following guidelines:

- Always provide multiple ways for students to learn the same material.
- Connect information to students' lives and to the world outside the classroom.
- Encourage students to be responsible for their learning.
- Connect lessons to other areas and topics students have studied.
- Encourage students' self-confidence by helping them be successful (Maxwell, Meiser, & McKnight, 2010).

The importance of recognizing students' learning styles in planning and teaching language arts is confirmed by research underlying the CCSS (NGA & CCSSO, 2010b). For instance, a discussion about vocabulary acquisition makes these recommendations:

> If students are going to grasp and retain words and comprehend text, they need **incremental, repeated exposure** in a variety of contexts to the words they are trying to learn. When students make multiple **connections between a new word and their own experiences,** they develop a nuanced and flexible understanding of the word they are learning. In this way, students learn not only what a word means but also how to **use that word in a variety of contexts,** and they can apply appropriate senses of the word's meaning in order to **understand the word in different contexts** (Landauer & Dumais, 1997; Landauer, McNamara, Dennis, & Kintsch, 2007; Nagy, Herman, & Anderson, 1985). (p. 32, emphasis added)

The bolded phrases in this passage identify recommendations that reiterate those made earlier for planning lessons for students with various learning styles. Providing repeated exposure to material, establishing connections to students' experiences, and extending learning to other topics and areas are particularly relevant to learning styles.

Multiple Intelligences

Another concept that underlies adolescents' learning is that of multiple intelligences, as described in a theory introduced by Harvard professor Howard Gardner (2011). Gardner suggests that we all have multiple ways of processing information, understanding material, and knowing the world.

Moreover, we have separate and equally valid types of intelligence, including verbal–linguistic intelligence, bodily–kinesthetic intelligence, and interpersonal intelligence, among others. Most of us have strengths in one or more types of intelligence.

Interestingly, both learning styles theory and multiple intelligences theory include elements of biology and psychology, anthropology and sociology, as well as art and culture (Silver, Strong, & Perini, 1997). However, learning styles theory addresses the different ways in which people think, whereas multiple intelligences theory "is an effort to understand how cultures and disciplines shape human potential" (p. 22). Moreover, whereas learning styles relate to differences in the process of learning, multiple intelligences relate to the content and products of learning.

This contrast identifies an important connection between multiple intelligences theory and the CCSS. Namely, teachers are expected to accept and build on students' differences by providing different materials and options for assignments and assessments. For example, it is not uncommon to have a ninth-grade class in which the students represent a wide variety of reading levels. Choosing texts that accommodate a range of reading levels is essential for building students' skills. At the core of the CCSS Reading standards is a "staircase" of text complexity, which represents the concept that students will read increasingly complex texts as they advance from grade to grade. As summarized in the introduction to the CCSS, "The Reading standards place equal emphasis on the sophistication of what students read and the skill with what they read" (NGA & CCSSO, 2010a, p. 8).

As teachers, we should also plan rich instructional tasks that engage students in developing several skills across the language arts and the content areas. In addition, we should provide students with regular opportunities to practice their skills and to demonstrate what they have learned. Like the CCSS Reading standards, the Writing standards take a "staircase" approach to skill development: "Each year in their writing, students should demonstrate increasing sophistication in all aspects of language use" (NGA & CCSSO, 2010a, p. 42). The Writing standards also emphasize the need to have students engage in a range of activities on a regular basis. Students are expected to use technology "to produce and publish writing as well as to interact and collaborate with others" (p. 43) and to complete both short-term and long-term projects "for a range of tasks, purposes, and audiences" (p. 47).

A second connection between multiple intelligences and the CCSS is the expectation for students to "understand other perspectives and cultures" (NGA & CCSSO, 2010a, p. 7). This expectation is stated in the introduction to the CCSS in discussing the qualities of students who meet the standards:

> Students appreciate that the twenty-first-century classroom and workplace are settings in which people from often widely divergent cultures and who represent diverse experiences and perspectives must learn and work together. Students actively seek to understand other perspectives and cultures through reading and listening, and they are able to communicate effectively with people of varied backgrounds. They evaluate other points of view critically and constructively. Through reading great classic and contemporary works of literature representative of a variety of periods, cultures, and worldviews, students can vicariously inhabit worlds and have experiences much different than their own. (p. 7)

This statement indicates the value that the CCSS place on students having opportunities to interact with people who think differently and live differently than they do.

Balanced Literacy

The balanced literacy framework is based on the idea that all students can read and write well. In every balanced literacy activity, the goal is to develop students' language arts skills while creating a shared authentic experience. Students engage in a collaborative environment and participate in a variety of literacy activities (Appleman, 2010; Beers, 2003; Fountas & Pinnell, 2008). In addition, differentiating instruction allows students to work at their own levels (Maxwell et al., 2011).

The notion of balanced literacy underlies the CCSS for the English language arts (ELA). The architecture of the ELA standards demonstrates that the language arts are interactive processes; they both influence and strengthen other processes in constructing meaning. Although the ELA standards are organized into four strands—Reading, Writing, Speaking and Listening, and Language—the development of skills and knowledge overlaps and reinforces learning across the individual language arts. The introduction to the CCSS offers two examples of these connections: one of the Writing standards "requires that students be able to write about what they read," and one of the Speaking and Listening standards "sets the expectation that students will share findings from their research" (NGA & CCSSO, 2010a, p. 4). Research and media skills are addressed throughout the CCSS.

In developing units and lessons, we can emphasize specific language arts, but overall, we should maintain a careful balance of listening, speaking, reading, and writing activities. Students should actively engage in all of the language arts on a continual basis and use the language arts to make sense of themselves and the world in which they live. Finally, we should guide students in constructing meaning, rather than provide them with meaning (Maxwell et al., 2011).

Students' Needs and Interests

Of course, English language arts teachers know about the best books. Books are our passion and our stock in trade. Nonetheless, teachers find it valuable to acknowledge the materials that students choose to read for entertainment.

Indeed, acknowledging students' needs and interests is a recurring element in the CCSS. Students can develop reading, writing, speaking and listening, and language skills by accessing a wide variety of literature and informational texts. The CCSS classroom includes not only works of classic literature and literary nonfiction but also young adult novels, graphic novels, and technology-based texts such as blogs. Texts should also relate to topics of special interest to students and to study in other content areas.

Planning a curriculum based on popular and technology-based texts is difficult and requires great flexibility, because students' needs and interests change rapidly during the course of the year. However, the rewards of teaching such a curriculum can be tremendous. Consider the many parallels that can be drawn between the plots of ancient Greek legends and those of recent superhero movies. Or imagine how students might compare their favorite celebrity tweets to *The Secret Diary of William Byrd* (Byrd, 1941/1972), the work of an eighteenth-century American aristocrat whose private writing offers readers detailed insights into his daily life.

Learning Language

When people use language in any form, they engage in an active, ongoing cognitive process (Maxwell et al., 2010). Teachers who recognize this principle of language use plan and implement lessons accordingly. Specifically, they allow students the time and experience needed to achieve competency or proficiency in each of the language arts.

The active nature of acquiring literacy skills is reflected in the CCSS. As mentioned earlier, the standards take a "staircase" approach, allowing students' skills to build from grade to grade. In the area of reading, in particular, texts are provided at different ability levels to facilitate students' progress. Reinforcement of learning through repeated exposure to materials is also central to the CCSS.

Another principle of language use and learning is that language processes occur holistically. In terms of language use, when people speak, listen, read, or write, they use multiple skills simultaneously. In terms of language learning, people reach competency or proficiency in different skills at different times (Maxwell et al., 2010).

These ideas run throughout the CCSS. As mentioned earlier, the development of skills and knowledge overlaps and reinforces learning across the standards. The developers of the CCSS recognize that "the processes of communication are closely connected" and refer to the standards as an "integrated model of literacy" (NGA & CCSSO, 2010a, p. 4). In the introduction to the standards, the developers state, "In short, students who meet the Standards develop the skills in reading, writing, speaking, and listening that are the foundation for any creative and purposeful expression in language" (p. 3).

Preparing Students to Be College and Career Ready

THE PRIMARY PURPOSE OF THE CCSS IS CLEARLY STATED in the introduction to the standards document: "to help ensure that all students are college and career ready in literacy no later than the end of high school" (NGA & CCSSO, 2010a, p. 3). A related purpose is stated, as well: "[to] lay out a vision of what it means to be a literate person in the twenty-first century" (p. 3). As teachers, we should have two purposes, as well: to help students meet the expectations of the CCSS and to help them develop into literate individuals.

In the introduction to the CCSS, the developers identify seven qualities in a "portrait" of students who meet the CCSS and are becoming literate individuals:

- They demonstrate independence.
- They build content knowledge.
- They respond to the varying demands of audience, task, purpose, and discipline.
- They comprehend as well as critique.
- They value evidence.
- They use technology and digital media strategically and capably.
- They come to understand other perspectives and cultures. (p. 7)

Demonstrating independence is a key quality of successful students. The introduction to the standards goes on to describe these students as follows:

Students can, without significant scaffolding, comprehend and evaluate complex texts across a range of types and disciplines, and they can construct effective arguments and **convey intricate or multifaceted information**. Likewise, students are able independently to discern a speaker's key points, request clarification, and **ask relevant questions.** They build on others' ideas, **articulate their own ideas**, and confirm they have been understood. Without prompting, they demonstrate command of standard English and acquire and **use a**

wide-ranging vocabulary. More broadly, **they become self-directed learners,** effectively seeking out and using resources to assist them, including teachers, peers, and print and digital reference materials. (p. 7, emphasis added)

The bolded phrases in this passage highlight specific skills that high school students must master to be career and college ready in today's world. Thus, the CCSS recognize the developmental needs of adolescents and apply this information in developing standards that support vital skills at the time students are becoming adults in a democratic society.

English Language Arts Standards

For high school, the ELA standards are divided into two grade levels: grades 9–10 and grades 11–12. As noted earlier, the standards are further divided into four strands that represent the language arts corpus: Reading, Writing, Speaking and Listening, and Language. In addition, the Reading strand is split to provide standards for two types of texts: Literature and Informational Texts. It is important to note that informational texts in ELA are literary nonfiction works. This will be further discussed and explained later in the text.

Underlying each strand of the ELA standards is a set of College and Career Readiness (CCR) Anchor Standards. Within each strand, the categories and numbers of the Anchor Standards correspond with the categories and numbers of the specific ELA standards. For example, within the Writing strand, CCR Anchor Standard 1 in the category Text Types and Purposes states, "Write arguments to support claims in an analysis of substantive topics or texts, using valid reasoning and relevant and sufficient evidence" (NGA & CCSSO, 2010a, p. 41). In the ELA Writing Standards for grades 9–10 and 11–12, standard 1 repeats this broad objective but also breaks out five specific skills that students are expected to master (see Table 2.1). The skills are very similar across the two grade-level groups, with the grades 11–12 skills building on and extending the grades 9–10 skills.

Interdisciplinary Literacy Standards

For grades 6–12, the CCSS provide not only the ELA Standards but also a second set of standards related to literacy in the content areas. These interdisciplinary standards were created to address the literacy needs of middle school and high school students in subjects other than English. To be clear, these are *literacy* standards, not *content* standards. Their focus is on developing students' skills in reading and writing within these content areas. In fact, the literacy standards are based on the same CCR Anchor Standards as the ELA Standards for reading and writing.

The CCSS Reading Standards for Literacy are divided into two sets: one for history/social studies and one for science and technical subjects. Students are expected to develop strong reading comprehension skills in working with informational texts, analyzing and synthesizing the texts to develop content knowledge. The need for these skills is clearly articulated by the developers of the CCSS:

Reading is critical to building knowledge in history/social studies as well as in science and technical subjects. College and career ready reading in these fields requires an appreciation of the norms and conventions of each discipline, such as the kinds of evidence used in history and science; an understanding of domain-specific words and phrases; an attention to precise details; and the capacity to evaluate intricate arguments, synthesize complex information, and follow detailed descriptions of events and concepts. In history/

TABLE 2.1 • *Writing Standard 1 for Grades 9–10 and 11–12*

Grades 9–10 students:	Grades 11–12 students:
1. Write arguments to support claims in an analysis of substantive topics or texts, using valid reasoning and relevant and sufficient evidence.	1. Write arguments to support claims in an analysis of substantive topics or texts, using valid reasoning and relevant and sufficient evidence.
a. Introduce precise claim(s), distinguish the claim(s) from alternate or opposing claims, and create an organization that establishes clear relationships among claim(s), counterclaims, reasons, and evidence.	a. Introduce precise, knowledgeable claim(s), establish the significance of the claim(s), distinguish the claim(s) from alternate or opposing claims, and create an organization that logically sequences claim(s), counterclaims, reasons, and evidence.
b. Develop claim(s) and counterclaims fairly, supplying evidence for each while pointing out the strengths and limitations of both in a manner that anticipates the audience's knowledge level and concerns.	b. Develop claim(s) and counterclaims fairly and thoroughly, supplying the most relevant evidence for each while pointing out the strengths and limitations of both in a manner that anticipates the audience's knowledge level, concerns, values, and possible biases.
c. Use words, phrases, and clauses to link the major sections of the text, create cohesion, and clarify the relationships between claim(s) and reasons, between reasons and evidence, and between claim(s) and counterclaims.	c. Use words, phrases, and clauses as well as varied syntax to link the major sections of the text, create cohesion, and clarify the relationships between claim(s) and reasons, between reasons and evidence, and between claim(s) and counterclaims.
d. Establish and maintain a formal style and objective tone while attending to the norms and conventions of the discipline in which they are writing.	d. Establish and maintain a formal style and objective tone while attending to the norms and conventions of the discipline in which they are writing.
e. Provide a concluding statement or section that follows from and supports the argument presented.	e. Provide a concluding statement or section that follows from and supports the argument presented.

Source: NGA & CCSSO (2010).

social studies, for example, students need to be able to analyze, evaluate, and differentiate primary and secondary sources. When reading scientific and technical texts, students need to be able to gain knowledge from challenging texts that often make extensive use of elaborate diagrams and data to convey information and illustrate concepts. Students must be able to read complex informational texts in these fields with independence and confidence because the vast majority of reading in college and workforce training programs will be sophisticated nonfiction. (NGA & CCSSO, 2010a, p. 60)

The point is made, as well, that the Reading standards are intended to complement the content standards of these subject areas—not to replace them (p. 60).

The CCSS Writing Standards for Literacy address students' ability to demonstrate what they know and understand through writing. Students are expected to write for a range of tasks, purposes, and audiences and to use a variety of resources in supporting and developing their ideas. The importance of writing in the content areas is stated in the CCSS document:

For students, writing is a key means of asserting and defending claims, showing what they know about a subject, and conveying what they have experienced, imagined, thought, and felt. To be college and career ready writers, students must take task, purpose, and audience into careful consideration, choosing words, information, structures, and formats deliberately. They need to be able to use technology strategically when creating, refining, and collaborating on writing. They have to become adept at gathering information, evaluating sources, and citing material accurately, reporting findings from their research and analysis of sources in a clear and cogent manner. They must have the flexibility, concentration, and fluency to produce high-quality first-draft text under a tight deadline and the capacity to revisit and make improvements to a piece of writing over multiple drafts when circumstances encourage or require it. To meet these goals, students must devote significant time and effort to writing, producing numerous pieces over short and long time frames throughout the year. (CCSS 2010, p. 63)

Although the ELA Standards and interdisciplinary literacy standards are quite similar, some differences should be noted. For instance, the literacy standards do not break out specific expectations related to Writing Anchor Standard 3, which addresses narrative writing. Narrative writing remains more closely aligned with the ELA Standards, although students are expected to incorporate narrative elements into their informative/explanatory and argumentative writing in the content areas (NGA & CCSSO, 2010a, p. 65). Similarly, reading literature is absent from the literacy standards but is a key part of the ELA Standards. Despite these minor differences, both the ELA standards and the interdisciplinary literacy standards address the urgent need for high school students to develop the literacy skills needed for college and career.

Content area literacy is not a new idea for educators. The concept of reading and writing across the curriculum has been embraced for decades. What is unique about the CCSS application of this concept is that all content area teachers are responsible for developing students' literacy skills—not just language arts teachers.

Most of us have likely heard the statement "We are all teachers of reading and writing," but content area high school teachers often respond to this statement with discomfort. In all fairness, most high school teachers have not received adequate training in teaching reading and writing. Yet the entire educational community is being called on to recognize that incorporating schoolwide reading and writing strategies is essential if students are to going to comprehend the material in content area classes.

Classroom Connection

Sample Lesson for Grades 9–10

The Family Story is an example of a ninth-grade language arts lesson that integrates the ELA Standards and the balanced literacy framework. The lesson is based on the novel *The Joy Luck Club*, by Amy Tan (1989), in which the author recounts the lives of four families and the relationships between the mothers and daughters. The mothers are all Chinese immigrants and have values, memories, and hopes that they want to pass on to their daughters. However, the daughters, as first-generation Chinese–Americans, realize that their lives are quite different from their mothers' lives. In portraying these mother–daughter relationships, Tan reveals the importance of heritage and family.

This lesson uses the balanced literacy model to help students develop specific skills. Through close reading, students will learn about the literary concept of *theme* and how an author develops a theme in crafting a story. Students will also use speaking and listening skills when they interview family members and friends to record a family story. Finally, students will write their own stories, which will relate to the theme of *The Joy Luck Club*.

ELA Standards

This lesson meets the following ELA standards for grades 9–10 (NGA & CCSSO [2010]):

Reading: Literature

- **RL.9-10.1** Cite strong and thorough textual evidence to support analysis of what the text says explicitly as well as inferences drawn from the text.
- **RL.9-10.2** Determine a theme or central idea of a text and analyze in detail its development over the course of the text, including how it emerges and is shaped and refined by specific details; provide an objective summary of the text.
- **RL.9-10.4** Produce clear and coherent writing in which the development, organization, and style are appropriate to task.

Writing

- **W.9-10.4** Produce clear and coherent writing in which the development, organization, and style are appropriate to task, purpose, and audience.

Speaking and Listening

- **SL.9-10.3** Evaluate a speaker's point of view, reasoning, and use of evidence and rhetoric, identifying any fallacious reasoning or exaggerated or distorted evidence.

Language

- **L.9-10.1** Demonstrate command of the conventions of Standard English grammar and usage when writing or speaking.
  a. Use parallel structure.
  b. Use various types of phrases (noun, verb, adjectival, adverbial, participial, prepositional, absolute) and clauses (independent, dependent; noun, relative, adverbial) to convey specific meanings and add variety and interest to writing or presentations.
- **L.9-10.2** Demonstrate command of the conventions of Standard English capitalization, punctuation, and spelling when writing.
  a. Use a semicolon (and perhaps a conjunctive adverb) to link two or more closely related independent clauses.
  b. Use a colon to introduce a list or quotation.
  c. Spell correctly.

Required Materials

- Copies of *The Joy Luck Club* (Tan, 1989)
- Handout: "Telling a Family Tale"
- Writing materials/computer
- Grade-sheet handout
- Recorder (optional)

NEW YORK INSTITUTE OF TECHNOLOGY

Figure 2.1 presents the handout "Telling a Family Tale," which describes the assignments students will complete in this lesson. In this figure, see the marginal notes that identify which ELA Standards are being addressed.

Student Instructions

Provide students with these instructions for preparing their final project:

1. Type the project using a 12-point font; also double-space the text and set standard margins.

2. Provide a complete heading and an original, creative title for the project.

FIGURE 2.1 ● The Joy Luck Club Telling a Family Tale

Prominent themes in Amy Tan's novel *The Joy Luck Club* are family, family relationships, and stories, along with intergenerational conflict and memories of the past. This theme of family, and the impact that heritage has on one's life, will serve as the focus of your writing assignment.

The Assignment Part 1

Talk to several members of your family and friends and uncover a family story that you will retell. There is no qualification to what this story should be, other than you should consider it a story worth retelling and it is part of your family's history. Consider the stories that were told throughout *The Joy Luck Club*; these stories have some impact on the lives of those who hear them and carry important memories and lessons. In addition, the story may be one with which you already have familiarity or it can be a story that you have never heard before.

In learning the story, talk to as many sources as possible and gather descriptive details. Think about the time, place, people involved, and specific details surrounding the event.   SL.9-10.3

The more specific that you can be and the more details you gather, the better the story will be.

Using the novel as a model, note how Amy Tan tells family stories that recreate events and place the reader in the moment. Keep in mind that stories are changed and embellished over time through tellings and retellings. Thus, you may choose to add details, as long as the story remains accurate.   RL.9-10.2

After you have interviewed several sources and recorded notes (either written or with a recorder) and you have included your own thoughts and memories, recreate the family story.   W.9-10.4

Use details, descriptive words, and vivid details to recreate the story and show it to the reader, do not simply tell the story.

The Assignment Part 2

After you have completed writing the story, now write a reflective page about what you learned and your reaction to this family story. Be honest and candid in describing your feelings.

3. Proofread your work.
4. Make sure to write in complete sentences and to use correct spelling and appropriate punctuation.
5. If you quote what someone has said, put quotation marks around that text.
6. Add illustrations, photographs, and artifacts as appropriate.

Evaluation

A sample form for use in evaluating students' projects is shown in Figure 2.2. Again, marginal notes identify the ELA Standards being addressed.

FIGURE 2.2 ● Telling a Family Tale Grade Sheet

Requirements
Typed, double-spaced, 12-point font, standard margins, complete heading, and creative and original title

1	2	3	4	5

Part 1 – The Story Itself

Focus and Organization
Retells a specific family story, each paragraph centers on one main idea, ideas presented in a logical manner   W.9-10.4

1	2	3	4	5	6	7	8	9	10

Development of Ideas
Incorporates specific and descriptive details, uses descriptive language and vivid imagery, recreates a story that the reader can envision

1	2	3	4	5	6	7	8	9	10	11	12	13	14	15	16	17	18	19	20

Mechanics
Correct spelling and appropriate punctuation, complete sentence structure (no run-ons or fragments), correct use of quotation marks and punctuation of dialogue
L.9-10.1   L.9-10.2

1	2	3	4	5

Part 2 – Personal Reflection

Quality of Writing
Honest and candid reaction, developed response, proofread and edited for mechanical and spelling errors

1	2	3	4	5	6	7	8	9	10

Additional comments:

Classroom Connection
Sample Unit for Grades 11–12

This three-week unit, designed for students in grades 11–12, explores the concept of beauty, as portrayed by authors and artists in literature and artwork. Activities in the lesson are aligned with the ELS Standards and represent a number of the reading goals articulated in the CCSS.

For this unit, it is assumed that the class meets five times a week and that class periods are 50 minutes long. It is also assumed that students will complete much of the assigned reading outside the classroom as homework.

Essential Question

- If beauty is in the eye of the beholder, can there be a standard of universal beauty?

Enduring Understandings

- Determine how the author's point of view about a topic affects the development of the text and its theme.
- Broaden your understanding by considering points of view that are different from your own.
- Explore what authors and artists have suggested about *beauty* in their writing and artwork.
- Consider how a concept such as *beauty* reflects individual and societal values.
- Make a claim and provide evidence and reasoning to support your argument through written and oral language.

Texts and Artworks

Students will read and evaluate a wide variety of works, including classic literature, literary nonfiction (i.e., informational text), and multicultural works. In addition, students will view and evaluate several paintings. The recommended texts and artworks for this unit are as follows:

- "Ode on a Grecian Urn," by John Keats (1819/1999)
- *Romeo and Juliet*, by William Shakespeare (1594–1595/2000)
- *The Bluest Eye*, by Toni Morrison (1970)
- *A Beautiful Mind*, by Sylvia Nasar (1998)
- "Beautifying the World Through Art," by Gary Witherspoon (1977)
- Paintings by Georgia O'Keefe (George O'Keefe Museum, 2011)

ELA Standards

The following ELA Standards for grades 11–12 are addressed in this unit (NGA & CCSSO [2010]):

Reading: Literature

- **RL.11-12.1** Cite strong and thorough textual evidence to support analysis of what the text says explicitly as well as inferences drawn from the text, including determining where the text leaves matters uncertain.

- **RL.11-12.2** Determine two or more themes or central ideas of a text and analyze their development over the course of the text, including how they interact and build on one another to produce a complex account; provide an objective summary of the text.
- **RL.11-12.3** Analyze the impact of the author's choices regarding how to develop and relate elements of a story or drama (e.g., where a story is set, how the action is ordered, how the characters are introduced and developed).
- **RL.11.10** By the end of grade 11, read and comprehend literature, including stories, dramas, and poems, in the grades 11-CCR text complexity band proficiently, with scaffolding as needed at the high end of the range.[*]
- **RL.12.10** By the end of grade 12, read and comprehend literature, including stories, dramas, and poems, at the high end of the grades 11-CCR text complexity band independently and proficiently.[*]

Reading: Informational Text

- **RI.11-12.2** Determine two or more central ideas of a text and analyze their development over the course of the text, including how they interact and build on one another to provide a complex analysis; provide an objective summary of the text.
- **RI.11-12.3** Analyze a complex set of ideas or sequence of events and explain how specific individuals, ideas, or events interact and develop over the course of the text.

Writing

- **W.11-12.1** Write arguments to support claims in an analysis of substantive topics or texts, using valid reasoning and relevant and sufficient evidence.

a. Introduce precise, knowledgeable claim(s), establish the significance of the claim(s), distinguish the claim(s) from alternate or opposing claims, and create an organization that logically sequences claim(s), counterclaims, reasons, and evidence.

b. Develop claim(s) and counterclaims fairly and thoroughly, supplying the most relevant evidence for each while pointing out the strengths and limitations of both in a manner that anticipates the audience's knowledge level, concerns, values, and possible biases.

c. Use words, phrases, and clauses as well as varied syntax to link the major sections of the text, create cohesion, and clarify the relationships between claim(s) and reasons, between reasons and evidence, and between claim(s) and counterclaims.

d. Establish and maintain a formal style and objective tone while attending to the norms and conventions of the discipline in which they are writing.

e. Provide a concluding statement or section that follows from and supports the argument presented.

---

[*]The College and Career Readiness (CCR) Anchor Standards for Reading will be discussed in greater detail in Chapter 3. At this point, it is important to note that CCR Anchor Standard 10 states the ultimate expectation of the Reading standards. Standards 1–9 identify the skills necessary to achieve Standard 10.

- **W.11-12.6** Use technology, including the Internet, to produce, publish, and update individual or shared writing products in response to ongoing feedback, including new arguments or information.

Speaking and Listening

- **SL11-12.1** Initiate and participate effectively in a range of collaborative discussions (one-on-one, in groups, and teacher-led) with diverse partners on grades 11–12 topics, texts, and issues, building on others' ideas and expressing their own clearly and persuasively.

  a. Come to discussions prepared, having read and researched material under study; explicitly draw on that preparation by referring to evidence from texts and other research on the topic or issue to stimulate a thoughtful, well reasoned exchange of ideas.

  b. Work with peers to promote civil, democratic discussions and decision making, set clear goals and deadlines, and establish individual roles as needed.

  c. Propel conversations by posing and responding to questions that probe reasoning and evidence; ensure a hearing for a full range of positions on a topic or issue; clarify, verify, or challenge ideas and conclusions; and promote divergent and creative perspectives.

  d. Respond thoughtfully to diverse perspectives; synthesize comments, claims, and evidence made on all sides of an issue; resolve contradictions when possible; and determine what additional information or research is required to deepen the investigation or complete the task.

- **SL11-12.5** Make strategic use of digital media (e.g., textual, graphical, audio, visual, and interactive elements) in presentations to enhance understanding of findings, reasoning, and evidence and to add interest.

Language

- **L.11-12.2** Demonstrate command of the conventions of standard English capitalization, punctuation, and spelling when writing.

  a. Observe hyphenation conventions.
  b. Spell correctly.

- **L.11-12.5** Demonstrate understanding of figurative language, word relationships, and nuances in word meanings.

  a. Interpret figures of speech (e.g., hyperbole, paradox) in context and analyze their role in the text.
  b. Analyze nuances in the meaning of words with similar denotations.

Development of the skills articulated in these ELA Standards is the primary focus of this unit. Nonetheless, other skills and even other content will undoubtedly be addressed in the unit, because that is the nature of a lesson or unit created using the balanced literacy framework.

Overview of Day-to-Day Lessons

Day 1

Prior to this class, each student will have selected five images of beauty. Students will bring their images to class and be prepared to review them in this unit-opening discussion.

In small groups, students take turns explaining their images and identifying how beauty is represented in each one. The students develop criteria for characterizing beauty by discussing the unit's essential question: *If beauty is in the eye of the beholder, can there be a standard of universal beauty?* The students' criteria will be applied to the texts and images explored throughout the unit.

Day 2

Using the criteria developed in the previous class, the students evaluate the following works of literature and art:

- "Ode on a Grecian Urn," by John Keats (1819/1999)
- Selected paintings by Georgia O'Keefe (George O'Keefe Museum, 2011)

Day 3

Students apply what they have discovered about *beauty* thus far in revising the criteria they developed on the first day. Students also continue to explore beauty in various poems, artworks, and songs.

Day 4

In their Literature Circles, students select one of the following plays or novels to read and discuss:

- *Romeo and Juliet*, by William Shakespeare (1594–1595/2000)
- *The Bluest Eye*, by Toni Morrison (1970)
- *A Beautiful Mind*, by Sylvia Nasar (1998)

Days 5–8

Students continue to meet in their Literature Circles to explore their plays and novels by focusing on the unit's essential question: *If beauty is in the eye of the beholder, can there be a standard of universal beauty?*

Day 9

In today's final meeting of the Literature Circles, each group develops an argument in support of one of the following positions:

- Beauty is in the eye of the beholder, so there cannot be a universal standard of beauty.
- Beauty is not in the eye of the beholder, so there can be a universal standard of beauty.

Each Literature Circle presents its argument to the class and is prepared to engage in a large-group discussion. Support for the argument should include specific examples from the play or novel read and discussed in the Literature Circle.

● *Day 10*

As a culminating activity, students once again revise the criteria for beauty that they created at the beginning of the unit, applying what they have learned. Each student also develops a written response, providing evidence and reasoning to support his or her criteria for beauty.

REFERENCES

Appleman, D. (2010). *Adolescent literacy and the teaching of reading: Lessons for teachers of literature.* Urbana, IL: National Council of Teachers of English.

Beers, K. G. (2003). *When kids can't read, what teachers can do: A guide for teachers, 6–12.* Portsmouth, NH: Heinemann.

Fountas, I., & Pinnell, G. S. (2008). *Guiding readers and writers: Teaching comprehension, genre, and content literacy.* Portsmouth, NH: Heinemann.

Gardner, H. (2011). *Frames of mind: The theory of multiple intelligences* (3rd ed.). New York, NY: Basic Books.

Landauer, T. K., & Dumais, S. T. (1997). A solution to Plato's problem: The latent semantic analysis theory of acquisition, induction, and representation of knowledge. *Psychological Review, 104,* 211–240.

Landauer, T. K., McNamara, D. S., Dennis, S., & Kintsch, W. (Eds.) (2007). *Handbook of latent semantic analysis.* London, England: Psychology Press.

Maxwell, R. S., Meiser, M., & McKnight, K. S. (2011). *Teaching English in middle and secondary schools* (5th ed.). Boston, MA: Allyn & Bacon.

Nagy, W. E., Herman, P., & Anderson, R. C. (1985). Learning words from context. *Reading Research Quarterly, 20,* 233–253.

National Governors Association Center for Best Practices & Council of Chief State School Officers (NGA & CCSSO). (2010a). *Common Core State Standards: English language arts and literacy in history/social studies, science, and technical subjects.* Washington, DC: Authors. Retrieved from www.corestandards.org/assets/CCSSI_ELA%20Standards.pdf.

National Governors Association Center for Best Practices & Council of Chief State School Officers (NGA & CCSSO). (2010b). Appendix A: Research supporting key elements of the standards and glossary of key terms. *Common Core State Standards.* Washington, DC: Authors. Retrieved from http://www.corestandards.org/assets/Appendix_A.pdf.

Silver, H., Strong, R., & Perini, M. (1997). Integrating learning styles and multiple intelligences. *Educational Leadership 55*(1), 22–27. Available online at www.ascd.org/publications/educational-leadership/sept97/vol55/num01/Integrating-Learning-Styles-and-Multiple-Intelligences.aspx.

LITERATURE CITED

Byrd, W. 1972. *The Secret Diary of William Byrd of Westover, 1709–1712.* New York, NY: Arno Press. (Original work published 1941)

Georgia O'Keefe Museum. (2011). Collections online. *OKeefeMuseum.org.* Available online at http://contentdm.okeeffemuseum.org.

Keats, J. (1999). "Ode on a Grecian Urn." *Bartleby.com.* Available online at www.bartleby.com/101/625.html. (Original work published 1819)

Morrison, T. (1970). *The bluest eye.* New York, NY: Random House.

Nasar, S. (1998). *A beautiful mind.* New York, NY: Simon & Schuster.

Shakespeare, W. (2000). *Romeo and Juliet. Bartleby.com.* Available online at http://www.bartleby.com/70/index38.html. (Original work published 1594–1595)

Tan, A. 1989. *The Joy Luck Club.* New York, NY: G. P. Putnam's Sons.

Witherspoon, G. (1977). Beautifying the world through art. Chapter 4 in, *Language and Art in the Navajo Universe.* Ann Arbor, MI: University of Michigan Press.

Reading Comprehension

I TRAVEL ALL ACROSS THE UNITED STATES, LEADING staff development programs, speaking about adolescent literacy, and teaching reading and writing strategies for grades 9–12. And everywhere I go, I hear similar stories from high school English teachers. Many teachers report that almost half of their students read below grade level—in some cases, several grades below grade level. Other teachers report that their students can decode texts effectively and understand letters and corresponding sounds but cannot go beyond the simple recall of information. Still other teachers report that many of their students are simply not interested in reading by the time they have reached high school.

For students to be prepared for adult life in the twenty-first century, they must have strong reading comprehension skills. In fact, as teachers, our single greatest opportunity to prepare students for college and career is to help them develop these skills. The Common Core State Standards (CCSS) provide a context for introducing students to a wide variety of texts while building important comprehension skills for career and college readiness.

Christian Schwier/Fotolia

Exploring the Reading Standards

AS NOTED IN CHAPTER 2, FOR HIGH SCHOOL, THE CCSS English Language Arts (ELA) Standards are divided into two grade-level bands: grades 9–10 and grades 11–12. Within the ELA Standards, the Reading standards set expectations for two types of texts: Literature and Informational Text. The Literature standards address the reading of stories, dramas, and poems, and the Informational Text standards address the reading of literary nonfiction (which includes historical, scientific, and technical texts written for a broad audience). Organizing the Reading standards according to these two types of texts makes the CCCS quite different from the standards previously developed and adopted by most states.

The Reading Standards for Literature and for Informational Text are both aligned with the Common Core Readiness (CCR) Anchor Standards for Reading. The same 10 Anchor Standards apply to reading both literature and informational text (see Table 3.1). In fact, the

TABLE 3.1 ● *Common Core Readiness (CCR) Anchor Standards for Reading, Grades 9–12**

Key Ideas and Details

1. Read closely to determine what the text says explicitly and to make logical inferences from it; cite specific textual evidence when writing or speaking to support conclusions drawn from the text.

2. Determine central ideas or themes of a text and analyze their development; summarize the key supporting details and ideas.

3. Analyze how and why individuals, events, and ideas develop and interact over the course of a text.

Craft and Structure

4. Interpret words and phrases as they are used in a text, including determining technical, connotative, and figurative meanings, and analyze how specific word choices shape meaning or tone.

5. Analyze the structure of texts, including how specific sentences, paragraphs, and larger portions of the text (e.g., a section, chapter, scene, or stanza) relate to each other and the whole.

6. Assess how point of view or purpose shapes the content and style of a text.

Integration of Knowledge and Ideas

7. Integrate and evaluate content presented in diverse formats and media, including visually and quantitatively, as well as in words.

8. Delineate and evaluate the argument and specific claims in a text, including the validity of the reasoning as well as the relevance and sufficiency of the evidence.

9. Analyze how two or more texts address similar themes or topics in order to build knowledge or to compare the approaches the authors take.

Range of Reading and Level of Text Complexity

10. Read and comprehend complex literary and informational texts independently and proficiently.

---

*These Anchor Standards apply to grades 6–12.
Source: NGA & CCSSO (2010).

same Anchor Standards underlie the Reading standards for all grade levels, beginning in kindergarten. Clearly, the developers of the CCSS believe that these enduring skills are at the heart of what makes students effective readers. Moreover, they believe that these skills are relevant regardless of the age of the student or the nature of the text he or she is reading.

The categories and numbers of the CCR Anchor Standards for Reading correspond with the categories and numbers of the Reading Standards for Literature and for Informational Text (see Tables 3.2 and 3.3 respectively). The developers of the CCSS describe the two levels of standards

TABLE 3.2 ● *Reading Standards for Literature: Grades 9–12*

Grades 9–10 students:	Grades 11–12 students:
Key Ideas and Details	
1. Cite strong and thorough textual evidence to support analysis of what the text says explicitly as well as inferences drawn from the text.	1. Cite strong and thorough textual evidence to support analysis of what the text says explicitly as well as inferences drawn from the text, including determining where the text leaves matters uncertain.
2. Determine a theme or central idea of a text and analyze in detail its development over the course of the text, including how it emerges and is shaped and refined by specific details; provide an objective summary of the text.	2. Determine two or more themes or central ideas of a text and analyze their development over the course of the text, including how they interact and build on one another to produce a complex account; provide an objective summary of the text.
3. Analyze how complex characters (e.g., those with multiple or conflicting motivations) develop over the course of a text, interact with other characters, and advance the plot or develop the theme.	3. Analyze the impact of the author's choices regarding how to develop and relate elements of a story or drama (e.g., where a story is set, how the action is ordered, how the characters are introduced and developed).
Craft and Structure	
4. Determine the meaning of words and phrases as they are used in the text, including figurative and connotative meanings; analyze the cumulative impact of specific word choices on meaning and tone (e.g., how the language evokes a sense of time and place; how it sets a formal or informal tone).	4. Determine the meaning of words and phrases as they are used in the text, including figurative and connotative meanings; analyze the impact of specific word choices on meaning and tone, including words with multiple meanings or language that is particularly fresh, engaging, or beautiful. (Include Shakespeare as well as other authors.)
5. Analyze how an author's choices concerning how to structure a text, order events within it (e.g., parallel plots), and manipulate time (e.g., pacing, flashbacks) create such effects as mystery, tension, or surprise.	5. Analyze how an author's choices concerning how to structure specific parts of a text (e.g., the choice of where to begin or end a story, the choice to provide a comedic or tragic resolution) contribute to its overall structure and meaning as well as its aesthetic impact.
6. Analyze a particular point of view or cultural experience reflected in a work of literature from outside the United States, drawing on a wide reading of world literature.	6. Analyze a case in which grasping point of view requires distinguishing what is directly stated in a text from what is really meant (e.g., satire, sarcasm, irony, or understatement).

(continued)

TABLE 3.2 ● *(continued)*

Grades 9–10 students:	Grades 11–12 students:
Integration of Knowledge and Ideas	
7. Analyze the representation of a subject or a key scene in two different artistic mediums, including what is emphasized or absent in each treatment (e.g., Auden's "Musée des Beaux Arts" and Breughel's *Landscape with the Fall of Icarus*).	7. Analyze multiple interpretations of a story, drama, or poem (e.g., recorded or live production of a play or recorded novel or poetry), evaluating how each version interprets the source text. (Include at least one play by Shakespeare and one play by an American dramatist.)
8. (Not applicable to literature)	8. (Not applicable to literature)
9. Analyze how an author draws on and transforms source material in a specific work (e.g., how Shakespeare treats a theme or topic from Ovid or the Bible or how a later author draws on a play by Shakespeare).	9. Demonstrate knowledge of eighteenth-, nineteenth- and early-twentieth-century foundational works of American literature, including how two or more texts from the same period treat similar themes or topics.
Range of Reading and Level of Text Complexity	
10. By the end of grade 9, read and comprehend literature, including stories, dramas, and poems, in the grades 9–10 text complexity band proficiently, with scaffolding as needed at the high end of the range.	10. By the end of grade 11, read and comprehend literature, including stories, dramas, and poems, in the grades 11-CCR text complexity band proficiently, with scaffolding as needed at the high end of the range.
By the end of grade 10, read and comprehend literature, including stories, dramas, and poems, at the high end of the grades 9–10 text complexity band independently and proficiently.	By the end of grade 12, read and comprehend literature, including stories, dramas, and poems, at the high end of the grades 11-CCR text complexity band independently and proficiently.

Source: NGA & CCSSO (2010).

TABLE 3.3 ● *Reading Standards for Informational Text: Grades 9–12*

Grades 9–10 students:	Grades 11–12 students:
Key Ideas and Details	
1. Cite strong and thorough textual evidence to support analysis of what the text says explicitly as well as inferences drawn from the text.	1. Cite strong and thorough textual evidence to support analysis of what the text says explicitly as well as inferences drawn from the text, including determining where the text leaves matters uncertain.
2. Determine a theme or central idea of a text and analyze in detail its development over the course of the text, including how it emerges and is shaped and refined by specific details; provide an objective summary of the text.	2. Determine two or more central ideas of a text and analyze their development over the course of the text, including how they interact and build on one another to produce a complex account; provide an objective summary of the text.
3. Analyze how the author unfolds an analysis or series of ideas or events, including the order in which the points are made, how they are introduced and developed, and the connections that are drawn between them.	3. Analyze a complex set of ideas or sequence of events and explain how specific individuals, ideas, or events interact and develop over the course of the text.

(continued)

TABLE 3.3 • *(continued)*

Grades 9–10 students:	Grades 11–12 students:

Craft and Structure

4. Determine the meaning of words and phrases as they are used in the text, including figurative, connotative, and technical meanings; analyze the cumulative impact of specific word choices on meaning and tone (e.g., how the language of a court opinion differs from that of a newspaper.

5. Analyze in detail how an author's ideas or claims are developed and refined by particular sentences, paragraphs, or larger portions of a text (e.g., a section or chapter).

6. Determine an author's point of view or purpose in a text and analyze how an author uses rhetoric to advance that point of view or purpose.

4. Determine the meaning of words and phrases as they are used in the text, including figurative, connotative, and technical meanings; analyze how an author uses and refines the meaning of a key term or terms over the course of a text (e.g., how Madison defines *faction* in *Federalist* No. 10).

5. Analyze and evaluate the effectiveness of the structure an author uses in his or her exposition or argument, including whether the structure makes points clear, convincing, and engaging.

6. Determine an author's point of view or purpose in a text in which the rhetoric is particularly effective, analyzing how style and content contribute to the power, persuasiveness, or beauty of the text.

Integration of Knowledge and Ideas

7. Analyze various accounts of a subject told in different mediums (e.g., a person's life story in both print and multimedia), determining which details are emphasized in each account.

8. Delineate and evaluate the argument and specific claims in a text, assessing whether the reasoning is valid and the evidence is relevant and sufficient; identify false statements and fallacious reasoning.

9. Analyze seminal U.S. documents of historical and literary significance (e.g., Washington's Farewell Address, the Gettysburg Address, Roosevelt's Four Freedoms speech, King's "Letter from Birmingham Jail"), including how they address related themes and concepts.

7. Integrate and evaluate multiple sources of information presented in different media or formats (e.g., visually, quantitatively) as well as in words in order to address a question or solve a problem.

8. Delineate and evaluate the argument and specific claims in a text, assessing whether the reasoning is valid and the evidence is relevant and sufficient; identify false statements and fallacious reasoning.

9. Analyze seventeenth-, eighteenth-, and nineteenth-century foundational U.S. documents of historical and literary significance (including The Declaration of Independence, the Preamble to the Constitution, the Bill of Rights, and Lincoln's Second Inaugural Address) for their themes, purposes, and rhetorical features.

Range of Reading and Level of Text Complexity

10. By the end of grade 9, read and comprehend literary nonfiction in the grades 9–10 text complexity band proficiently, with scaffolding as needed at the high end of the range.

    By the end of grade 10, read and comprehend literary nonfiction at the high end of the grades 9–10 text complexity band independently and proficiently.

10. By the end of grade 11, read and comprehend literary nonfiction in the grades 11-CCR text complexity band proficiently, with scaffolding as needed at the high end of the range.

    By the end of grade 12, read and comprehend literary nonfiction at the high end of the grades 11-CCR text complexity band independently and proficiently.

Source: NGA & CCSSO (2010).

as "necessary complements—the former providing broad standards, the latter providing additional specificity—that together define the skills and understandings that all students must demonstrate" (NGA & CCSSO, 2010a, p. 35). Also, by applying the same broad standards to two basic types of texts, the developers created a unifying structure with the Reading standards. The CCSS place an equal emphasis on reading literature and reading informational text.

In both the CCR Anchor Standards and the ELA Reading Standards, Standards 1–9 embody the knowledge and skills necessary to achieve Standard 10. Standard 10 is the sole standard in the cluster Range of Reading and Level of Text Complexity and represents the culmination of knowledge and skill development. As described by the developers of the CCSS, "Standard 10 defines a grade-by-grade 'staircase' of increasing text complexity that rises from beginning reading to the college and career readiness level" (NGA & CCSSO, 2010a, p. 8). Students' ability to read texts of various types and difficulties is a particular focus of the CCSS for Reading. Being able to comprehend increasingly challenging texts becomes even more critical in high school, as students prepare for college or career. (The issue of text complexity is explored in more detail in Chapter 4.)

Reading Comprehension and the CCSS

The Focus on Comprehension Skills

Reading consists of four components: alphabetics (also known as *phonemic awareness* or *phonics*), fluency, comprehension, and vocabulary. Of these components, comprehension warrants the greatest amount of attention at the high school level. In fact, many of the reading challenges frequently encountered among high school students are related to comprehension. Common difficulties are as follows:

- difficulty monitoring understanding while reading
- difficulty making sense of new or unfamiliar content
- difficulty making sense of content-specific language and terminology (i.e., academic language)
- difficulty making sense of familiar words being used with different meanings

The CCSS for Reading address these and other concerns related to high school students' lack of comprehension skills—specifically, the fact that many high school students can decode a text but cannot derive its meaning. High school readers need support to develop their comprehension skills and exercise their ability to glean important information and make complex interpretations through close reading. In addition, high school readers need access to texts that are diverse in terms of rigor and subject matter. In many cases, high school students' disinterest in reading has resulted from being expected to read texts that are too difficult for them or about topics that are of no interest to them.

As high school teachers, we need to focus on developing students' reading comprehension skills by teaching them strategies to derive meaning from a text. Instruction should address the specific skills that underlie comprehension, such as previewing the text, activating prior knowledge, understanding text structures, and performing after-reading or metacognitive tasks. We also need to recognize, however, that a one-size-fits-all approach to instruction will not be effective, given the tremendous differences in reading ability among the students in a typical classroom.

The Focus on Informational Text

Being adept readers of informational texts, along with related literacy skills, is particularly important for individuals entering college and career during the twenty-first century. A vast amount of information is available during this so-called Information Age, and processing it requires good reading and critical-thinking skills.

Darling-Hammond et al. (2008) have pointed out that the quantity of new information produced in the period 1997–2002 was equal to that produced over the entire history of humankind up to that point. Perhaps even more importantly, this abundance of information has affected society in unexpected ways. Changes in the employment landscape have been particularly dramatic. In the early 1980s, 95% of all U.S. jobs were in manufacturing, compared to only 10% today. In years past, most jobs involved the repetition of simple physical tasks, but today, jobs require high-level thinking. Workers are expected to process large amounts of information quickly and routinely—usually, by reading text. And based on that information, they are expected to analyze situations and promptly adapt their response strategies.

Educators must recognize this cultural shift and adjust both their expectations and their approach to instruction. For high school students to compete successfully as adults, they must be able to comprehend complex informational texts.

This mandate does not apply solely to English language arts teachers. The developers of the CCSS are quite clear in stating that the responsibility for building students' comprehension and other literacy skills is shared by teachers in the content areas. Content area teachers are expected to use a wide variety of texts (including literature) to help students acquire content knowledge. Reading in content area classes is also necessary for students to meet the rigorous expectations of the CCSS. Students cannot develop reading skills exclusively through their work in English language arts classes; they must read in their content area classes, as well.

The developers of the CCSS state that this interdisciplinary approach to literacy instruction is motivated in part by "extensive research establishing the need for college and career ready students to be proficient in reading complex informational text independently in a variety of content areas" (NGA & CCSSO, 2010a, p. 4). The developers also note that the reading framework for the 2009 National Assessment of Educational Progress (NAEP) requires an increasingly greater use of informational text in assessing students across the grades (National Assessment Governing Board, 2009).

This greater focus on informational texts in the CCSS does not mean that English language arts teachers are no longer expected to teach literature. (This is one of the greatest misconceptions about the CCSS!) On the contrary, it means that language arts teachers cannot be alone in teaching literature.

The CCSS Versus Other Reading Standards and Theories

No Child Left Behind   The No Child Left Behind (NCLB) Act of 2001 and NCLB-influenced reading standards relied heavily on the recommendations of the National Reading Panel (NRP) (Calkins, Ehrenworth, & Lehman, 2012). Those recommendations were based on a model of reading that includes five equally important components: phonemic awareness, phonics, fluency, vocabulary, and comprehension (NRP, 2000).

Granting these five components equal importance is where the NCLB-related standards went wrong. In fact, not all five components are taught throughout students' educational careers. The first two components—phonemic awareness and phonetics—are covered mainly during the early elementary years and rarely revisited during high school. By that time, most students have proficient decoding skills and are able to "sound out" unfamiliar words. They may struggle, however, to incorporate new words into their working vocabularies. In addition, many high school students lack reading comprehension skills (Beers, 2002).

The NRP recommendations and the resulting structure of NCLB streamlined the teaching and learning of phonemic awareness, phonetics, fluency, vocabulary, and comprehension. NCLB-based instruction was characterized by timed readings and multiple-choice tests and required little demonstration of high-level comprehension. This approach to reading instruction sharply contrasts the balanced literacy approach advocated by the CCSS, in which readers are encouraged to experience a wide variety of texts and to integrate literary knowledge.

Indeed, comprehension is the cornerstone of the CCSS Reading standards. The very architecture of the CCSS requires students to read not only literature but also historical documents, technology-based texts, and other materials to hone their comprehension skills. Beyond that, students are encouraged to make claims about what they have read through both writing and speaking. And in addition to working independently, students work in small groups, where they learn to challenge each other's assumptions and conclusions. The expectations outlined in the CCSS represent a bold paradigm shift from the recommendations of the NRP and NCLB.

Reader-Response Theory   In the CCSS, close reading and textual analysis is considered the primary means of developing high-level comprehension and interpretive skills. Some educators view the focus on close reading as a rejection of the highly regarded reader-response theory.

Reader-response theory suggests that while meaning resides in the text, the interaction of the reader and the text is what actually creates that meaning. This theory, founded by Louise Rosenblatt (1938/1995, 1978/1994), grew out of the mid-twentieth-century debate over the New Criticism movement, which encouraged readers to glean all meaning from the text itself, without regard for external filters such as race/ethnicity, gender, socioeconomic status, political beliefs, and the like.

Even though the CCSS emphasize close reading and textual analysis—an approach commonly associated with the New Criticism movement—it does not completely exclude the concept at the heart of reader-response theory. The importance of the reader's schema (i.e., background knowledge and experiences) on his or her comprehension of a specific text has been well documented by reading theorists (Appleman, 2010; Bransford, 2010; Smith, 1971). The reader's existing body of knowledge and experience create a cognitive framework through which he or she organizes thought and interprets information.

The CCSS, then, accept elements of both New Criticism and reader-response theory. Namely, close reading–textual analysis and reader schema must work together to develop high-level comprehension skills.

Reading Comprehension in the CCSS Curriculum and Classroom

TO IMPROVE HIGH SCHOOL STUDENTS' READING COMPREHENSION, WE must create a curriculum that addresses three realities:

1. In terms of complexity, there is a significant gap between the texts typically assigned to students in grades 11 and 12 and those encountered in college and career (NGA & CCSSO, 2010b, pp. 2–3). If high school students are not provided with more complex texts, many of them will be prevented from achieving their full potential in the workplace.

2. High school classes are composed of diverse readers who perform at varied grade levels. Some of them read above grade level, but far more of them read below grade level.

3. The more adolescents read, the more proficient they become at developing comprehension skills and fulfilling the expectations of the CCR Anchor Standards for Reading.

Our goal, therefore, is to provide all students with a wide variety of texts that will challenge them but not overwhelm them.

To achieve this goal, we cannot use as the sole source of reading material excerpts from abbreviated texts, such as those often found in literature anthologies. In large part, anthologies fall short because they are generally written and selected to target specific grade levels; given this, they are inappropriate for students who read above or below grade level.

Selecting Appropriate Texts

To provide the appropriate levels of text complexity for our classrooms of diverse readers, we must use multiple texts. Moreover, those texts must include both literature and informational text. Table 3.4 describes these two types of texts, using definitions from the CCSS, and provides examples of both types of texts, as well.

TABLE 3.4 ● *Types of Texts, as Defined by the CCSS*

	Literature	**Informational Text (Literary Nonfiction)**
Definition	Includes the subgenres of adventure stories, historical fiction, mysteries, myths, science fiction, realistic fiction, allegories, parodies, satire, and graphic novels Includes one-act and multi-act plays, both in written form and on film Includes the subgenres of narrative poems, lyrical poems, free verse poems, sonnets, odes, ballads, and epics (p. 57)	Includes the subgenres of exposition, argument, and functional text in the form of personal essays, speeches, opinion pieces, essays about art or literature, biographies, memoirs, journalism, and historical, scientific, technical, or economic accounts (including digital sources) written for a broad audience. (p. 57)
Examples	*Stories:* Homer. *The Odyssey* Gogol, Nikolai. "The Nose." Achebe, Chinua. *Things Fall Apart* Shaara, Michael. *The Killer Angels* Zusak, Marcus. *The Book Thief* *Plays:* Sophocles. *Oedipus Rex* Shakespeare, William. *The Tragedy of Macbeth* Ibsen, Henrik. *A Doll's House* Williams, Tennessee. *The Glass Menagerie* Ionesco, Eugene. *Rhinoceros* *Poems:* Donne, John. "Song." Poe, Edgar Allan. "The Raven.	Walker, Alice. "Women." Baca, Jimmy Santiago. "I Am Offering This Poem to You." Henry, Patrick. "Speech to the Second Virginia Convention." Lincoln, Abraham. "Gettysburg Address." Smith, Margaret Chase. "Remarks to the Senate in Support of a Declaration of Conscience." King, Jr., Martin Luther. "Letter from Birmingham Jail." Reagan, Ronald. "Address to Students at Moscow State University." Quindlen, Anna. "A Quilt of a Country."

Consider how a teacher might select texts while planning a unit on American Freedom Writers. Literary texts for this unit might include poems by Langston Hughes, such as "Dreams" (1926) and "I, Too, Sing America" (1926). Corresponding informational texts might include "Letter from Birmingham Jail," by Dr. Martin Luther King (1963), along with articles from newspapers reporting on King's arrest in Birmingham and the text of the Civil Rights Act of 1968. Providing students with this diverse set of texts will ensure they have access to a wide variety of materials at different ability levels.

In this kind of unit, students read literature and examine literary elements such as theme, point of view, and mood through the close reading of texts. They also read informational texts and examine the nature and structure of argumentative and expository texts. As students apply what they know about these different types of texts, they become more proficient readers—able to read and analyze many types of rigorous texts. This, in turn, builds students' comprehension skills and overall reading ability for college and career readiness.

Certainly, in choosing materials, we must also consider both the existing availability of books and the limitations of our schools' financial resources. Figure 3.1 lists teachers'

FIGURE 3.1 ● Examples of Available Texts for Consideration in Curriculum Planning

Literature

Pride and Prejudice, by Jane Austen
Fahrenheit 451, by Ray Bradbury
Jane Eyre, by Charlotte Brontë
Wuthering Heights, by Emily Brontë
The Good Earth, by Pearl S. Buck
Alice's Adventures in Wonderland, by Lewis Carroll
My Antonia, by Willa Cather
A House on Mango Street, by Sandra Cisneros
The Hunger Games trilogy, by Suzanne Collins
The Red Badge of Courage, by Stephen Crane
A Tale of Two Cities, by Charles Dickens
The Great Gatsby, by F. Scott Fitzgerald
Lord of the Flies, by William Golding
Princess Academy, by Shannon Hale
A Raisin in the Sun, by Lorraine Hansberry
The Scarlet Letter, by Nathaniel Hawthorne
One Flew Over the Cuckoo's Nest, by Ken Kesey
Ophelia, Lady Macbeth's Daughter, by Lisa M. Klein
To Kill a Mockingbird, by Harper Lee
The Giver, by Lois Lowry
The Life of Pi, by Yann Martel
The Host, by Stephanie Meyer

(continued)

FIGURE 3.1 ● (*continued*)

Twilight series, by Stephanie Meyer
Cry, the Beloved Country, by Alan Paton
The Wee Free Men, by Terry Pratchett
All Quiet on the Western Front, by Erich Marie Remarque
Frankenstein, by Mary Shelley
The Grapes of Wrath, by John Steinbeck
Of Mice and Men, by John Steinbeck
The Pearl, by John Steinbeck
Dracula, by Bram Stoker
Uncle Tom's Cabin by Harriet Beecher Stowe
Gulliver's Travels, by Jonathan Swift
The Joy Luck Club, by Amy Tan
The Hobbit, by J. R. R. Tolkien
Lord of the Rings trilogy, by J. R. R. Tolkien
The Adventures of Huckleberry Finn, by Mark Twain
Slaughterhouse Five, by Kurt Vonnegut Jr.
The Picture of Dorian Gray, by Oscar Wilde
Native Son, by Richard Wright

Informational Text

"Letter on Thomas Jefferson," by John Adams
I Know Why the Caged Bird Sings, by Maya Angelou
"Take the Tortillas Out of Your Poetry," by Rudolfo Anaya
In Cold Blood, by Truman Capote
"The Fallacy of Success," by G. K. Chesterton (1909)?
"Blood, Toil, Tears and Sweat: Address to Parliament on May 13th, 1940," by Winston Churchill
Narrative of the Life of Frederick Douglass, an American Slave, by Frederick Douglass
"Society and Solitude," by Ralph Waldo Emerson
Black Like Me, by John Howard Griffin
The Autobiography of Malcolm X, by Alex Haley
"Speech to the Second Virginia Convention," by Patrick Henry
Farewell to Manzanar, by Jeanne Wakatsuki Houston
The Story of My Life, by Helen Keller
"Letter from Birmingham Jail," by Martin Luther King Jr.
"Gettysburg Address," by Abraham Lincoln
Circle of Children, by Mary MacCracken
Lovey: A Very Special Child, by Mary MacCracken
Black Elk Speaks, by John C. Neihardt
"Politics and the English Language," by George Orwell

(*continued*)

FIGURE 3.1 ● *(continued)*

Common Sense, by Thomas Paine
Harriet Tubman: Conductor on the Underground Railroad, by Ann Petry
"State of the Union Address," by Franklin Delano Roosevelt
Travels with Charley: In Search of America, by John Steinbeck
Walden, by Henry David Thoreau
Up From Slavery, by Booker T. Washington
"Farewell Address," by George Washington
"Hope, Despair and Memory," by Elie Wiesel
Night, by Elie Wiesel
Black Boy, by Richard Wright

suggestions of books that may already be available and thus lend themselves to inclusion in curriculum planning. Note that this list is intended only as a starting point; teachers should explore other options, as well. For instance, many online resources provide booklists and other recommendations of texts to integrate into the curriculum (see Figure 3.2).

Asking Essential Questions

In many schools and districts, English language arts teachers develop instructional units as two- or three-week modules that are built on essential questions. These questions, described by Wiggins and McTighe (2005) aren't simple questions that can be answered with brief responses. Instead, the objective of essential questions is to provoke further inquiry. A well-crafted essential question triggers thoughtful student reflection instead of a simple answer. These "big questions" pique students' curiosity and motivate them to explore new information.

According to Wiggins and McTighe, essential questions usually have some or all of these qualities:

● They are timeless and thus relevant across the lifespan.
● They point to the core ideas and questions within a field.
● They help make sense of complicated ideas.
● They engage a diverse range of learners (pp. 108–109).

These authors also suggest that essential questions can be framed in two ways: (1) as *overarching questions,* which are useful for providing a focus to a course or program of study, and (2) as *topical questions,* which lead to understanding about a particular topic in a unit or lesson (p. 114).

The fundamental purpose of asking essential questions is to engage students in inquiry—to search for answers and insights using a wide variety of texts. This inquiry-type model is effective in meeting the CCSS because it **encourages the integration** of both literature and informational texts to explore deeper meanings. Moreover, this approach supports the development of reading comprehension skills.

In planning units, we should select and organize texts around essential questions. Doing so will make it easier to include a suitable range of texts that develop students' comprehension

FIGURE 3.2 ● Online Booklists and Other Resources for Selecting Texts

Popular Paperbacks for Young Adults (Young Adult Library Services Association/American Library Association)—Lists of popular and topical titles that are widely available and represent a range of accessible themes and genres.
www.ala.org/yalsa/popular-paperbacks-young-adults

Middle/High School Literature (Awesome Library)—Lists of books and authors of literature commonly studied in high school.
www.awesomelibrary.org/Classroom/English/Literature/Middle_High_School_Literature.html

Children's Literature (Millikin University)—Resources for finding children's and young adult literature.
http://millikin.libguides.com/childrens-literature

The Alan Review (Virginia Tech)—Discussion and lists of young adult literature for young adult males.
http://scholar.lib.vt.edu/ejournals/ALAN/winter99/gill.html

Booklists for Young Adults on the Web—Compiled from young adult–related webpages of librarians, teachers, and others working with young adults.
www.seemore.mi.org/booklists

Reading Suggestions (TeachersFirst)—Teacher- and editor-maintained website listing books that are being used in classrooms.
www.teachersfirst.com/read-sel.cfm

Booklists (VOYA Magazine)—A range of lists and reviews of young adult literature.
www.voyamagazine.com/topics/health

Booklists: Young Adult Fiction Index (Library Booklists)—Lists of books by genre and topic.
http://librarybooklists.org/fiction/ya/yaindex.htm

skills, motivate them to read more, and help them to meet the expectations of the CCSS. As stated by the developers of the CCSS:

> To become college and career ready, students must grapple with works of exceptional craft and thought whose range extends across genres, cultures, and centuries. Such works offer profound insights into the human condition and serve as models for students' own thinking and writing. Along with high-quality contemporary works, these texts should be chosen from among seminal U.S. documents, the classics of American literature, and the timeless dramas of Shakespeare. Through wide and deep reading of literature and literary nonfiction of steadily increasing sophistication, students gain a reservoir of literary and cultural knowledge, references, and images; the ability to evaluate intricate arguments; and the capacity to surmount the challenges posed by complex texts. (NGA & CCSSO, 2010a, p. 34)

Table 3.5 provides examples of essential questions along with corresponding works of literature and informational texts and online resources. In short, essential questions should form the backbone of effectively designed curriculum.

TABLE 3.5 ● *Examples of Essential Questions and Corresponding Texts and Technology Resources*

Essential Question(s)	Literature	Informational Texts	Technology Resources
What creates friendship? What does friendship mean?	*To Kill a Mockingbird,* by Harper Lee* *The Outsiders,* by S. E. Hinton *Of Mice and Men,* by John Steinbeck *Tomo: Friendship through Fiction, An Anthology of Japan Teen Stories,* ed. by Holly Thompson	*Chicken Soup for the Teenage Soul on Love and Friendship,* by Jack Canfield, Mark Victor Hansen and Kimberly Kirberger "Citizen Kate," by Allison Pearson, (*Newsweek Magazine Online,* April 3, 2011)	StoryStar: www.storystar .com
How do stories make us human?	"The Gift of the Magi," by O. Henry* "The Scarlet Ibis," by James Hurst "Everyday Use," by Alice Walker "The Tell-Tale Heart," by Edgar Allan Poe	"Letter from Birmingham Jail," by Martin Luther King Jr.* *The Absolutely True Diary of a Part-Time Indian,* by Sherman Alexie* *Claudette Cloven: Twice Toward Justice,* by Phillip M. Hoose*	National Storytelling Network: www.storynet .org International Storytelling Center: www .storytellingcenter.net
How are paths to freedom influenced by society?	*Things Fall Apart,* by Chinua Achebe *Night,* by Elie Wiesel *The House on Mango Street,* by Sandra Cisneros	*There Are No Children Here,* by Alex Kotlowitz *Motorcycle Diaries: Notes on a Latin American Journey,* by Ernesto Che Guevara	Teaching Tolerance: www .tolerance.org
Is the "American dream" a myth or reality?	*The Great Gatsby,* by F. Scott Fitzgerald "A Summer Tragedy," by Arna Bontemps "I Hear America Singing," by Walt Whitman *A Raisin in the Sun,* by Lorraine Hansberry* *Fences,* by August Wilson "Dreams," by Langston Hughes "Legal Alien," by Pat Mora	"Letters to John Adams," by Abigail Adams "Speech in the Virginia Convention," by Patrick Henry* "What Is an American?" by Hector St. Jean de Crevecoeur "The Declaration of Independence" "Rethinking the American Dream," by David Kamp (*Vanity Fair,* April 2009)	Ellis Island: www .ellisisland.org Civil Rights in the U.S.: www .civilrights.org

(continued)

TABLE 3.5 • *(continued)*

Essential Question(s)	Literature	Informational Texts	Technology Resources
Why do people explore and leave their homelands?	"On Being Brought from Africa to America," by Phillis Wheatley* *The Odyssey,* by Homer *The Last Summer of the Death Warriors,* by Francisco Stork	"The Selling of Joseph: A Memorial," by Samuel Sewall *A Narrative of the Captivity and Restoration of Mrs. Mary Rowlandson,* by Mary Rowlandson	National Humanities Center: www .nationalhumanitiescenter .org/pds/amerbegin/ exploration/exploration .htm
How is individual identity created?	*The Astonishing Life of Octavian Nothing,* by M. T. Anderson *Marcelo in the Real World,* by Francisco Stork *How I Made It to Eighteen,* by Tracy White	*The Autobiography of Benjamin Franklin* *Janis Joplin: Rise Up Singing,* by Ann Angel *John Lennon: All I Want Is the Truth,* by Elizabeth Partridge	What Color Is Your Parachute? http://parachute .capella.edu
How is seventeenth-century English literature a reflection of the people and events of that time?	*The Merchant of Venice,* by William Shakespeare* *The Pilgrim's Progress,* by John Bunyan "Holy Sonnet 10," by John Donne*	"An Essay Concerning Human Understanding," by John Locke	Shakespeare's Globe Theatre: www .shakespearesglobe.com Poetry resources for teens: www.poets.org Seventeenth-century recipes: www.godecookery.com

*CCSS Exemplar Text

Guiding Principles

As we consider what classroom instruction looks like under the CCSS, we should keep in mind the following principles:

- The more students read, the greater their reading proficiency.
- Allowing students to have some choices in reading materials has several benefits. It allows for differentiating instruction and meeting the needs of different levels of readers, and it increases students' motivation. If we want students to read more, we must provide them with materials that they find engaging.
- Students should have access to a range of texts that are complex and rigorous. Being able to process increasingly difficult texts is necessary for success beyond high school, whether in college or career.
- Reading should be arranged around essential questions, not specific authors or novels. Exploring essential questions and complex ideas provides a context for meaningful

exploration. It also has the added benefit of motivating students to read and to ponder what it means to be human.

● A curriculum that builds comprehension skills should include strategies that promote active reading. Mastering these strategies will encourage students to read and help them to comprehend with greater independence. Being able to use these strategies will support students throughout their academic experiences and careers.

Strategies for Developing Reading Comprehension

HIGH SCHOOL TEACHERS HAVE DESIGNED MANY STRATEGIES AND techniques to foster the development of students' comprehension skills. When students learn these strategies and are given opportunities to apply them while reading a wide variety of texts, reading proficiency improves dramatically. Research supports the teaching of these, because they have been proven effective in helping students to make real achievements in comprehension skills for reading both inside and outside school (Beach, 2010; Langer 2011; NRP, 2000).

Reading strategies are generally categorized according to when they are used: before reading, during reading, and after reading. For all kinds of reading comprehension strategies, however, the goal is for students to develop a "toolbox" for support in reading complex texts throughout high school and beyond.

Before-Reading Strategies

Before-reading (or prereading) strategies are frequently taught in elementary English language arts classrooms, but high school teachers sometimes overlook their value. Considering the large number of high school students who read below grade level, we should find value in any reading strategy that will help transition students from reluctant, struggling readers to proficient, independent readers.

Before-reading strategies are useful when students are trying to comprehend either literature or informational text. These strategies are especially effective in supporting struggling readers as they "unpack" particularly challenging texts. Designed to draw out students' prior knowledge (or schema), prereading activities can help individuals to make personal connections with the text. Also, previewing new information allows students to predict what the text is about, further supporting their comprehension.

Anticipation Guides   When good readers pick up a text, they tend to anticipate what it will be about. This is not true, however, of struggling readers. Providing students with an Anticipation Guide can help them develop this skill.

An Anticipation Guide previews the key themes and ideas that will be presented in an upcoming text. It provides students with an opportunity to draw on their prior knowledge and experiences and to recognize how their personal points of view influence the opinions they form about the text. Figure 3.3 shows a sample Anticipation Guide for the short story "Everyday Use," by Alice Walker (1973).

To create an Anticipation Guide, write a series of statements (10 is usually manageable) that relate to the text students are about to read. The statements should be about the themes, beliefs, conflicts, and other ideas that will be presented in the text (not the facts of the text). For each statement, provide a checkbox or other means for students to agree or disagree with the

FIGURE 3.3 ● Sample Anticipation Guide for Short Story

ANTICIPATION GUIDE
"Everyday Use," by Alice Walker

Directions: Put an X in the appropriate column to indicate whether you agree or disagree with each statement.

Agree	Disagree	Statement
_____	_____	1. It is important to remember where you have come from.
_____	_____	2. Family heirlooms are important to everyone.
_____	_____	3. You can't judge a book by its cover.
_____	_____	4. Your upbringing will determine your values.
_____	_____	5. Every person in a family has the same values.
_____	_____	6. Things are more important than relationships.
_____	_____	7. People can change.

statement. Responding to these statements triggers students to anticipate what the text is about and gets them thinking about its key ideas.

ABC Brainstorm   The ABC Brainstorm strategy helps students to organize their thoughts about a topic or text prior to reading and studying the new information. The student scans the text, looking for words or terms that begin with A, B, C, etc. The student records those words in alphabetical order. Then they go back and actually read the same text. While they read, they attempt to uncover the meaning of their list of ABC words. The list of words, created before actual reading, serves as a guide for exploration and actually helps the student focus on discovering the meaning of the full text.

During-Reading Strategies

During-reading strategies help students to become more active and engaged readers. Because many students struggle to engage with the text, we need to teach strategies that prompt them to make connections, monitor their understanding, and keep focused on the text.

Most during-reading strategies provide a structure for students to create meaning as they read, with the intention of making these behaviors become more natural and automatic. Some during-reading strategies also involve visualization techniques. Teaching students to visualize what they are thinking about is one of the most effective ways to support their comprehension (Boardman et al., 2008).

Story Trails   Story Trails offers a structure for students to use in arranging information in sequential order—perhaps the events from a story, stages of a historical event, or steps in a scientific or mathematical process. Visualizing and then representing the key events, stages, or steps facilitates greater exploration of the newly learned content.

When introducing Story Trails, brainstorm with students in a large-group discussion about the key events, stages, or steps. As students recall the information, arrange it in sequential order. Then have students reexamine the information to identify specific details that can be illustrated.

Graphic Organizers   Learning theory suggests that the human mind naturally organizes and records information, creating structures to store newly acquired information and connect it to previous knowledge (Piaget, 1923/2001). Graphic organizers serve as physical representations of these mental storage systems and thereby support students in remembering and connecting information (Vygotsky, 1962/1986). When students can remember and assimilate information by using a graphic organizer, they can delve into more critical thinking and greater comprehension (McKnight, 2010).

After-Reading Strategies

After-reading (or postreading) strategies direct students to think reflectively about what they have read, and as they consider particular elements of the text, they explore deeper levels of meaning. After-reading strategies prompt students to do the following:

- to extend the meaning of the text by going beyond the literal meaning and considering inferences and metaphorical meanings
- to question what they do not understand about the text
- to make a personal connection to the text
- to have additional opportunities to visualize the text
- to perform close reading and analysis of the text
- to summarize information and use the summary in discussing and writing about the text
- to develop final conclusions about the text, including the theme, author's message, and inferential meanings

Summary Organizers   Summarizing information leads students to greater understanding of it. When students summarize the ideas and information from a text, they demonstrate how well they understand the content. Also, when students can summarize what they have learned, they are better positioned to reflect on it and relate it to their own knowledge and beliefs. Students begin to explore what this newly learned information means and connect it what they may already know. Figure 3.4 is an example of a summary organizer that asks students to identify the main ideas and supporting details.

Literature Circles   Literature Circles, which are essentially book clubs or reading clubs, engage students in genuine and authentic reading experiences (Daniels & Steineke, 2004). Participating in Literature Circles is a common activity in middle school classrooms and should be a regular activity in high school classrooms, as well.

The following list identifies the basic elements of Literature Circles. Note how closely these elements align with the CCSS Anchor Standards for Reading (see standard numbers in parentheses:

- Different groups of students choose and read different books. (10)
- Members write down notes to help guide their reading and discussion. (1, 10)

FIGURE 3.4 ● Sample Summary Organizer

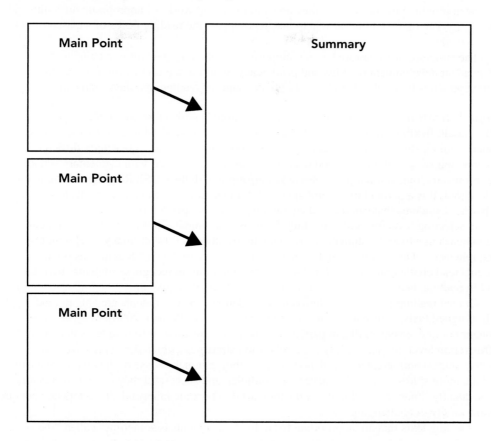

- The teacher does not lead discussion of any book; rather, he or she serves as a facilitator, fellow reader, and observer.
- Personal responses, connections, and questions provide the starting points for discussions. (2, 3, 10)
- When groups complete their books, the students present final projects that celebrate what they have read and discovered. (5, 6)
- Assessment involves teacher observations, student self-evaluations, and both formative and summative (usually the final project) activities/assessments. (2, 3, 4, 5, 6—depending on assessment focus)
- Groups meet for two or three weeks, not longer.
- Teacher-led mini-lessons cover a wide range of topics that support students' group work, such as literary analysis, reading strategies, and social strategies. Mini-lessons also support students' development of skills for reading and analyzing texts. (3, 4, 5, 6, 7, 8, 9—depending on focus and objective of mini-lesson)

Working in Literature Circles gives students the opportunity to experience a wide variety of texts that align with the expectations of the CCSS. Because students choose from texts that have been provided by the teacher, they are certain to read works of appropriate difficulty and complexity. Literature Circles also help teachers support the reading needs of a classroom of diverse readers.

The structure of Literature Circles supports students' engagement in reading and independent development of skills and proficiency. Working within this rigorous reading context prepares high school students for the demands of reading in college and career.

Guided Reading   Guided reading is an instructional approach in which the teacher meets with a small, flexible group of students that have a common reading goal or focus. During guided reading, students develop strategies that allow them to read increasingly difficult texts on their own. Although guided reading is typically associated with elementary school classrooms, its foundational principles are compatible with the CCSS Reading standards for high school. It is a particularly useful approach for teaching comprehension skills to the many high school students that cannot read challenging texts independently.

In selecting texts for guided reading, Fountas and Pinnell (2008) recommend student–text matches in which the student can read the text at about a 90% accuracy level with high comprehension. This recommendation may seem contrary to the CCSS emphasis on having students read challenging texts. Nonetheless, it is important to recognize students' frustration level in reading, because once they reach that level, they often give up.

Guided reading provides a solution to this dilemma. When students are able to read their assigned texts, their reading skills improve (Fountas & Pinnell, 2008). They develop stronger comprehension skills, in particular, when they are allowed to read texts that are not at frustration level. Students apply comprehension strategies (which they may have been directly taught) with greater confidence, because they can make sense of the text more easily. And the more students read, the more their confident and successful they become as readers. Consequently, students develop the skills they need to become independent readers and conquer a wide variety of challenging texts.

Selecting texts that are appropriate for individual students is sometimes called "the Goldilocks approach," because it requires each student's assigned text to be "just right." In addition to helping struggling students approach difficult texts, teachers must also recognize when a selected text is too easy for a student. Under those circumstances, the teacher has to raise the level and complexity of the reading. Doing so is necessary to ensure that selections remain aligned with the CCSS call for rigor and challenge.

Teachers must also recognize when a selected text is too easy for a student and then raise the level and complexity of the reading. Doing so is necessary to ensure that selections remain aligned with the CCSS call for rigor and challenge.

The practice of assigning students texts appropriate for their reading skills is certainly not new; in fact, it is widely accepted in reading instruction. Moreover, the CCSS do not advocate or endorse guided reading or any specific instructional approach. As stated in the introduction to the CCSS, teachers and curriculum specialists know how best to meet the needs of students as they develop the skills articulated in the standards. In fact, however, students can make substantial progress in reading comprehension when they are matched with a variety of increasingly challenging texts. (Textual complexity will be discussed in greater detail in Chapter 4.)

Classroom Connection
CCSS-Based Reading in a Ninth-Grade English Classroom

Ellie is a ninth-grade English teacher, and in one of her classes, she teaches 25 students. According to reading test data, 5 of these students read at a fifth-grade level, 8 read at a seventh-grade level, 6 read at a ninth-grade level, and 6 read above a ninth-grade level.

The next instructional unit Ellie has planned for her students is centered on the essential question *What are the limits of friendship?* Ellie's curriculum will focus on meeting the following CCR Anchor Standards for Reading:

1. Read closely to determine what the text says explicitly and to make logical inferences from it; cite specific textual evidence when writing or speaking to support conclusions drawn from the text.

2. Determine central ideas or themes of a text and analyze their development; summarize the key supporting details and ideas.

3. Analyze how two or more texts address similar themes or topics in order to build knowledge or to compare the approaches the authors take.

Table 3.6 shows how Ellie will organize her students so that all of them work at reading levels that are challenging but not frustrating. Each student selects a novel to read from the three listed in the column that corresponds to his or her reading level. Note that the list represents a wide variety of texts at different reading levels and interests and that all of them address the essential question: *What are the limits of friendship?* Ellie will teach students close reading and textual analysis skills (which are addressed in the following section) as they read the texts they have selected. She also plans to use mini-lessons, small-group instruction, and learning centers to help her students develop the skills outlined in the CCSS.

TABLE 3.6 ● *Lesson Texts Provided for Students at Different Reading Levels*

Student's Reading Level			
Grade 5	**Grade 7**	**Grade 9**	**Above Grade 9**
Scorpions, by Walter Dean Myers (1988)	*The Boy in the Striped Pajamas,* by John Boyne (2006)	*The Fault in Our Stars,* by John Green (2012)	*Of Mice and Men,* by John Steinbeck (1973/1993)
Bridge to Terabithia, by Katherine Paterson (1977)	*The Sisterhood of the Traveling Pants,* by Ann Brashares (2001)	*The Color Purple,* by Alice Walker (1982)	*Their Eyes Were Watching God,* by Zora Neale Hurston (1937/2013)
Stargirl, by Jerry Spinelli (2000)	*Freshman Year and Other Unnatural Disasters,* by Meredith Zeitlin (2012)	*The Outsiders,* by S. E. Hinton (1967/1997)	*The Perks of Being a Wallflower,* by Stephen Chbosky (1999)

Close Reading and Textual Analysis   Many high school students cannot complete a simple analysis of a text. When asked comprehension questions, they readily share their personal thoughts and feelings about the text but cannot support their impressions with concrete examples.

Some educators link this focus on personal responses with students' participating in Literature Circle activities based on reader-response theory. Although such activities have been tremendously successful in engaging young readers with texts, in some ways, they have reduced the value of close reading and textual analysis. Similarly, the rigor involved in textual analysis has been lost in recent years as a consequence of NCLB, under which reading comprehension was often taught using multiple-choice tests and similar activities. Now, with the CCSS, we are acknowledging once again that close reading is a vital skill in preparing adolescents for the critical thinking that is necessary for success in both career and college.

What exactly is close reading? It involves an intensive analysis of a text to better understand not only what it says but also how it creates that message and what it means. Close reading requires students to use a variety of tools, such as questioning, discussing, and rereading. Students need to reread challenging texts to understand them well.

There are several different levels of close reading. As outlined in the following list, each level has corresponding questions and prompts that promote close reading and build students' skills as they engage in increasingly complex texts:

First Impressions/First Read

- What is the first thing you notice about the passage?
- What is the second thing you notice about the passage?
- Do the two things you notice complement each other or contradict each other?
- What mood does the passage create in you? Why?

Vocabulary and Diction

- Which words do you notice first? Why? What is noteworthy about this diction?
- How are the important words related to one another?
- Do any words seem used in an odd manner? Why?
- Do any words have double meanings? Do they have several connotations?
- Look up any unfamiliar words.

Text Patterns

- Does any image here remind you of an image elsewhere in the book? Where? What is the connection?
- How might this image fit into the pattern of the book as a whole?
- Could this passage symbolize the entire work?
- What is the sentence rhythm like: short and choppy? long and flowing? Does the rhythm build or stay at an even pace? What is the style like?
- Look at the punctuation. Is there anything unusual about it?

- Is there any repetition within the passage? What is the effect of the repetition?
- How many types of writing are in the passage (for example, narration, description, argument, dialogue, rhymed or alliterative poetry, etc.)?
- Can you identify paradoxes in the author's thoughts or styles?
- What has the author left out or remained silent about?

Point of View and Characterization

- How does the passage make you react or think about characters or events within the narrative?
- Are there colors, sounds, and physical descriptions that appeal to your senses?
- Who speaks in the passage? To whom does he or she speak?
- Who narrates the piece? Does the narrator have a limited or partial point of view?

Symbolism and Metaphorical Meanings

- Are there metaphors in the text? What kinds?
- Is there one controlling metaphor? If not, how many different metaphors are there and in what order do they occur? How might this be significant?
- What objects might be symbols and represent other things?
- Do any of the objects, colors, animals, or plants appearing in the passage have traditional connotations or meanings?

The CCSS state the clear expectations that for students to be career and college ready, they must be able to determine the meanings of complex texts and to create thoughtful, effective arguments about what they know and understand from reading. Close reading and textual analysis teach students how to be both skillful readers and critical thinkers.

Strategies for Developing Close Reading and Analytical Skills   The most effective means of developing students' close reading and analytical skills is to engage them in increasingly rigorous tasks with a wide variety of texts. To accomplish this complex goal, we must lead students through the focused activities and processes involved in analyzing a text.

Think-Aloud Strategies   In a think-aloud strategy, the teacher narrates his or her own thought processes while approaching a text. Teaching students think-aloud strategies can help them develop close reading skills, as can many of the activities that involve paraphrasing and argument analysis.

Sticky Notes   An example of a think-aloud strategy is Sticky Notes (Burke, 2000). In using this strategy, students stop as needed while reading to record their insights, personal connections, and questions about the text. Students record these details on sticky notes and post them at the relevant points in the text. Students then use these notes as prompts in small- and large-group discussions.

To model the Sticky Notes strategy or another think-aloud strategy, display a page from a text that students are currently reading using an overhead, LCD, or other projector. For the following example, the teacher displays the opening passage from *The Scarlet Letter*, by

Nathaniel Hawthorne (1850/1999). The teacher begins the activity by thinking aloud for her students, as follows:

> One of the things that good readers do is pay attention to the voices and pictures in their heads when they read. I'm a good reader, and I listen to the voices in my head as I read. Those voices comment about what I'm reading, ask questions about what I'm reading, and sometimes make connections to what I'm reading. The pictures that pop into my head when I'm reading are important, too. When the author describes a place, I imagine what it looks like. When the author describes a character, I imagine what he or she looks like.
>
> Right now, we are going to read together a passage from *The Scarlet Letter*. While we read, we are going to practice a close reading strategy called Sticky Notes. Using these sticky notes [holds up small "tablet" of notes], I'm going to record the comments, questions, and connections and maybe the pictures that are in my head and then stick these notes on the text. Each note will contain a piece of information about the text that I'm thinking about now and want to come back to later.

At this point, the teacher begins to read the passage aloud. Each time she stops, she states what idea or image has come into her head while jotting it down on a sticky note, and then she posts the note at that place in the text. Figure 3.5 shows a sample of the teacher's annotated text. After demonstrating the Sticky Note strategy to students, the teacher asks them to practice the strategy with *The Scarlet Letter* and then later with the other texts they are currently reading.

FIGURE 3.5 ● Sample of a Text Annotation Using the Sticky Notes Strategy

The door of the jail being flung open from within, there appeared, in the first place, like a black shadow emerging into sunshine, the grim and grisly presence of the Town Beadle, with a sword by his side and his staff of office in his hand.

This personage prefigured and represented in his aspect the whole dismal severity of the Puritanic code of law, which it was his business to administer in its final and closest application to the offender. Stretching forth the official staff in his left hand, he laid his right upon the shoulder of a young woman, whom he thus drew forward until, on the threshold of the prison-door, she repelled him, by an action marked with natural dignity and force of character, and stepped into the open air, as if by her own free-will. She bore in her arms a child, a

> Town Beadle. I'm not sure that I know what that means. Is it a police officer?

> Why would a pregnant woman be put in jail? How did she get there? I think she's a strong woman. Author uses words like *natural dignity*.

(continued)

FIGURE 3.5 ● (*continued*)

baby of some three months old, who winked and turned aside its little face from the too vivid light of day; because its existence, heretofore, had brought it acquainted only with the gray twilight of a dungeon, or other darksome apartment of the prison.

When the young woman—the mother of this child—stood fully revealed before the crowd, it seemed to be her first impulse to clasp the infant closely to her bosom; not so much by an im- pulse of motherly affection, as that she might thereby conceal a certain token, which was wrought or fastened into her dress.

> I think this woman is a nonconformist. Her smile is "haughty."

, wisely judging that one token of her shame would but poorly she took the baby on her arm, and, with a burning blush, and d a glance that would not be abashed, looked around at her hbours. On the breast of her gown, in fine red cloth, surround- embroidery and fantastic lourishes of gold thread, appeared rtistically done, and with so much fertility and gorgeous luxu- riance of fancy, that it had all the effect of a last and fitting decoration to the apparel which she wore; and which was of a splendor in accordance with the taste of the age, but greatly beyond what was allowed by the sumptuary regulations of the colony.

> Why does she have an ornate A on her clothes? I want to know what she did.

> I see a beautiful woman, brunette, who challenges conformity. I think she's misunderstood by her community.

Stop and Write   Another strategy for developing close reading and textual analysis skills is Stop and Write. The teacher should introduce this strategy by modeling it for students, thinking aloud about the process and demonstrating how to use the graphic organizer that is provided.

In Stop and Write, as the student reads, he or she decides when to stop and records notes about the text—as well as his or her own questions, connections, predictions, and ideas—on a two-column graphic organizer. The student records facts and specific details from the text in column 1 and adds personal connections, questions, predictions, and so on in column 2. See Figure 3.6 for an example.

FIGURE 3.6 ● Sample of Stop and Write Graphic Organizer

What I read . . . . (record facts and details about the text)	What I think . . . (personal connections, questions and predictions.)

Paraphrasing and Analyzing Arguments   Mastering strategies such as Sticky Notes and Stop and Write enables students to use their own impressions, questions, and predictions to analyze texts. However, as the texts and therefore the analyses become more challenging, teachers need a variety of strategies for developing students' skills. A catalog of strategies for developing close reading and textual analysis skills using poetry is provided in the book *360 Degrees of Text*, by Eileen Murphy Buckley (2011).

Using the poem "To His Coy Mistress," by Andrew Marvel (c. 1650s/1999), Buckley demonstrates a strategy that involves paraphrasing and argument analysis. After students have participated in an activity aimed at activating their background knowledge, they practice a close reading technique. Using a two-column graphic organizer, students record the original language of the poem in the first column (couplet by couplet) and then paraphrase and write questions about the text in the second column (Buckley, 2011, p. 47). Figure 3.7 shows a completed graphic organizer based on reading Marvel's poem.

Completing this activity teaches students to apply important close reading skills, such as paraphrasing and active questioning, while they are reading. It also teaches students to organize information visually, which has been proven to be a particularly effective strategy for struggling readers.

FIGURE 3.7 ● Sample of Graphic Organizer for Paraphrasing Text

Original	Paraphrase
Had we but world enough, and time, This coyness, lady, were no crime.	If we had all the time in the world Acting shy would not be a bad thing to do to me (Think aloud: Crime? That's an interesting word choice! Is it against the law to resist his advances?)
We would sit down and think which way To walk, and pass out long love's day.	We would sit together thinking about what to do with our time together.
Thou by the Indian Ganges' side Shouldst rubies find;	You could be by that big river in India finding rubies (Think aloud: I had to look up what the Indian Ganges was. I found out . . .)
I by the tide Of Humber would complain.	I could be here by the shore in England complaining that you are gone. (Think aloud: I am picturing a drama came here... Is he really overwhelmed with grief as he imagines being away from her? I'm not sure if I trust him yet. I'll give him the benefit of the doubt until I read on.)

Classroom Connection

Lesson for Annotating Text

This lesson studying the novel *The House on Mango Street,* by Sandra Cisneros (1984), demonstrates how a traditionally structured lesson can be expanded to meet three of the CCSS for reading comprehension.

Grade Level:

Grades 9–12

Common Core State Standards:

This lesson meets these three standards (NGA & CCSSO [2010]):

Reading: Literature

- **RL9-10.1:** Cite strong and thorough textual evidence to support analysis of what the text says explicitly as well as inferences drawn from the text.
- **RL9-10.4:** Determine the meaning of words and phrases as they are used in the text, including figurative and connotative meanings; analyze the cumulative impact of specific word choices on meaning and tone (e.g., how the language evokes a sense of time and place; how it sets a formal or informal tone).

Speaking and Listening

- **SL.9-10.3:** Evaluate a speaker's point of view, reasoning, and use of evidence and rhetoric, identifying any fallacious reasoning or exaggerated or distorted evidence.

Time Needed:

This lesson requires five or six class periods of 45 minutes each.

Learning Outcomes:

During this lesson, students will:

- Read, summarize, analyze, and annotate a text.
- Identify poetic devices and themes in a text.
- Reinforce their group cooperation and oral presentation skills.

Materials Needed:

- Copies of *The House on Mango Street* (Cisneros, 1984)
- Copies of the five vignettes described in the handout "Practice Annotating the Text and Presenting to the Class" (see Figure 3.8)

FIGURE 3.8 ● Student Handout Describing the Lesson

Practice Annotating the Text and Presenting to the Class
The House on Mango Street, by Sandra Cisneros
    You will be assigned to a group and then complete this project together. You will choose a vignette, follow the steps below to study and annotate it, and then prepare a presentation to share this information with the rest of the class.

Schedule

Day 1: Introduce the activity.
Day 2: Work on the activity in class.
Days 3–5: Deliver presentations to class.

Vignettes

"Hairs," pp. 6–7
"Boys and Girls," pp. 8–9
"My Name," pp. 10–11
"Cathy, Queen of Cats," pp. 12–13
"Laughter," pp. 17–18

Steps

1. Read the vignette.
2. Discuss the vignette with your group members. Make sure everyone understands what the text is about.
3. Annotate the vignette in your book. Identify the poetic devices and themes within it.

Poetic Devices to Consider

simile
metaphor
symbolism
repetition
rhyme
alliteration
imagery
personification
onomatopoeia

Themes to Consider

culture
identity

(continued)

FIGURE 3.8 ● (*continued*)

> loneliness
> family
> socioeconomics
> race and discrimination
> hopes and dreams
> ways to escape
> growing up and fitting in
>
> 4. Annotate the vignette on the transparency or digital version of the text. (You will use this version to show the annotated vignette to the class.) Be prepared to share with the class the poetic devices and themes you have identified.
> 5. Summarize the vignette in three or four sentences using your own words.
> 6. Select one significant quote from the vignette. Explain why you chose it.
> 7. What lesson(s) does this vignette teach? Explain how.
> 8. Write one question that you can ask the class. (The question should not have a yes/no answer.)
> 9. Practice the presentation with your group members. Also practice reading the vignette aloud. (You will do this as part of our presentation to the class.)
>
> **Grading**
>
> Your group will be assigned a grade based on these criteria:
>
> - accuracy in following directions
> - ability to answer questions (Hand in a copy of the responses.)
> - quality of the presentation
>
> To receive credit for this project, you must participate in the group work and the presentation. The group must turn in one copy of the responses (steps 4–8), but each member should have a copy, as well, to be prepared for the presentation.
>
> Write all responses in complete sentences. Make sure that the copy of the responses that the group hands in includes a complete heading, identifying the title of the vignette and the names of all group members.

Each student will need:

- Copy of the handout "Reading Instructions" (see Figure 3.9)
- Copy of the handout "Practice Annotating the Text and Presenting to the Class"

- Class handout (see Figure 3.10)
- Copy of the "Grade Sheet" (see Figure 3.11)
- Writing materials or computer

FIGURE 3.9 ● Student Handout Providing Reading Instructions

The House on Mango Street is a collection of vignettes that are connected by themes, symbols, characters, style, and the use of poetic devices. Keep these connectors in mind as you read the vignettes.

Everyone should read the vignettes, make notes and markings in the margin, and be prepared to discuss them in class.

You must complete the following steps in order to receive full credit for the reading assignments. Prepare for each due date by completing the following:

STEP 1: Read each vignette.

STEP 2: Annotate the text.

- Read actively and take notes
- Underline poetic devices and significant words and phrases
- Label these devices in the margin
- Write the major themes that arise in each vignette
- Make connections with other parts of the book
- Find evidence in the text to help you prepare for discusses and tests

Consider poetic devices such as:

simile	metaphor	symbolism
repetition	rhyme	alliteration
imagery	personification	onomatopoeia

Consider themes such as:

culture	socio-economics	race and
family	ways to	discrimination
hopes and dreams	escape	growing up and
identity	loneliness	fitting in

I will check your books periodically to make sure that you are doing this. You **MUST** annotate the text if you want to receive credit!

Get in the habit of writing in your books and taking notes; it will help you under-stand the book and prepare you for discusses and tests.

FIGURE 3.10 ● Student Handout

Grading:
You will be assigned a grade based on

- following directions
- how well you answer all the questions (hand in the copy of the responses)*
- quality of the presentation

You will receive credit only if you participate in your group work and presentation.

The group needs to turn in one copy of the responses (steps 4–8) for the entire group, but each member should have a copy of this as well in order to be prepared for the presentation.**

*Write the responses in complete sentences.
**Make sure that this copy includes a complete heading with the name of each group member and the title of the vignette.

Activities:

Setup
Before beginning this lesson, students should be able to define and identify poetic devices and understand the concept of *theme*. Review these topics, if necessary, to ensure understanding.

Day 1

1. Distribute the handout "Reading Instructions" (one per student).
2. Explain how to annotate a text while students follow along with step 2 on the handout.
3. Read aloud as a class the first vignette from *The House on Mango Street*.
4. Ask students to brainstorm a list of themes from the vignette. Model how to annotate the text as students volunteer their responses.
5. Ask students to annotate the vignette in their own books by recording the themes that are mentioned.

Day 2

1. While referring to the previous day's work on the model vignette, explain the group project to the class.
2. Distribute the handouts "Practice Annotating the Text and Presenting to the Class" and "Grade Sheet" (one of each per student). Answer questions, as needed.
3. Divide the class into small groups, and assign each group one vignette. Be sure to provide each group with a transparency or digital version of the text that they can mark up and use in their presentation to the class.

FIGURE 3.11 ● Grade Sheet

Grade Sheet
Annotating the Text and Group Presentation
The House on Mango Street, by Sandra Cisneros

Group members' names:
Vignette title:
Oral Reading of the Vignette

1	2	3	4	5
Needs much improvement		Fair	Good	Great

Quality of Annotation (poetic devices, themes, lessons learned)

1	2	3	4	5
Needs much improvement		Fair	Good	Great

Summary of Vignette

1	2	3	4	5
Needs much improvement		Fair	Good	Great

Important Quote and Explanation

1	2	3	4	5
Needs much improvement		Fair	Good	Great

Question Posed to Class

1	2	3	4	5
Needs much improvement		Fair	Good	Great

Lessons Vignette Teaches

1	2	3	4	5
Needs much improvement		Fair	Good	Great

TOTAL: _____ / 30

4. Have group members read their vignette and then discuss it to identify poetic devices and themes.

5. Have groups begin to prepare their oral presentations. Each group member should play a specific role in the presentation.

Note: An additional class period can be devoted to group work, or this work can be assigned as homework.

● **Days 3–5**

Groups deliver their presentations to the class.

Evaluation:

Practice annotations will be evaluated using the following criteria:

- accuracy in following directions
- quality of written responses to steps 4–8 on the handout "Practice Annotating" (Responses must be written in complete sentences.)

Presentations will be evaluated using the following criteria (see "Grade Sheet"):

- oral reading of the vignette
- quality of the annotation (identifying poetic devices and themes)
- summary of the vignette
- important quote and explanation
- question posed to the class
- lessons that the vignette teaches

A wide variety of strategies can be used with high school students to develop reading comprehension skills. Table 3.7 provides an extensive catalog of strategies that includes brief descriptions and identifications of before-, during-, and after-reading strategies. Two additional resources that teachers will find useful are Cris Tovani's *I Read It, But I Don't Get It: Comprehension Strategies for Adolescent Readers* (2000) and Kylene Beers's *When Kids Can't Read: What Teachers Can Do. A Guide for Teachers 6–12* (2002). Both books offer student–teacher case studies and strategies to support reading comprehension in adolescent readers.

TABLE 3.7 ● *Catalog of Reading Strategies*

Name of Strategy	Description of Strategy	Before Reading	During Reading	After Reading
ABC Brainstorm	Students brainstorm ideas about a given topic corresponding to the letters of the alphabet (i.e., one idea per letter). Can be used to record previous knowledge before reading or new knowledge after reading.	X		X
Analysis Notes	Students record main ideas and details from a narrative text on a two-column chart. Prompts readers to identify important information while studying elements of literature.		X	

(continued)

TABLE 3.7 ● *(continued)*

Name of Strategy	Description of Strategy	Before Reading	During Reading	After Reading
Anticipation Guide	Before reading the text, students read a statement and write down whether they agree with it. After reading the text, students write about whether their opinion has changed and share their thinking with the class.	X		
Bookmarks for Questions	Students use bookmarks to mark their places while reading and answer questions on the bookmarks as they go (e.g., "The main character wants to . . .").		X	
Character Traits Web	Students record details about a character (e.g., appearance, actions, thoughts, words) and how others react to him or her. Details can be recorded in a learning log or graphic organizer.		X	X
Collaborative Strategic Reading	Before reading the text, students brainstorm ideas about the topic and write down predictions about the text. During reading, students write about the gist of the text. After reading, students write down questions about the main ideas of the text and what they learned from reading it.	X	X	X
Concept Sorts	Students sort words into categories by their meanings. The categories can be determined by the teacher or students. Used to introduce students to the vocabulary associated with a new topic or book.	X		X
Cornell Notes	Students create a two-column chart and use it to take notes while they read. Students record their notes about a text in the right-hand column and questions, main points, and other ideas about the text in the left-hand column.		X	
Directed Reading and Thinking Activity (DRTA)	This DRTA organizer prompts students to preview the text and make predictions about it. In the left-hand column, students write preview notes; in the center column, they write direct notes from the text; and in the right-hand column, they review the text by writing a written summary. The summary should support students' predictions from the first column with information from the second column.	X	X	X

(continued)

TABLE 3.7 ● (continued)

Name of Strategy	Description of Strategy	Before Reading	During Reading	After Reading
Exit Slips	Students write a summary of the text. Using this organizer prompts students to think about what they have learned and why it is important.			X
First Lines	Students write down the first line of the text, along with their prediction of its meaning, before continuing to read. After reading, students write an explanation of the first line and revise their prediction, as needed.	X		X
Fishbone	A cause-and-effect diagram used to determine causal relationships within a complex idea or event. Students begin with the result and analyze the various contributing causes.		X	X
Five Ws	Students read a text and then respond to the five W prompts to explore different elements of their reading: What happened? Who was there? Why did it happen? When did it happen? Where did it happen?			X
Fix-Up Strategies	An organizer that helps students address comprehension problems while reading a text. Includes these prompts: Preview, Predict, Set a Purpose, Visualize, Connect, Monitor, Use Prior Knowledge, and Make Inferences.		X	
Gist	Students preview a text and write down key words and phrases. Then students use as many of the key words/phrases as they can to write a 20-word sentence that summarizes the text.			X
Herringbone	Students use this graphic organizer to establish supporting details for a main idea. The supporting details branch out from main idea.		X	X
Inference Prompter	A three-column organizer that helps students develop skills in predicting and inferring. In the first column, students write what they know about the topic, in the second column, they write what they learned from the reading; and in the third column, they make inferences using the information from the first two columns.	X		X

(continued)

TABLE 3.7 ● *(continued)*

Name of Strategy	Description of Strategy	Before Reading	During Reading	After Reading
Journalist Graphic Organizer	A chart that covers the five Ws of journalistic writing: who? what? when? where? and why? Helps students communicate their understanding of the text.			X
KWL	Students use this three-column chart to record information from the before, during, and after stages of reading: K = what they already know about the topic, W = what they want to know about the topic, and L = what they learn from reading the text.	X	X	X
KWHL	A modified KWL that incorporates primary and secondary resources for research: H = How am I going to find out?	X	X	X
KWLT	A modified KWL that includes a fourth step: T = talking to peers about what they learned and teaching this information to others.	X	X	X
KWLS	A modified KWL that incorporates sources for researching the topic and question: S = possible sources.	X	X	X
Learning Logs	Used to help students keep track of learning during the collaboration process. Students think about what they read and write down questions/reflections about their learning, draw pictures, and make diagrams. The completed log can be used as a guide for follow-up activities and evaluation.	X	X	X
Listen–Read–Discuss	This technique helps students increase their knowledge about a topic before reading. Students listen to a lecture and complete a graphic organizer before reading the text. After reading, students form small groups and discuss what they have learned.	X		X
List–Group–Label	Students list all of the words they can think of related to a given topic. Then students group the words based on their similarities and label each group.	X		

(continued)

TABLE 3.7 ● *(continued)*

Name of Strategy	Description of Strategy	Before Reading	During Reading	After Reading
PACA	A predicting and confirming activity that encourages active reading. On the left side of the chart, students write predictions about the text (before reading); in the center, they mark a "+" for each supported prediction and a "−" for each unsupported prediction (during reading); and on the right side, they write notes from the text that support or contradict their predictions about the text (after reading).	X	X	X
Paragraph Shrinking	Students pair off to read together and take turns being the "Coach" and the "Player." Each student reads as the "Player" and stops to summarize each paragraph. If the "Player" makes a mistake, the "Coach" asks him or her to go back, skim the paragraph, and answer again.		X	
PLAN	A horizontal organizer that helps students visualize their learning. Students predict what the text will be about, locate important information while reading, record information and details from the text, and write down what they learned from reading.	X	X	X
Possible Sentences	Working in groups, students define a set of vocabulary words and then select pairs of related words. Next, students write a sentence for each pair of words that could appear in the text, using what they know from the subject and title.	X		
Power Notes	Teaches students to organize information from a text. Main ideas and supporting details are displayed vertically: Power 1 = Main idea, Power 2 = Details to support 1, Power 3 = Details to support 2, Power 4 = Details to support 3.		X	X
Prior Knowledge	An organizer that prompts students to think about what they already know about a topic and then apply it to a reading. In the first column, students write what they already know about the topic, and in the second column, they write what they learned from the reading.	X		X

(continued)

TABLE 3.7 ● *(continued)*

Name of Strategy	Description of Strategy	Before Reading	During Reading	After Reading
Question–Answer–Relationship (QAR)	Students create questions of specific types based on the text and their previous knowledge about the topic, including questions that can be answered directly from the text and questions that can be answered after doing research. Students also record answers to the questions.			X
Questioning the Author	Students use a series of questions to determine the author's purpose and the extent to which the author achieved that purpose. Helps students develop a more complex and deeper comprehension of the text.			X
Reading Connections	Prompts students to make four types of personal connections to the text: Personal Experiences, Current Events and Prior Knowledge, Other Subjects, Other Texts. Helps students comprehend and relate to the text.			X
REAP	A hierarchical strategy similar to Gist. Students read the text, encode the text in their own language, annotate the text by writing its message, and ponder the meaning of the text.			X
Reference Frames	An organizer that incorporates students' personal knowledge with new information. Students are given a topic written in a small square. They write down their current knowledge about the topic around it within a medium square, and they write down newly acquired information in a larger square containing the topic and current knowledge squares.	X	X	X
ReQuest	Students read to a determined stopping point in the text and then write down as many questions as they can to ask the teacher about it. The teacher answers students' questions without referring to the text and then asks students prepared questions about the text. Then the cycle of reading–questioning repeats.		X	

(continued)

TABLE 3.7 ● *(continued)*

Name of Strategy	Description of Strategy	Before Reading	During Reading	After Reading
Selective Highlighting	Used to help students organize what they have read by identifying what is important. Teaches students to highlight/underline only the key words, phrases, vocabulary, and ideas that are central to understanding the reading.		X	
Six-Column Vocabulary Organizer	A learning log that helps students categorize words they encounter in the text by etymology. Students provide a definition, synonym, antonym, part of speech, picture, and sentence using the word.			X
Spider	A free-form graphic organizer that allows students to think about information visually and metaphorically. Students complete the organizer working in groups. Helps students visualize how information and ideas are connected to a central idea and understand that people think somewhat differently about the same ideas and information.			X
Sticky Notes	Students stop at self-selected points in the text and record their thinking on stick-on notes. Prompts students to record questions, connections, and comments while they read.		X	
Storyboard Notes: Three Frame	Boxes prompt students to create pictures for scenes, ideas, and events in the text. Helps students focus on the beginning, middle, and ending or the situation, problem, and solution.			X
Storyboard Notes: Six Frame	A six-frame version of the Storyboard Notes organizer that has students record more details from the text.			X
Story Trails/ History Trails	Provides a structure for students to use in putting events of a story or historical occurrence in chronological order and to illustrate specific details. Students' understanding of key events facilitates their understanding of the structure of the story or occurrence.			X
Summarizing	After reading, students identify the essential ideas of the text along with important details to support them. Teaches students to condense a lengthy text to its main points, thereby clarifying their understanding.			X

(continued)

TABLE 3.7 ● *(continued)*

Name of Strategy	Description of Strategy	Before Reading	During Reading	After Reading
Summary Organizer	A chart that prompts students to create main categories, supply relevant details, and write a summary.			X
Survey, Question, Read, Recite, Review (SQ3R)	Students survey the text they will read (S), turn the headings into questions (Q), read the text and work on answering the questions (R), orally summarize what they have read and take notes (R), and finally study the notes and use them to recall the reading (R).	X	X	X
Survey, Question, Read, Recite, Relate, Review (SQ4R)	Students complete an SQR3 with one added step: Reflect/Relate. In this added step, students write about what the information means to them and how it contributes to their understanding of the text.	X	X	X
T-Notes	Using this T-shaped graphic organizer facilitates students' ability to compare ideas. On the left side, students record problems related to the topic, and on the right side, they record potential solutions. Students can use the bottom area of the chart to record their ideas and opinions.			X
Text–Think–Connect (TTC)	A reading tool that graphically represents students' responses to learning in three columns: "Text Facts," "Thoughts about the Text," and "Connections."		X	X
Text Structures	An organizer used to exam the format and structure of a text. Prompts students with questions about the title, author, cover art, and table of contents.	X		
Think Aloud	Students follow a series of questions that they think about and answer aloud while reading. Students eventually learn to generate their own questions to guide comprehension. Helps students monitor their thinking as they read.		X	
Think–Pair–Share	Students work with partners to share and record their knowledge on a given topic. Partners record their information in separate columns.	X		X

(continued)

TABLE 3.7 ● *(continued)*

Name of Strategy	Description of Strategy	Before Reading	During Reading	After Reading
Three-Column Notes	In the first column, students record the topic of the text; in the second column, they record what they learned while reading it; and in the third column, they write their ideas and opinions as they reflect on the text.		X	X
Vocabulary Slides	Students create vocabulary slides from assigned or self-selected words in the text. Students draw around the word a picture, synonym, antonym, part of speech, and sentence using the word. Helps students to contextualize vocabulary words.			X
Y-Diagram	A simplified version of the Herringbone and Fishbone strategies. The main idea of the text forms the base of the Y, and supporting ideas/details create the stems. Helps students to visual how ideas/details support the main idea.		X	X

REFERENCES

Appleman, D. (2010). *Adolescent literacy and the teaching of reading: Lessons for teachers of literature.* Urbana, IL: National Council of Teachers of English.

Beach, R. (2010). *Literacy tools in the classroom: Teaching through critical inquiry, grades 5–12.* New York, NY: Teachers College Press.

Beers, K. (2002). *When kids can't read: What teachers can do. A guide for teachers 6–12.* Portsmouth, NH: Heinemann.

Boardman, A. G., Roberts, G., Vaughn, S., Wexler, J., Murray, C. S., & Kosanovich, M. (2008). *Effective instruction for adolescent struggling readers: A practice brief.* Portsmouth, NH: RMC Research, Center on Instruction.

Bransford, J. (2000). *How people learn: Brain, mind, experience, and school.* Washington, DC: National Academies Press.

Burke, J. (2000). *Reading reminders: Tools, tips, and techniques.* Portsmouth, NH: Boynton/Cook.

Calkins, L., Ehrenworth, M., & Lehman, C. (2012). *Pathways to the Common Core: Accelerating achievement.* Portsmouth, NH: Heinemann.

Daniels, H., & Steineke, N. (2004). *Mini-lessons for literature circles.* Portsmouth, NH: Heinemann.

Darling-Hammond, L., Barron, B., Pearson, P. D., Schoenfeld, A. H., Stage, E. K., Zimmerman, T. D., Cervetti, G. N., & Tilson, J. L. (2008). *Powerful learning: What we know about teaching for understanding.* San Francisco, CA: Jossey-Bass.

Fountas, I., & Pinnell, G. S. (2008). *Guiding readers and writers: Teaching comprehension, genre, and content literacy.* Portsmouth, NH: Heinemann.

Langer, J. A. (2011). *Envisioning knowledge: Building literacy in the academic disciplines.* New York, NY: Teachers College Press.

McKnight, K. S. (2010). *The teacher's big book of graphic organizers: 100 reproducible organizers that help kids with reading, writing, and the content areas.* San Francisco, CA: Jossey-Bass.

Murphy Buckley, E. (2011). *360 degrees of text: Using poetry to teach close reading and powerful writing.* Urbana, IL: National Council of Teachers of English.

National Assessment Governing Board. (2009). *Reading framework for the 2009 National Assessment of Educational Progress.* Washington, DC: US Department of Education. Retrieved from www.nagb.org/content/nagb/assets/documents/publications/frameworks/reading09.pdf.

National Governors Association Center for Best Practices & Council of Chief State School Officers (NGA & CCSSO). (2010a). *Common Core State Standards: English language arts and literacy in history/social studies, science, and technical subjects.* Washington, DC: Authors. Retrieved from www.corestandards.org/assets/CCSSI_ELA%20Standards.pdf.

National Governors Association Center for Best Practices & Council of Chief State School Officers (NGA & CCSSO). (2010b). Appendix A: Research supporting key elements of the standards and glossary of key terms. *Common Core State Standards.* Washington, DC: Authors. Retrieved from www.corestandards.org/assets/Appendix_A.pdf.

National Reading Panel (NRP). (2000). *Report of the National Reading Panel: Teaching children to read* (00–4769). Washington, DC: US Department of Health and Human Services, National Institutes of Health, Eunice Kennedy Shriver National Institute of Child Health and Human Development.

Piaget, J. (2001). *The language and thought of the child* (M. Gabain and R. Gabain, trans.). New York, NY: Routledge. (Original work published 1923; translation first published 1959)

Rosenblatt, L. M. (1994). *The reader, the text, and the poem: The transactional theory of the literary work.* Carbondale, IL: Southern Illinois University Press. (Original work published 1978)

Rosenblatt, L. M. (1995). *Literature as exploration* (5th ed.). New York: Barnes & Noble. (Original work published 1938)

Smith, F. (1971). *Understanding reading: A psycholinguistic analysis of reading and learning to read.* New York, NY: Holt, Rinehart, & Winston.

Tovani, C. (2000). *I read it, but I don't get it: Comprehension strategies for adolescent readers.* Portland, ME: Stenhouse.

Vygotsky, L. S. (1986). *Thought and language* (rev. ed.), edited by A. Kozulin. Cambridge, MA: MIT Press. (Original work published 1962)

Wiggins, G., & McTighe, J. (2005). *Understanding by design* (2nd ed.). Alexandria, VA: Association for Supervision and Curriculum Development.

LITERATURE CITED

Boyne, J. (2006). *The boy in the striped pajamas.* Oxford, UK: David Fickling Books.

Brashares, A. (2001). *The sisterhood of the traveling pants.* New York, NY: Delacorte Press.

Chbosky, S. (1999). *The perks of being a wallflower.* New York, NY: Pocket Books.

Cisneros, S. (1984). *The house on Mango Street.* Houston, TX: Arte Público Press.

Civil Rights Acts of 1968. (1968). Public Law 90–284, 82 Stat. 73. Available online at www.house.gov/legcoun/Comps/civil68.pdf.

Green, J. (2012). *The fault in our stars.* New York, NY: Dutton Books.

Hinton, S. E. (1997). *The outsiders.* New York, NY: Viking Press. (Original work published 1967)

Hughes, L. (1926). Dreams. *Poets.org.* Retrieved from www.poets.org/viewmedia.php/prmMID/16075.

Hughes, L. (1926). I, too, sing America. *Poets.org.* Retrieved from www.poets.org/viewmedia.php/prmMID/15615.

Hurston, Z. N. (2013). *Their eyes were watching God.* New York, NY: Harper. (Original work published 1937)

King, M. L. (1963). Letter from Birmingham jail. *Stanford.edu.* Retrieved from www.stanford.edu/group/King/frequentdocs/birmingham.pdf.

Myers, W. D. (1988). *Scorpions.* New York, NY: HarperCollins/Amistad.

Patterson, K. (1977). *Bridge to Terabithia.* New York, NY: Crowell.

Spinelli, J. (2000). *Stargirl.* New York, NY: Scholastic.

Steinbeck, J. (1993). *Of mice and men.* New York, NY: Penguin Books. (Original work published in 1937)

Walker, A. (1973). Everyday use. In *In love and trouble: Stories of black women.* New York, NY: Harcourt Brace Jovanovich.

Walker, A. (1982). *The color purple.* New York, NY: Harcourt Brace Jovanovich.

Zeitlin, M. (2012). *Freshman year and other unnatural disasters.* New York, NY: Speak/Penguin Group.

Text Complexity

THE ISSUE OF TEXT COMPLEXITY AND ITS EMPHASIS in the Common Core State Standards (CCSS) is troubling to many of the teachers I have met. They recognize that many, if not most, of their students read below grade level, so the idea of expecting students to read even more challenging texts seems unrealistic. Likewise, considering how few students are motivated to read, teachers wonder how they will be able to turn their students into successful independent readers, capable of reading and understanding texts about a range of topics and written at various levels of difficulty.

Students must meet both of these expectations to be prepared for college and career, according to the CCSS, and for us to help students achieve these expectations will require skillful teaching. As stated by the developers of the CCSS, "Many students will need careful instruction—including effective scaffolding—to enable them to read at the level required by the Common Core State Standards" (Coleman & Pimentel, 2012, p. 8).

Lithian/Fotolia

Key Observations about Reading

RESEARCH AND DATA ABOUT READING OVERWHELMINGLY CONFIRM TWO points: Students need to read more, and they need to read more frequently. In fact, reading ability is the "secret sauce" for academic achievement. Krashen (2004) demonstrated this in his review of reading research, concluding that children who read more at home and at school perform better on assessments of reading comprehension than students who do not read the same volume of material. Similarly, a report by the National Assessment of Educational Progress (NAEP) on U.S. students' reading performance found a correlation between high reading scores and reading more at school and at home (Donahue et al., 1999).

So, while it is well accepted that adolescent readers must read more frequently to be prepared for college and career, two questions remain: How can they be motivated to read? and What kinds of texts should they read?

Motivation for Reading

Students who are motivated to read in school will likely be motivated to read on their own, as well. As teachers, we have limited influence on our students' lives outside the classroom, so it makes sense for us to focus our efforts on reading in the school environment.

Schools and classrooms with high levels of student achievement, in terms of text complexity and reading rigor, commonly share these four qualities:

1. Students have access to high-interest texts.
2. Students have some choice in reading materials.
3. Students have input into how and what they learn.
4. Classrooms provide many books of varied levels of textual complexity (Beers, 2013; Beers 2003; Fisher, 2012; Gallagher, 2009; Miller 2009; Moeller, 2007).

By giving students access to texts about a range of subjects and written by a range of authors and by offering students some choice in what they read, we demonstrate that their personal tastes and opinions matter. As adolescents prepare for adulthood, they have a strong need to express individual preferences. In the classroom, students often use their choices of reading materials to indicate group identification and to stimulate peer interaction. When we give students these opportunities for self-expression, we embrace this aspect of adolescent development, rather than fight it.

Giving students choices about their learning makes them feel that their voices are heard and their opinions are valued. Students who do not receive this recognition simply do not have the same motivation for academic achievement.

Texts for Reading

A second concern is that even when students do read, they do not read sufficiently rigorous texts. Data from the NAEP consistently demonstrate that the majority of students entering high school are not proficient readers (U.S Department of Education; 2012). Specifically, most students cannot comprehend grade-level texts and understand content information in written materials. A 2006 report issued by American College Testing (ACT) confirmed that many high school students lack basic reading skills, such as identifying main ideas and determining the meanings of words and phrases in context.

As discussed in Chapter 3, during the era of the No Child Left Behind Act, there was a heavy emphasis on standardized testing and the data it produced. Entire programs focused on skill-and-drill at the expense of developing students' strategies for reading comprehension and independent reading of challenging texts. This isn't to say that developing basic skills is unimportant. Rather, the point is that overemphasizing the learning of skills loses sight of the fact that skills are tools or strategies, not objectives. Moreover, testing students primarily or exclusively on skill sets detracts from the overreaching goal of having them learn to read and comprehend grade-level texts.

Text Complexity and the CCSS

IN APPENDIX A OF THE CCSS, THE DEVELOPERS state that one of the key requirements of the English Language Arts (ELA) Standards for Reading is that "all students must be able to comprehend texts of steadily increasing complexity as they progress through school" (NGA & CCSSO, 2010b, p. 2). By the time students complete high school, they should be able to read and comprehend the kinds of texts they will encounter in college and career. Standard 10 of the College and Career Readiness (CCR) Anchor Standards for Reading clearly states the expectation for students to "read and comprehend complex literary and informational text independently and proficiently" (NGA & CCSSO, 2010a, p. 35).

In Appendix A, the developers of the CCSS also explain that the focus on text complexity is intended to address an alarming development in reading achievement (ACT, 2006). Namely, although the demands of reading associated with college, career, and citizenship have remained constant or increased over the past 50 years, the texts used in kindergarten through grade 12 have become less demanding. In addition, reading instruction has neglected the importance of students being able to read complex texts independently. As a result, there is a "serious gap between many high school seniors' reading ability and the reading requirements they will face in college" (NGA & CCSSO, 2010b, p. 2).

Measuring Text Complexity

To help close this gap, the developers of the CCSS have provided guidelines for how text complexity can be measured and integrated as a regular part of reading instruction. Those guidelines are based on a model that uses three factors to measure text complexity: qualitative measures, quantitative measures, and reader and task considerations (see Figure 4.1) (NGA & CCSSO, 2010a, p. 57). These three factors are considered equally important in assessing text complexity and balance one another in certain ways, as noted in the following discussion.

Qualitative Measures   Qualitative measures of text complexity include the following:

1. levels and specificity of meaning or purpose
2. difficulty and conventionality of structure, including use of graphics
3. conventionality and clarity of language use
4. demands or assumptions about knowledge and prior experiences (NGA & CCSSO, 2010b, pp. 5–6)

FIGURE 4.1 ● Measuring Text Complexity

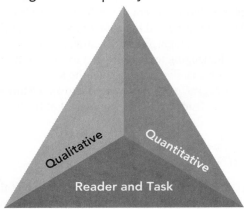

Source: NGA & CCSSO, 2010a, p. 57.

Evaluations of texts using qualitative measures are often performed by teachers and curriculum specialists: attentive readers who are capable of making informed decisions about how these measures affect the difficulty of a text. In analyzing a given text, the evaluator should consider each of the four measures along a continuum of difficulty, not as being present or absent. Figure 4.2 shows a basic rubric for evaluating an informational text along qualitative dimensions. Note the use of arrows to indicate degrees or levels of each measure, ranging from "High" to "Low."

Quantitative Measures   Quantitative measures include word length and frequency, sentence length, and text cohesion—readability factors that are more efficiently measured by a computer than a human reader (NGA & CCSSO, 2010b, p. 4). Well-known examples of quantitative tools that are used to determine readability include the Flesch-Kincaid tests, the Dale-Chall formula, and the Lexile Framework for Reading.

The developers of the CCSS suggest that the Lexile Framework, when used in conjunction with qualitative measures, is among the most useful quantitative tools, because it places both

FIGURE 4.2 ● Rubric for Evaluating an Informational Text Using Qualitative Measures

Levels of Purpose			
High ⟵⟶			Low
The **purpose** is implied and difficult to determine.	Implied **purpose** is relatively easy to infer.	The **purpose** is implied, but the reader can identify the purpose using the context or source.	The **purpose** is explicitly stated.

(continued)

FIGURE 4.2 ● *(continued)*

Structure			
High ◄────────────────► Low			
Text features are necessary to understand content.	**Text features** support the reader's understanding of the content.	**Text features** enhance the reader's understanding of the content.	**Text features** help the reader understand the content but are not necessary for comprehension.
Graphics are essential to understand the text.	**Graphics** may sometimes be necessary to understand the text.	**Graphics** are supplemental to understanding the text.	**Graphics** aren't necessary to understand the text.
Organization (main ideas and details) is complex and not explicit—demands inferencing from the reader.	**Organization (main ideas and details)** is mostly explicit— uses organization found in the subject or content area.	**Organization (main ideas and details)** is clearly stated and logically sequenced.	**Organization (main ideas and details)** is clearly stated.

Language Conventionality and Clarity			
High ◄────────────────► Low			
Meaning may include extensive figurative language and is often ambiguous.	**Meaning** is complex and can include abstract and figurative language.	**Meaning** is mostly explicit but may include instances of metaphorical or abstract meanings.	**Meaning** is straightforward and easy to understand.
Dialect is unfamiliar and/or archaic.	**Dialect** is characteristically unfamiliar.	**Dialect** is conversational and mostly contemporary.	**Dialect** is contemporary and familiar.

Knowledge Demands			
High ◄────────────────► Low			
Extensive, specialized **knowledge of subject matter** is required.	Some specialized **knowledge of subject matter** is required.	Requires some generalized **knowledge of subject matter**.	**Knowledge of subject matter** is not required. Requires only practical knowledge.

readers and texts on the same scale (NGA & CCSSO, 2010b, p. 7). The developers also note, however, that quantitative tools are not always reliable when used in isolation. For example, *To Kill a Mockingbird* (Lee, 1960) has a readability range of fourth–fifth grade, according to the Lexile Framework. However, most English teachers know that this novel is not appropriate for fourth-graders when language, themes, and demands of prior knowledge are considered.

This example illustrates why text complexity isn't determined solely using quantitative measures. Factoring in qualitative measures demonstrates that *To Kill a Mockingbird* is more suitable for students in grades 9 or 10—the grades in which this novel in usually taught. To assist teachers in balancing the use of quantitative and qualitative measures of text complexity, the CCSS developers offer this advice:

> Until widely available quantitative tools can better account for factors recognized as making such texts challenging, including multiple levels of meaning and mature themes, preferences should likely be given to qualitative measures of text complexity when evaluating narrative fiction for students in grade 6 and above. (NGA & CCSSO, 2010b, p. 8)

Reader and Task Considerations   The final component of the CCSS model for measuring text complexity doesn't focus on the text but rather on the reader and the task he or she is expected to perform. Reader variables include motivation, knowledge, and experiences, and task variables include the purpose and complexity of the assigned task and the questions posed (NGA & CCSSO, 2010b, p. 4). Together, these variables involve "Matching reader to text and task" (NGA & CCSSO, 2010a, p. 57). Given the professional knowledge that teachers have of their students and the subject matter, they are in the best position to assess reader and task considerations. Figure 4.3 presents a checklist that teachers can use to evaluate these variables when measuring the complexity of a text.

FIGURE 4.3 ● Checklist for Evaluating Reader and Task Considerations

Reading Skills

1. Does the reader have the inferencing skills needed to make connections that may not be explicit in this text?
2. Does the reader have the visualization skills needed to picture what is being described in the text?
3. Does the reader have the active questioning stance needed to explore the ideas in the text?
4. Does the reader have the comprehension strategies needed to actively read this text?
5. Does this text support the development of inferencing skills, visualization skills, active questioning, and comprehension strategies in the reader?

Motivation and Engagement

1. Is the reader interested in the specific context of this text?
2. Is the reader motivated to actively engage with this text?

Types of Texts

As discussed in Chapter 3, the ELA Reading standards set expectations for two types of texts: literature and informational text. The Literature standards address the reading of stories, dramas, and poems, and the Informational Text standards address the reading of literary nonfiction (which includes historical, scientific, and technical texts written for a broad audience) (NGA & CCSSO, 2010a, p. 57). In terms of text complexity, students are expected to read both literature and literary nonfiction to develop "the capacity to surmount the challenges posed by complex texts" (NGA & CCSSO, 2010a, p. 34).

Although the developers of the CCSS use the term *literary nonfiction* in discussing the standards, this term does not appear in the actual ELA Standards for Reading. Instead, the term *informational text* is used in the standards, because it is applicable across all content areas. Using the same term throughout the Reading standards establishes coherence and consistency across all grade levels and content areas: English language arts, history/social studies, science, and technical subjects.

Examples of informational texts that might be read in several content areas include *The Autobiography of Benjamin Franklin* (Franklin, 1791/1994) and *Narrative of the Life of Frederick Douglass, an American Slave* (Douglass, 1845/1995). Even Jonathan Swift's satirical essay "A Modest Proposal" (1729/1997) can be considered an informational text because of its many political and social references and its clear use of argumentative structure and language.

Exemplar Texts

To further assist teachers in evaluating text complexity, the developers of the CCSS have provided so-called text exemplars that illustrate "the complexity, quality, and range of reading appropriate for various grade levels" (NGA & CCSSO, 2010a, p. 8). These exemplars, which are provided in Appendix B of the CCSS (NGA & CCSSO, 2010c), are intended to serve as guideposts for teachers as they select texts for use in their own classrooms. Teachers will also find useful the performance tasks that supplement the text exemplars; these tasks identify specific applications of the ELA Standards for Reading for given texts.

Figure 4.4 provides a list of texts for students in grades 9–12 that illustrates the levels of complexity, quality, and range recommended by the ELA Standards for Reading. Both literary works and informational texts are included. To be clear, the CCSS do not mandate the use of any specific texts. The developers note that this list is intended to be representative of suitable texts and suggest that teachers select texts based on topics or themes relevant to their courses and students (NGA & CCSSO, 2010a, p. 58).

Strategies for Addressing Text Complexity

HIGH SCHOOL ENGLISH LANGUAGE ARTS TEACHERS ARE QUITE knowledgeable. By using the exemplar texts and other tools provided by the CCSS, they can develop a reading curriculum that challenges students of various proficiency levels. To implement that curriculum, teachers can apply a range of strategies in their classrooms. As stated in the introduction to this chapter, helping students meet the CCSS expectations for text complexity requires skillful teaching.

FIGURE 4.4 ● Examples of Texts That Illustrate the Complexity, Quality, and Range of Student Reading for Grades 9–12

Literature

Grades 9–10

The Tragedy of Macbeth, by William Shakespeare (1592)

"Ozymandias," by Percy Bysshe Shelley (1817)

"The Raven," by Edgar Allan Poe (1845)

"The Gift of the Magi," by O. Henry (1906)

The Grapes of Wrath, by John Steinbeck (1939)

Fahrenheit 451, by Ray Bradbury (1953)

The Killer Angels, by Michael Shaara (1975)

Grades 11–12

"Ode on a Grecian Urn," by John Keats (1820)

Jane Eyre, by Charlotte Brontë (1848)

"Because I Could Not Stop for Death," by Emily Dickinson (1890)

The Great Gatsby, by F. Scott Fitzgerald (1925)

Their Eyes Were Watching God, by Zora Neale Hurston (1937)

A Raisin in the Sun, by Lorraine Hansberry (1959)

The Namesake, by Jhumpa Lahiri (2003)

Informational Text

Grades 9–10

"Speech to the Second Virginia Convention," by Patrick Henry (1775)

"Farewell Address," by George Washington (1796)

"Gettysburg Address," by Abraham Lincoln (1863)

"State of the Union Address," by Franklin Delano Roosevelt (1941)

"Letter from Birmingham Jail," by Martin Luther King Jr. (1964)

"Hope, Despair and Memory," by Elie Wiesel (1997)

Grades 11–12

Common Sense, by Thomas Paine (1776)

Walden, by Henry David Thoreau (1854)

"Society and Solitude," by Ralph Waldo Emerson (1857)

"The Fallacy of Success," by G. K. Chesterton (1909)

Black Boy, by Richard Wright (1945)

"Politics and the English Language," by George Orwell (1946)

"Take the Tortillas Out of Your Poetry," by Rudolfo Anaya (1995)

Source: NGA & CCSSO (2010).

Schoolwide Literacy Plans, Data Records, and Assessment Tools

Every school needs a clearly articulated literacy plan to guide the development of consistent, high-quality instruction and assessment. Having a literacy plan also makes it easier for all teachers to share the same rigorous expectations and to provide information to individuals outside the school, such as families and community members.

Many schools already have assessment and data plans in place to monitor students' progress in reading. Teachers should continue to use these tools to monitor students' development of comprehension skills and then, when appropriate, move them to more challenging texts in all content areas.

To scaffold instruction in text complexity, English language arts teachers should maintain running records of students' reading skills. Several assessment tools are available to fill this need, such as Fluency Snapshots (Blachowicz, Sullivan, & Cieply, 2001). Many additional free/open access assessments are available at The Reading & Writing Project website (http://readingandwritingproject.com). (See also Online Resources, later in this section.)

Fluency

Fluency is one of the most important contributors to and indicators of text complexity (Rasinksi, 2010). To check for fluency, the teacher should have the student read aloud sections of a text. If the student can read aloud with the appropriate selection and intonation, then the text is most likely at a level that matches his or her reading ability.

Another useful strategy is based on the Five Finger Rule. To determine readability, the teacher should have a student read aloud one page of selected text. For each miscue, stumble, or incidence of inappropriate intonation, the teacher puts down one finger. If the teacher has put down all five fingers by the time the student has finished reading the page, then the text is most likely too challenging for him or her.

Literal Comprehension

The CCSS clearly state that students should be able to understand the explicit meaning of a text. The term *literal comprehension* is used to refer to a reader's understanding of straightforward information, such as facts, dates, locations, vocabulary, and so on. Students who cannot comprehend a text at this basic level will be unable to analyze it at a deeper level and will certainly be unable to meet the demands of college.

The ability to understand a text at this level involves what Coleman and Pimentel (2012) refer to as the "four corners of the text." The four corners are the students' ability to (1) analyze the text, (2) understand the literal meaning of the text, (3) cite the text, and (4) retell and explain the text to others.

Support Students' Efforts

Teachers can support students' efforts at reading complex texts by using some of the following strategies:

1. Have students study a text working in Literature Circles or pairs. Students can learn from and support each other as they read challenging passages and share strategies.

2. Do teacher read-alouds to demonstrate how a skilled reader thinks about and works toward comprehending a complex text.

3. Have students listen to an audio version of a text. (This isn't cheating!) In many cases, hearing a text read gives students the additional support they need to comprehend a challenging text.

4. If the student is motivated and keenly interested in the subject of a specific book, encourage him or her to read it, even if doing so may be challenging at first. Use other supportive strategies to lead the student to a successful reading experience with a challenging text.

Online Resources

Teachers should become familiar with the online resources provided about the Lexile Framework for Reading (www.Lexile.com). The following resources will be useful when creating a curriculum that meets the expectations of the CCSS:

- Lexile overview video (www.lexile.com/about-lexile/lexile-video/)
- "What does the Lexile measure mean?" (http://lexile.com/m/uploads/downloadablepdfs/WhatDoestheLexileMeasureMean.pdf)
- "Common Core State Standards" (www.lexile.com/using-lexile/lexile-measures-and-the-ccssi/)

Another valuable resource is the website of The Reading & Writing Project (http://readingandwritingproject.com), a research and staff organization founded by Lucy Calkins and based at Teachers College, Columbia University. Under the "Resources" tab is a subsection labeled "Common Core Resources." The CCSS expectations for textual complexity closely resemble The Reading & Writing Project recommendations.

Classroom Connection

Putting the Strategies to Work

Motivated, inspired teachers are already using CCSS-based strategies with great results. To illustrate, I would like to share the success stories of two incredible and dynamic teachers.

Mary Green

The first teacher, Mary Green, teaches ninth-grade language arts in the Chicago Public Schools. She has more than 32 students in each class, and they represent a wide range of reading levels. In addition, the majority of these students do not speak English as their first language. Undaunted by these challenges, Mary uses the Literature Circle model and Writing Workshop as the foundation of instruction in her language arts classroom.

Like many teachers, Mary has very few resources available to her and therefore finds it difficult to provide materials for the students in her language arts classes. Most of the novels available to students have been donated, but Mary has also found books by scrounging around resale shops and even purchasing many books herself.

To determine students' progress in improving their reading comprehension skills, Mary regularly administers reading assessments (usually Fluency Snapshots). She also regularly suggests that students read more challenging books. Mary's classrooms are always filled with joy and excitement, as the students devour the books. Any visitor will recognize that her students are excited about reading.

I was fortunate enough to work with Mary and her students over the course of a full school year. That year, Mary's students read more than they had during their entire educational careers. By the end of the year, on average, each student had read more than 20 novels.

Of course, the results of Mary's approach to reading instruction are not surprising. Her students outperformed students of every grade level in the school. Mary had such success with her students and promoted such tremendous growth in their reading comprehension skills that she was promoted to the school reading coach the following year.

Brooke Cray

Brooke Cray is an eleventh-grade teacher in South Carolina. In the school where she teaches, students are organized into different ability tracks. Brooke teaches the lowest level of eleventh-grade students in a course called Reading Workshop.

At the beginning of the school year, all of the approximately 20 students in Brooke's class were reading significantly below grade level. Even so, the students demonstrated real enthusiasm for reading. The first time I visited the class, I was stunned to see students enter the room and eagerly ask, "Ms. Cray, what new books do you have today?" And Ms. Cray herself was passion personified. Brooke talked excitedly about all of the books on her desk, in her bin, and on her cart.

Brooke does her best to surround herself and her students with a wide variety of reading materials. A range of authors, subject matters, genres, and levels of complexity are available in the ever-changing collection she makes available to students in her classroom.

As Brooke explained to me, some of her students had started the year reading books from the *Goosebumps* series (by R. L. Stine), which are on a fourth-grade reading level. By year's end, they were reading books such as *Scorpions* (Myers, 1988) and novels in the *Harry Potter* series (by J. K. Rowling). This progression represented about a two-year gain in students' reading comprehension.

I wasn't surprised to learn that Brooke's students made the largest gains on the state reading assessment in the entire school that year and among the largest gains of all of the schools in the district. Her students advanced, on average, more than two grade levels, and there was every indication that they would continue the progression toward higher-level reading and comprehension.

The CCSS in Action

Both Ms. Green and Ms. Cray exemplify the kind of teaching that is needed for students to meet the expectations of the CCSS. First, they recognize students' current reading level and match them with texts they are able to read independently. Then, as students improve their skills and can handle more complex texts, they make those texts available. Both teachers consistently steer their students toward more complex texts.

These are not random feel-good stories of teachers with superhuman skills who single-handedly pull their students up from the bottom of the testing heap. Rather, they are examples of motivated educators who have adapted the CCSS to their students' individual needs. These teachers acknowledge their students' actual reading levels and then move them forward, on their own unique paths, by offering them choices of interesting texts of increasing complexity.

REFERENCES

American College Testing (ACT). (2006). *Reading between the lines: What the ACT reveals about college readiness in reading.* Retrieved from www.act.org/research/policymakers/pdf/reading_report.pdf.

Beers, G. Kylene. *Notice & Note: Strategies for Close Reading.* Portsmouth, NH: Heinemann, 2012. Print.

Beers, G. Kylene. *When Kids Can't Read, What Teachers Can Do: A Guide for Teachers, 6-12.* Portsmouth, NH: Heinemann, 2003. Print.

Blachowicz, C. L. Z., Sullivan, D. M., & Cieply, C. (2001). Fluency snapshots: A quick screening tool for your classroom. *Reading Psychology 22,* 95–109. Retrieved from www.reading.ccsu.edu/demos/Courses/RDG%20502%20Jamaica%20Winter%202008/Articles/Fluency%20Snapshot%20Quick%20Screen.pdf.

Coleman, D., & Pimentel, S. (2012). *Revised publishers' criteria for the Common Core State Standards in English language arts and literacy, grades 3–12.* Washington, DC: National Assessment of Educational Progress. Retrieved from http://nces.ed.gov/nationsreportcard/pubs/main1998/1999500.asp.

Donahue, P. L., Voelkl, K. E., Campbell, J. R., & Mazzeo, J. (1999). *NAEP 1998 Reading report card for the nation.* Washington, DC: National Center for Education Statistics, U.S. Dept. of Education, Office of Educational Research and Improvement, 1999. Print.

Fisher, Douglas, Nancy Frey, and Diane Lapp. *Teaching Students to Read like Detectives: Comprehending, Analyzing, and Discussing Text.* Bloomington, IN: Solution Tree, 2012. Print.

Gallagher, Kelly, and Richard L. Allington. *Readicide: How Schools Are Killing Reading and What You Can Do about It.* Portland, Me.: Stenhouse, 2009. Print.

Krashen, S. D. (2004). *The power of reading: Insights from the research* (2nd ed.). Westport, CT: Libraries Unlimited.

Miller, Donalyn, and Jeff Anderson. *The Book Whisperer: Awakening the Inner Reader in Every Child.* San Francisco, CA: Jossey-Bass, 2009. Print.

Moeller, Victor J., and Marc V. Moeller. *Literature Circles That Engage Middle and High School Students.* Larchmont, NY: Eye On Education, 2007. Print.

National Governors Association Center for Best Practices & Council of Chief State School Officers (NGA & CCSSO). (2010a). *Common Core State Standards: English language arts and literacy in history/social studies, science, and technical subjects.* Washington, DC: Authors. Retrieved from www.corestandards.org/assets/CCSSI_ELA%20Standards.pdf.

National Governors Association Center for Best Practices & Council of Chief State School Officers (NGA & CCSSO). (2010b). Appendix A: Research supporting key elements of the standards and glossary of key terms. *Common Core State Standards.* Washington, DC: Authors. Retrieved from www.corestandards.org/assets/Appendix_A.pdf.

National Governors Association Center for Best Practices & Council of Chief State School Officers (NGA & CCSSO). (2010c). Appendix B: Text exemplars and sample performance tasks. *Common Core State Standards.* Washington, DC: Authors. Retrieved from www.corestandards.org/assets/Appendix_B.pdf.

Rasinski, T. V. (2010). *The fluent reader: Oral and silent reading strategies for building fluency, word recognition, and comprehension.* New York, NY: Scholastic.

The Nation's Report Card: Trends in Academic Progress 2012 NCES Number: 2013456 Release Date: June 27, 2013 (U.S. Department of Education, Institute of Education Sciences, National Center for Education Statistics) http://nces.ed.gov/pubsearch/getpubcats.asp?sid=031-017.

LITERATURE AND INFORMATIONAL TEXTS CITED

Douglass, F. (1995). *Narrative of the life of Frederick Douglass, an American slave.* Mineola, NY: Dover Publications. (Original work published 1845)

Franklin, B. (1994). *The autobiography of Benjamin Franklin. Project Gutenberg.* Retrieved from www.gutenberg.org/ebooks/148. (Original work published 1791)

Lee, H. (1960). *To kill a mockingbird.* New York, NY: Lippincott.

Myers, W. D. (1988). *Scorpions.* New York, NY: HarperCollins.

Swift, J. (1997). A modest proposal. *Project Gutenberg.* Retrieved from www.gutenberg.org/ebooks/1080. (Original work published 1729)

Language:
Grammar and Vocabulary

WHEN I THINK ABOUT HOW I "LEARNED" VOCABULARY, I recall being given long lists of words. For each list, my teacher required me to do the same three things. First, I wrote each word five times. Then, I looked up each word and recorded the definition. Finally, I wrote a sentence using each word to prove that I understood its meaning. And that was it! Three easy steps, and those words were mine for life.

When I think about "learning" grammar, I recall completing an endless number of worksheets. Over the years, I circled my share of nouns and underlined plenty of verbs. I could identify basic parts of speech in the sentences that were given to me, and so I understood grammar.

Goodluz/Fotolia

Of course, I didn't really learn much about vocabulary and grammar using these methods. In fact, in the years since I was a student, extensive research has shown that teaching language using passive methods is perhaps the worst approach possible (National Institute for Literacy, 2007). Language learning, at its most effective, is active and engaging. And while there is a time and place for writing sentences and doing worksheets, these activities will never be as effective as tapping a student's simple but overwhelming wish to communicate.

Key Observations about Learning and Teaching Language

THE DESIRE TO USE THE PERFECT WORD TO express a particular thought is the reason we need to know vocabulary. Similarly, being able to craft a sentence that captures exactly what we want to say, whether in speech or in writing, is the reason we need to know grammar. Learning language skills is not an end unto itself. The purpose of learning language skills is to support our ability to communicate.

Students aren't likely to grasp this purpose when instruction in language skills is limited to discrete lessons or units in a sequentially ordered curriculum. The development of language skills is an ongoing process—one that begins during our preschool years and continues through our student years and beyond.

As high school teachers, our concern is that we are at the end of the K–12 journey. By the time students reach us, they have already spent years developing their language skills. According to the expectations stated in the Common Core State Standards (CCSS), by high school, students should be able to apply their language skills in reading and writing complex texts. We know, however, that many students fall short of these expectations, especially upon entering high school. We have just a few years to "get them up to speed" before they graduate. And the expectations in college and the workplace are higher than ever.

To meet these high expectations for language skills, as is the case for meeting the other English Language Arts (ELA) Standards, teachers across the content areas must be involved, not only language arts teachers. Asking for this level of participation issues a great challenge. Teaching students about language (especially grammar) is perhaps the most challenging task that language arts teachers face. By nature, language embodies nuances and exceptions. (After all, language is the means for human expression, and humans are complex creatures.) Despite the difficulty of the task, however, involving our colleagues from the content areas offers them an opportunity to model the skills that students must develop to continue their own language development after they leave high school. Who better to demonstrate life-long learning than teachers?

Exploring the Language Standards

IN THE INTRODUCTION TO THE ELA STANDARDS FOR LANGUAGE, the developers of the CCSS make this statement about the skills and knowledge students must master to be ready for college and career:

To be career and college ready in language, students must have firm control over the conventions of standard English. At the same time, they must come to appreciate that language is as at least as much a matter of craft as of rules and be able to choose words, syntax, and punctuation to express themselves in achieved particular functions and rhetorical effects. They must also have extensive vocabularies, built through reading and study, enabling them to comprehend complex texts and engage in purposeful writing about and conversations around content. They need to become skilled in determining or clarifying the meaning of words and phrases they encounter, choosing flexibility from an array of strategies to aid them. They must learn to see an individual word as part of the network of other words—words, for example, that have similar denotations but different connotations. The inclusion of Language standards in their own strand should not be taken as an indication that skills related to conventions, effective language use, and vocabulary are unimportant to reading, writing, speaking, and listening; indeed, they are inseparable from such contexts. (NGA & CCSSO, 2010, p. 51)

Like the other strands of ELA Standards (e.g., Reading, Writing), the Language strand is founded on a set of College and Career Readiness (CCR) Anchor Standards, and the same Anchor Standards underlie the specific grade-level standards for students from grades K–12 (NGA & CCSSO, 2010, p. 51). Both sets of standards outline the skills and knowledge that students are expected to demonstrate. However, the Anchor Standards provide broad objectives, whereas the grade-level standards identify specific expectations.

Table 5.1 presents the grade-level Language standards for high school students. Note that for high school, the ELA Standards are organized into two grade-level bands: grades 9–10 and grades 11–12. The Language standards are further organized into three categories, or clusters: Conventions of Standard English, Knowledge of Language, and Vocabulary Acquisition and Use.

Conventions of Standard English

The first cluster, Conventions of Standard English, is where the expectations for grammar knowledge and skills are articulated. At these grade levels, Standards 1 and 2 don't outline an extensive list of required skills. Rather, grammar is recognized as a way of thinking

TABLE 5.1 ● *Language Standards for Grades 9–12*

Grades 9–10 students:	Grades 11–12 students:
Conventions of Standard English	
1. Demonstrate command of the conventions of standard English grammar and usage when writing or speaking.	1. Demonstrate command of the conventions of standard English grammar and usage when writing or speaking.
a. Use parallel structure.*	a. Apply the understanding that usage is a matter of convention, can change over time, and is sometimes contested.
b. Use various types of phrases (noun, verb, adjectival, adverbial, participial, prepositional, absolute) and clauses (independent, dependent; noun, relative, adverbial) to convey specific meanings and add variety and interest to writing or presentations.	b. Resolve issues of complex or contested usage, consulting references (e.g., *Merriam-Webster's Dictionary of English Usage*, Garner's *Modern American Usage*) as needed.

(*continued*)

TABLE 5.1 ● *(continued)*

Grades 9–10 students:	Grades 11–12 students:
2. Demonstrate command of the conventions of standard English capitalization, punctuation, and spelling when writing.	2. Demonstrate command of the conventions of standard English capitalization, punctuation, and spelling when writing.
a. Use a semicolon (and perhaps a conjunctive adverb) to link two or more closely related independent clauses.	a. Observe hyphenation conventions.
b. Use a colon to introduce a list or quotation.	b. Spell correctly.
c. Spell correctly.	

Knowledge of Language

3. Apply knowledge of language to understand how language functions in different contexts, to make effective choices for meaning or style, and to comprehend more fully when reading or listening.	3. Apply knowledge of language to understand how language functions in different contexts, to make effective choices for meaning or style, and to comprehend more fully when reading or listening.
a. Write and edit work so that it conforms to the guidelines in a style manual (e.g., *MLA Handbook*, *Turabian's Manual for Writers*) appropriate for the discipline and writing type.	a. Vary syntax for effect, consulting references (e.g., Tufte's *Artful Sentences*) for guidance as needed; apply an understanding of syntax to the study of complex texts when reading.

Vocabulary Acquisition and Use

4. Determine or clarify the meaning of unknown and multiple-meaning words and phrases based on *grades 9–10 reading and content*, choosing flexibly from a range of strategies.	4. Determine or clarify the meaning of unknown and multiple-meaning words and phrases based on *grades 11–12 reading and content*, choosing flexibly from a range of strategies.
a. Use context (e.g., the overall meaning of a sentence, paragraph, or text; a word's position or function in a sentence) as a clue to the meaning of a word or phrase.	a. Use context (e.g., the overall meaning of a sentence, paragraph, or text; a word's position or function in a sentence) as a clue to the meaning of a word or phrase.
b. Identify and correctly use patterns of word changes that indicate different meanings or parts of speech (e.g., *analyze, analysis, analytical; advocate, advocacy*).	b. Identify and correctly use patterns of word changes that indicate different meanings or parts of speech (e.g., *conceive, conception, conceivable*).
c. Consult general and specialized reference materials (e.g., dictionaries, glossaries, thesauruses), both print and digital, to find the pronunciation of a word or determine or clarify its precise meaning, its part of speech, or its etymology.	c. Consult general and specialized reference materials (e.g., dictionaries, glossaries, thesauruses), both print and digital, to find the pronunciation of a word or determine or clarify its precise meaning, its part of speech, its etymology, or its standard usage.
d. Verify the preliminary determination of the meaning of a word or phrase (e.g., by checking the inferred meaning in context or in a dictionary).	d. Verify the preliminary determination of the meaning of a word or phrase (e.g., by checking the inferred meaning in context or in a dictionary).

(continued)

TABLE 5.1 ● *(continued)*

Grades 9–10 students:	Grades 11–12 students:

5. Demonstrate understanding of figurative language, word relationships, and nuances in word meanings.
 	
  a. Interpret figures of speech (e.g., euphemism, oxymoron) in context and analyze their role in the text.
 	
  b. Analyze nuances in the meaning of words with similar denotations.
	5. Demonstrate understanding of figurative language, word relationships, and nuances in word meanings.
	
	  a. Interpret figures of speech (e.g., hyperbole, paradox) in context and analyze their role in the text.
	
	  b. Analyze nuances in the meaning of words with similar denotations.

6. Acquire and use accurately general academic and domain-specific words and phrases, sufficient for reading, writing, speaking, and listening at the college and career readiness level; demonstrate independence in gathering vocabulary knowledge when considering a word or phrase important to comprehension or expression.	6. Acquire and use accurately general academic and domain-specific words and phrases, sufficient for reading, writing, speaking, and listening at the college and career readiness level; demonstrate independence in gathering vocabulary knowledge when considering a word or phrase important to comprehension or expression.

*This skill is likely to require continued attention in higher grades as it is applied to increasingly sophisticated writing and speaking.
Source: NGA & CCSSO (2010).

about language and exploring options for constructing effective expressions. For instance, Standard 1b states the expectation of using different types of phrases and clauses "to convey specific meanings and add variety and interest to writing or presentations" (NGA & CCSSO, 2010, p. 54).

The standards in this cluster also recognize that students may be at very different levels in terms of language and, more specifically, grammar development. As English language arts teachers know, it is quite common for students to write with great clarity and focus yet demonstrate poor grammar and spelling skills. The standards acknowledge that keen ability in one language area doesn't always directly correlate with ability in another area.

Knowledge of Language

In the second cluster, Knowledge of Language, Standard 3 states expectations for applying knowledge and incorporates such elements as purpose and context, meaning and style, and comprehension. Again, it is the contextual application of language skills that matter, not the knowledge of rules. Even in high school, students may be able to recite the definitions of various parts of speech, but not know how those parts of speech actually function in language. For example, a noun can show quantity or number as singular or plural, it can demonstrate ownership by being possessive, and it can be common or proper in terms of type. Also, sometimes, phrases can function as nouns. Only by understanding these various functions will students be able to make effective choices for style and meaning and to fully comprehend spoken and written language. To meet the expectation of Language Standard 3, students must be able to apply what they know in multiple contexts. Furthermore, assessment will involve analysis of students' written work, not a set of multiple-choice items about grammar.

As mentioned earlier, passive methods of instructions—such as having students memorize rules and then apply them to sentences and paragraphs on worksheets—have been proven ineffective (National Institute for Literacy, 2007). In recognition of this, the CCSS are markedly different from the previous generation of English language arts standards. The CCSS focus on the students' ability to use and apply skills in real-world applications.

Standard 3 also recognizes the contextual and societal influences on language conventions. Once again, by not focusing on rules and definitions, the CCSS acknowledge that language is fluid and malleable and thus greatly influenced by the contexts and eras in which it's used. Recent research in language and literacy development supports the notion that people learn language most effectively when it is taught in context (Weaver, 1998; Hillocks and Smith, 2003). Students learn grammar best while manipulating language in an effort to communicate. They need to "mess" with language to develop a deep understanding of how it works. Only then can they be expected to use it effectively to express their complex ideas and original thoughts.

Vocabulary Acquisition and Use

Language Standards 4–6 state expectations for students to develop a deep understanding of words. Standard 4 addresses strategies and tools for determining and clarifying the meanings of words likely to be found in grade-level reading and content. Standard 5 addresses more sophisticated vocabulary skills, such as figurative language, word relationships, and nuances in meaning. Standard 6 addresses the academic and domain-specific language necessary for success in college and career, as well as the need for students to choose appropriate words and phrases on their own.

In this cluster of standards, as well as in previous clusters, memorizing word lists and performing skill-and-drill activities is not sufficient for mastery. The emphasis is on application of skills and knowledge in specific contexts. These standards also address the need for thoughtful consideration of the choices involved in effective language use and the ability to work independently in making these choices. To be college and career ready, students must be able to draw on a well-developed vocabulary and use it to accurately interpret and express ideas.

Strategies for Developing Language Skills

IN SHORT, WHAT THE ELA STANDARDS FOR LANGUAGE mean for high school English language arts teachers is that they must help students develop strategies for understanding and applying knowledge of grammar and vocabulary. The Language Standards are consistent with those in the other ELA strands in expecting students not only to acquire skills and knowledge but to be able to apply their skills and knowledge appropriately and independently in reading, writing, speaking, and listening.

Vocabulary Strategies

Perhaps the best way to expose students to new vocabulary is to increase both the amount of reading they do and the variety of materials they read. By encountering new words in authentic texts, students will get experience in using context clues. This is a skill that will serve them well into college and career.

In addition to increasing the amounts and levels of reading, students need to interact and "play" with words. Interactive and hands-on activities provide a means by which students can internalize new vocabulary and consider qualities of and relationships among words—for instance, examining word structures, morphemes, root words, influences from other languages, and so on. Table 5.2 is a catalog of strategies for developing students' vocabulary.

TABLE 5.2 ● *Strategies for Developing Vocabulary*

Strategy Name	Description
Concept or Vocabulary Map I	The student creates a concept or vocabulary map for each word. Each map contains five fields: one each for the word itself, important characteristics or key elements of the word, wrong/incorrect characteristics of the word, examples of the word, and crossed out examples of the word. Students' vocabulary maps can be displayed on a Word Wall to create a shared learning experience.
Concept or Vocabulary Map II	Compared to Concept or Vocabulary Map I, this version is more explicit about the placement of information and requires an exact definition for the vocabulary word or concept. Each map contains eleven fields: one for the word itself, one for the definition, three called "What is it like?" three called "What is it not like?" and three for "Examples." Again, vocabulary maps can be displayed on a Word Wall to create a shared learning experience.
Concept or Vocabulary Map III	This version requires the student to include an illustration or visualization. Each map contains nine fields: one for the word itself, one for the definition, three called "Examples," three called "Not Examples," and one for an illustration. This version of the map is particularly helpful with concrete nouns similar to those found in a science textbook.
Concept or Vocabulary Map IV	This version requires making a personal connection with the new vocabulary word or concept. Each map contains ten fields: one for the word itself, one for the definition, three called "Examples," three called "Not Examples," one called "I can find this word...," and one called "This word reminds me of...." In the last two fields, the student writes personal connections and ideas about where he or she would encounter the word or concept. Making these kinds of connections helps the student connect to prior knowledge, thus promoting retention into long-term memory.
Concept Sorts*	The teacher provides students with a list of terms or concepts from reading material. Students place words into different categories based on their meanings. After introducing the book or topic to be read, the teacher chooses relevant vocabulary terms and writes them on cards (one word per card), making several sets. The teacher creates and labels the categories or assists students as they sort the cards into their own categories.
Cyber Vocabulary Detective	Students are prompted to find assigned vocabulary words on the Internet and to use this information to determine the words' meanings. Each "Detective Sheet" includes three columns for students to fill out: "Vocabulary Word," "Sentence That Includes the Vocabulary Word," and "What Might the Vocabulary Word Mean?" The teacher gives students a list of Internet sites for use in their research (Dictionary.com, etymonline.com, and Word.com, for example). Audio-supported sites often provide pronunciations.

(continued)

TABLE 5.2 ● *(continued)*

Strategy Name	Description
Double-Entry Journals*	Students record their responses to the text as they read, writing down phrases or sentences from their text and then noting their reaction to each passage. This strategy activates prior knowledge and present feelings and promotes collaborative learning. It also fosters the connection between reading and writing, as students are able to "reply" to the author or speaker as they write their responses.
Frayer Model*	The student creates a vocabulary chart for each word. Each chart contains five fields: one each for the word itself, a definition, facts about the word, examples, and nonexamples. The teacher has students read the assigned text and carefully define the target concepts. Then the student completes the Frayer Model chart for each concept.
List–Group–Label*	Students engage in a three-step process to actively organize their understanding of content area vocabulary and concepts. First, the teacher selects a main concept in a reading passage and has students brainstorm words they think relate to the topic. Then the teacher divides the class into small groups and tells each group to divide the list of words into subcategories. The teacher challenges students to explain their reasoning. Finally, the teacher invites students to suggest a title or label for the groups of words they have formed.
Mnemonics*	A *mnemonic* is a strategy designed to help improve the memory of important information. This technique connects new learning to prior knowledge through the use of visual and/ or acoustic cues. The basic types of mnemonic strategies rely on the use of key words, rhyming words, and acronyms.
Possible Sentences*	Before reading, students are provided a short list of vocabulary words from their reading, which they group and eventually use to create meaningful sentences. After reading, students check to see if their "possible sentences" are accurate or need revising.
Selective Highlighting*	This strategy teaches students to highlight/underline *only* the key words, phrases, and vocabulary that are central to understanding the reading. Students should be instructed to read through the selection first. Then, as they reread, they should begin to highlight only the key vocabulary, not the entire sentence in which the words appear.
Six-Column Vocabulary Organizer Chart	This organizer/chart is actually a log that allows students to catalogue the etymologies of vocabulary words they encounter in their reading. Each chart consists of six columns: "Vocabulary Word," "Dictionary Definition," "Part of Speech," "Synonym," "Antonym," and "Picture That Represents the Word." Five to seven rows (vocabulary words) usually fit on each page. This chart is especially helpful for keeping a log or history of vocabulary words from a particular unit or chapter.
Vocabulary Slide	The student creates a vocabulary "slide" for each word. Each slide contains six fields: one each for the word itself, a synonym, an antonym, an icon or illustration of the word, part of speech, and a sample sentence. Students can also use the slides as flashcards for review.

(continued)

TABLE 5.2 • *(continued)*

Strategy Name	Description
Vocabulary Tree	This highly visual aid requires the student to specify a root word and then find related words—a strategy that supports students in learning and understanding new vocabulary. Each sheet contains an outline of a tree. At the bottom or on the trunk, the student writes the root word. Above, on the branches or among the leaves, the student writes words that are derived from the root word.
Word Detective	In this version, the student fills out a "Detective Sheet" for each word and is then prompted to research the etymology and connect a visual image to the word. Each sheet contains eight fields: one each for the word itself, the text or quote where the word was originally found, context clue #1, context clue #2, the actual definition, the part of speech, the word used in an original sentence, and an illustration that represents the student's understanding of the word. Students can save these sheets and compile their own "Word Detective" notebooks.
Word Hunts*	The teacher asks students to look for words and patterns in reading materials based on selected features. A Word Hunt focuses on the structure and meaning of words by turning students' attention to spelling patterns and root words. To begin, the teacher should demonstrate how to locate words that fit the patterns under study and how to sort those words into categories. Then, as students read and reread a text, the teacher asks them to find words that fit a particular pattern. Finally, students write down words that fit the desired patterns in journals or on charts.

*From "Classroom Strategies," *All About Adolescent Literacy* (www.adlit.org/strategy_library/).

The Frayer Model   The Frayer model is a vocabulary strategy in which a graphic organizer is used to develop students' word knowledge. In the basic strategy, students define a vocabulary word or term and then provide examples and nonexamples of it, recording this information in four different sections of the organizer. The Frayer model, which is often referred to as a *vocabulary slide*, prompts student to examine a few words in great depth. As mentioned earlier, the more students manipulate and use a new word, the more likely it will become part of their vocabulary. This is the kind of direct teaching of vocabulary that works.

The Frayer model can also be adapted in several ways to extend its use (Frayer et al., 1969). Figures 5.1 through 5.4 demonstrate how students can manipulate words using several versions of a basic graphic organizer. In each example, students play with the word at least five times. In several of the organizers, students are prompted to visualize the meanings of the words by providing illustrations, which deepens their understanding and comprehension of language.

FIGURE 5.1 ● Student's completed Frayer model graphic organizer for the word *might.*

Name: *Dan Olson*   Class: *Language Arts*

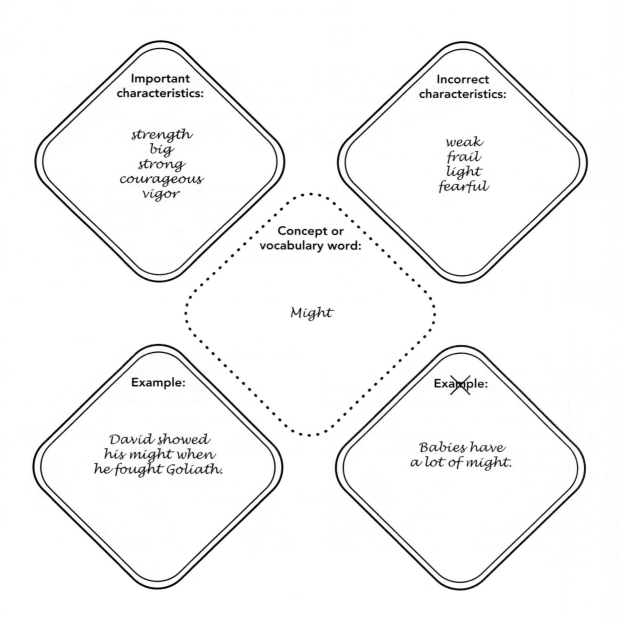

FIGURE 5.2 ● Student's completed Frayer model graphic organizer for the word *ability*. Note that the student was asked to provide an illustration of the word, along with a definition, examples, and nonexamples.

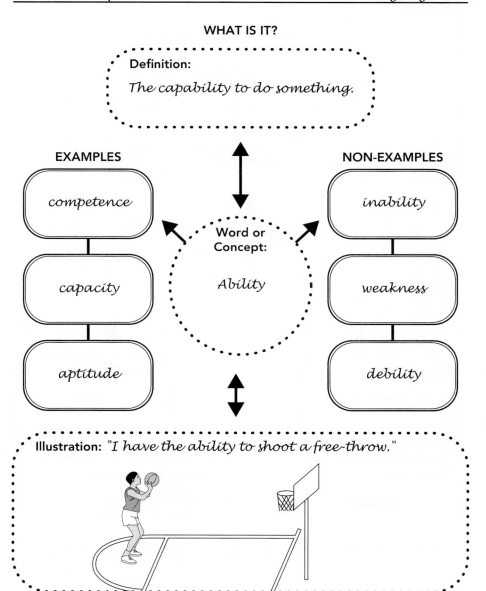

Name: *Jeni Pope*   Class: *Language Arts*

WHAT IS IT?

Definition:

The capability to do something.

EXAMPLES

competence

capacity

aptitude

Word or Concept:

Ability

NON-EXAMPLES

inability

weakness

debility

Illustration: *"I have the ability to shoot a free-throw."*

FIGURE 5.3 ● Student's completed Frayer model graphic organizer for the word *discourage*. In addition to an illustration, this organizer asks for a synonym, antonym, part of speech, and sentence.

Name: *Susan Anderson*   Class: *Language Arts*

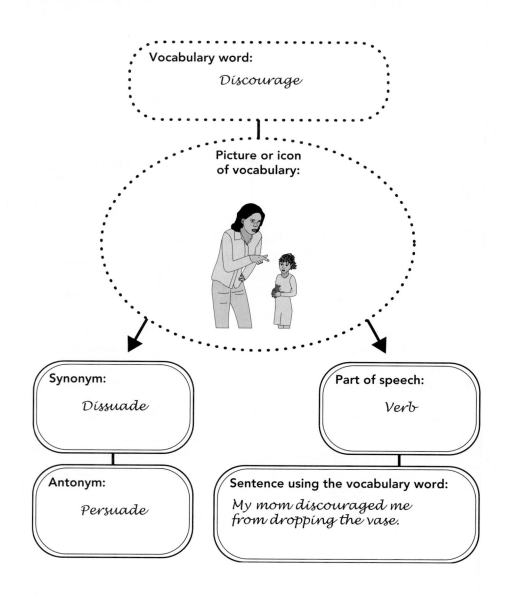

FIGURE 5.4 ● Student's completed Frayer model graphic organizer for the word *melancholy*. In addition to a definition, examples, and nonexamples, this version of the organizer asks the student to record where to find the word and to write a personal reflection about it.

Name: *Ellie Wilson*   **Class:** *Language Arts*

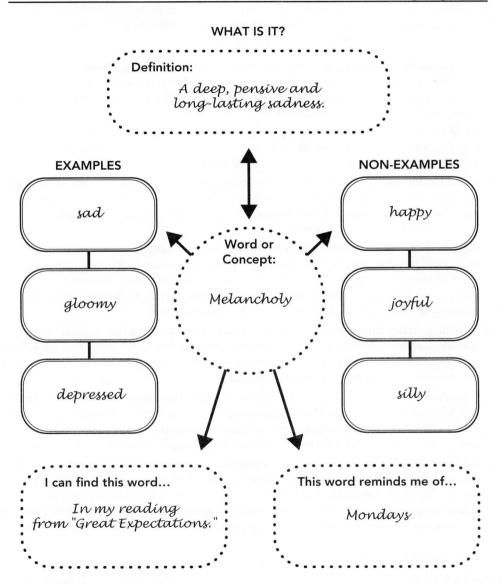

WHAT IS IT?

Definition:
A deep, pensive and long-lasting sadness.

EXAMPLES

sad

gloomy

depressed

Word or Concept:

Melancholy

NON-EXAMPLES

happy

joyful

silly

I can find this word...
In my reading from "Great Expectations."

This word reminds me of...
Mondays

Grammar Strategies

Short, focused mini-lessons provide the ideal format for introducing and reinforcing grammar concepts and conventions such as punctuation. Mini-lessons provide opportunities to offer traditional instruction on the conventions of standard English while allowing students to apply the newly acquired knowledge of language, as specified in the CCSS. As students gain experience in using and applying what they know about language, they develop greater expertise. Also, as Hillocks and Smith (2003) have noted, teaching grammar and language in isolation doesn't work. Students need to work with language on an ongoing basis and interact with others (as in Writing Workshop) to develop the kinds of skills the CCSS articulate.

Here is an overview of the mini-lesson format:

- **Determine the content need.** It might be appropriate for a ninth-grade student to learn about the seven rules for using commas (Strunk, 1918/1999) in a series of seven mini-lessons. However, when reinforcing the seven comma rules for a group of twelfth-graders, all seven rules can likely be covered in one mini-lesson.

- **Keep the lessons short.** The whole point of grammar mini-lessons is to break down concepts into small, easily digestible chunks. Any mini-lesson that will take more than 10 minutes is too long and should be reviewed and revised.

- **Make the lessons simple.** A mini-lesson is most effective when the grammar or writing concept is presented in the smallest digestible chunk. Covering common nouns, proper nouns, and collective nouns in one lesson may be too much. It may be more effective to cover each type of noun in a separate mini-lesson.

- **Engage students and provide for interaction.** Now more than ever, teachers must discover highly engaging and interesting instructional experiences for their technologically savvy students. Twenty-first-century students have unlimited access to information. Classrooms, then, must provide more than information; they must provide hands-on educational activities that approximate real-world experiences.

- **Provide practice time.** Before students are ready to transfer what they learn about grammar and writing to their writing, they need practice. In general, teach the concept and then allow for practice. The third stage, which is the most important, is transference of the new concept to the students' individual writing.

- **Consider what's next.** It's important to plan ahead and follow the curriculum, but be flexible depending on students' needs. For maximum impact, link current mini-lessons with previous mini-lessons. For example, mini-lessons on common nouns, proper nouns, and collective nouns can be logically followed by mini-lessons on possessive apostrophes and adjectives.

- **Evaluate.** The best way to assess whether students understand the grammatical and writing concepts that have been taught is to determine whether they have applied those concepts to their writing. To monitor individual mastery, use writing rubrics and checklists that include the successful application of grammatical and writing concepts as a criterion. As with all classroom activities, students benefit tremendously when provided with both verbal and written directions.

Curriculum Planning

In many school- and district-wide English language arts curriculum maps, vocabulary goals and grammar elements are articulated in great detail. Teachers are instructed to teach sentence structure, agreement, types of verbs, and so on at specific times during specific grade levels.

In many schools, full grammar programs are purchased or created by teachers and form the basis of the curriculum.

Despite being expensive and labor intensive to produce, those curriculum maps are not essential for effective language instruction. Schools and teachers can be sure to meet all curriculum requirements and to teach language skills and knowledge in context by applying these strategies:

1. Take a "skills snapshot" at the beginning of the school year. Use data from standardized tests in addition to audits of student writing. Based on what you observe, create a list of skills that must be addressed.

2. Integrate language skills (vocabulary and grammar) into all areas of English language arts, and encourage your colleagues in the content areas to do the same.

3. Remember that students need to mess with language. Provide regular opportunities for them to work on their language skills in situations in which they will not be penalized for making mistakes.

4. Immerse students in oral and written language. Grant them permission to talk more in class for the purpose of rehearsing and practicing language skills. Collaborative group work is ideal for this purpose.

Classroom Connection

This feature provides three sample grammar mini-lessons and tips for implementing them in the classroom. Note that in each mini-lesson, students are encouraged to play with and manipulate language.

Sample Grammar Mini-Lesson: Adjectives Abound

Overview and Tips for Classroom Implementation:

Students can find it challenging to add descriptive language to their writing. This mini-lesson incorporates strong visuals to prompt students to use adjectives and to incorporate figurative language in narrative writing.

Step-by-Step Instructions:

Prepare for this lesson by collecting pictures from different sources. To conduct the lesson, follow these steps:

1. Allow students to work in pairs. Each student pair selects a picture from the teacher's collection.

2. Ask students to record all of the adjectives they can think of to describe the selected picture. Give student pairs three minutes to complete their lists. Use a timer as the students work on this part of the mini-lesson.

3. Once students have completed their lists, instruct them to use a thesaurus to add more words.

4. Using the completed adjective lists, have each student pair write a narrative paragraph about their picture. Each pair's final product should include the picture, the adjective list, and the narrative paragraph.

● **Additional Tips:**

Scour new and used bookstores and garage sales for pictures. Old coffee table books and calendars contain better photos for this activity than magazines and the Internet. Pictures of nature, landscapes, locations, buildings, and everyday people are more interesting for this activity than pictures of celebrities and famous events.

Sample Grammar Mini-Lesson: Apostrophe Errors in Public Print

Overview and Tips for Classroom Implementation:

Encourage students to find errors in apostrophe use on signs and in printed media—for instance, using apostrophes in forming plurals (*the Smith's, it's*). Finding errors is a favorite activity of students who are developing their own writing and grammar skills. In most cases, they are astounded at the number of errors they find, and they are delighted to find that their proofreading skills are superior to those of professional typesetters.

Step-by-Step Instructions:

Prepare for this mini-lesson by collecting examples of incorrect apostrophe use. Some online sources of examples are listed later in this lesson, but try to find examples from students' own neighborhood or community. Local examples will be more interesting to students.

1. Have students form small groups of two to four. Then distribute among the groups a variety of pictures and samples of printed media that contain errors.
2. Distribute the graphic organizer for this assignment, one per student (see Figure 5.5). Working with group members, students should examine the pictures and printed media examples, identify the apostrophe errors, explain what is incorrect, and provide the correct language.

FIGURE 5.5 ● Graphic organizer for use in mini-lesson about apostrophe use

Directions: For each picture and media example, record the following information in this graphic organizer:

Picture or Media Example (Write down the sentence, statement, or signage with the apostrophe error.)	Explain (What is the apostrophe error?)	Fix It! (Rewrite the sentence or statement correctly.)

Additional Tips:

One of the essential requirements of language learning at any age is to use authentic examples. Providing students with examples that are found in the real world (especially their immediate world) grounds the language learning experience in authenticity. As a result, students will develop a heightened awareness of how language is used in real-world applications.

The graphic organizer can be used as a formative assessment to determine if students are internalizing the concepts associated with correct apostrophe use (e.g., formation of plurals versus possessives, contractions, and so on).

Here are some websites that feature pictures and texts with apostrophe errors:

- Sharon Colon: Apostrophe Picture Galleries (www.sharoncolon.com/pictures.htm)
- Apostrophe Abuse (www.apostropheabuse.com/)
- Grocer's Apostrophe (www.flickr.com/groups/77173807@N00/)

Finally, this particular mini-lesson is not exclusive to errors in using apostrophes. It can easily be adapted to feature any kind of punctuation, grammar, or word usage error.

Sample Grammar Mini Lesson: Colons

Overview and Tips for Classroom Implementation:

In this mini-lesson, students will learn how to use colons correctly and effectively in writing.

Step-by-Step Instructions:

1. Provide the following information about colons to students:

   A colon (:) is a punctuation mark that is used to introduce a series of items. Here are some reminders about how to use colons:

   - Do not use a colon directly after a verb or preposition.

   Example: The winter months are: December, January, and February.

   - Use a colon after the salutation of a business letter.

   Example: Dear Professor:

   - Use a colon between the hour and the minute in writing a time.

   Example: School starts at 8:00 a.m.

   - Use a colon between a title and subtitle:

   Example: Frankenstein: or, the Modern Prometheus.

2. Write each of the following phrases on a piece of heavy paper or card stock. Make the print large enough for all of the students in class to see. Note that the colons are missing (for now):

   Set 1

   Did you go

   to the store

   S McKnight

   8 9

   at 5 00 p.m.?

Set 2

The following students

Tayesha, Will, and Sophie

for the spelling bee.

Set 3

My friend gave me the book,

Frankenstein or the Modern Prometheus

to read.

In addition to these sets of phrase cards, make punctuation cards with colons on them (one colon per card, enough cards for all of the students). It will be helpful to students if the punctuation cards are a different color than the phrase cards.

3. Divide the class into small groups of four students. Give each student a phrase card and a punctuation card. Each group of four students should have four phrase cards and four punctuation cards that will make a full sentence that includes a colon.

4. Ask each group of students to arrange their phrase cards and punctuation cards in a complete sentence. Once the group has completed their sentence, have them present it to their classmates.

Additional Tips:

Before beginning this activity, post the "rules" for colon use at the front of the classroom so students can easily refer to them. Also, as noted earlier, consider using different colors for the phrase cards and the punctuation cards. Using different colors helps students arrange the cards into a cogent sentence.

REFERENCES

Frayer, D., Frederick, W. C., & Klausmeier, H. J. (1969). *A schema for testing the level of cognitive mastery.* Madison, WI: Wisconsin Center for Education Research.

Hillocks, G., & Smith, M. (2003). Grammar and literacy learning. In J. Flood, D. Lapp, J. Squire, & J. Jensen (Eds.), *Handbook of research on teaching the English language arts* (2nd ed., pp. 721–737). Mahwah, NJ: Erlbaum.

National Governors Association Center for Best Practices & Council of Chief State School Officers (NGA & CCSSO). (2010). *Common Core State Standards: English language arts and literacy in history/social studies, science, and technical subjects.* Washington, DC: Authors. Retrieved from www.corestandards.org/assets/CCSSI_ELA%20Standards.pdf.

National Institute for Literacy. (2007). *What content-area teachers should know about adolescent literacy.* Retrieved from http://www.nifl.gov/nifl/publications/adolescent_literacy07.pdf.

Strunk, W., Jr. (1999). *The elements of style. Bartleby.com.* Retrieved from www.bartleby.com/141/. (Original work produced 1918)

Weaver, Constance. (1996). *Teaching grammar in context.* Portsmouth: Boynton/Cook.

Writing

IN A TYPICAL DAY, YOU LIKELY WRITE DOZENS of e-mails, text messages, tweets, and Facebook posts. You may also read a lot of text on the Internet, whether for work or pleasure. I read newspapers and magazines almost exclusively on the Internet, and although I don't always like to admit it, I use Wikipedia on occasion. What's particularly exciting about reading materials such as newspapers and magazines on the Internet is that in many cases, we can respond to them directly in writing. Whenever I feel passionate about a story I've read, I respond in the "Comment" area. I also enjoy reading what other people write, because knowing what others think and believe challenges my own thinking and beliefs.

Our adolescent students are doing all of these things and more. They have rich online lives that many adults are just beginning to understand. In addition to being active with social media, many students read and write blogs and conduct research online (especially about gaming).

Monkey Business/Fotolia

Students frequently post their own writing on the Internet, presenting their views for the entire world to see. Gone are the days in which students shared their writing exclusively with teachers and received feedback only from graded papers with comments written in the margins.

I'll admit that when I consider all of this, I sometimes feel overwhelmed. Today's students are writing for a worldwide audience before they have had the opportunity to read our comments in the margins! And when I think about the fast pace of technology, my excitement is sometimes tempered by dread. How will I ever keep up? When I work with teachers who are learning to use educational technology, I sense their trepidation—and I sympathize.

These are the realities of teaching writing in the twenty-first century. As teachers, we must embrace the fact that our students are writing, even if they are writing in different contexts than we had ever imagined. We must also take "baby steps" to develop our knowledge about using technology to help our students develop literacy skills. In fact, our students may be the best guides for helping us learn these new technologies. We should show similar patience as we guide them in becoming coherent and inspired writers in today's world.

Key Observations about Teaching and Learning Writing

IN THE 1980S, THE WORK OF WRITING GURUS such as Nancy Atwell, Lucy Calkins, Donald Murray, and Tom Romano led to a paradigmatic shift in writing instruction, in which the focus changed from the *product* to the *process*. Since then, English language arts teachers have worked with students across all grade levels to approach writing as a multistage, recursive process. This paradigmatic shift gave us the familiar elements of writing instruction that we all know today, such as *prewriting, drafting, revising, editing,* and *publishing.*

The work of these experts, along with contemporaneous research, also firmly established that adolescent students develop writing skills when they do the following:

1. write often
2. rethink and revise their writing
3. work together as a community of writers
4. recognize the importance of expressing what they know and understand through writing.

Now, we find ourselves in the second decade of a new century. We are emerging from a period during which significantly more emphasis was placed on reading than writing. Indeed, during the era of No Child Left Behind, the five essential components of reading (phonemic awareness, phonics, vocabulary, fluency, and comprehension) were the focus of both instruction and testing (NRP, 2000). Writing, on the other hand, wasn't tested in many states and school districts and therefore received little attention in the classroom. Frankly, because it wasn't tested, it didn't count. Not only was this policy misguided, but it was also illogical. The research corpus on the development of literacy strongly demonstrates the connections between reading and writing (Heller, 2007; National Institute for Literacy, 2007; Flood, 2003).

The developers of the Common Core State Standards (CCSS) read the research and recognized the need to focus equally on reading and writing. Writing, from the view of the developers, is the means through which we express what we know and understand from reading. Moreover, writing skills are foundational to college and career readiness.

Exploring the Writing Standards

IN THE CCSS DOCUMENT, THE INTRODUCTION to the Writing standards includes the following note about the range and content of students' writing:

> For students, writing is a key means of asserting and defending claims, showing what they know about a subject, and conveying what they have experienced, imagined, thought, and felt. To be college- and career-ready writers, students must take task, purpose, and audience into careful consideration, choosing words, information, structures, and formats deliberately. They need to know how to combine elements of different kinds of writing—for example, to use narrative strategies within argument and explanation within narrative—to produce complex and nuanced writing. They need to be able to use technology strategically when creating, refining, and collaborating on writing. They have to become adept at gathering information, evaluating sources, and citing material accurately, reporting findings from their research and analysis of sources in a clear and cogent manner. They must have the flexibility, concentration, and fluency to produce high-quality first-draft text under a tight deadline as well as the capacity to revisit and make improvements to a piece of writing over multiple drafts when circumstances encourage or require it. (NGA & CCSSO, 2010a, p. 41)

This note outlines the knowledge and skills that students today need to be prepared for college and career. Toward that goal, the CCSS define what students should know and be able to do by the end of each grade.

For high school, the CCSS English Language Arts (ELA) Standards outline expectations for two grade-level bands: grades 9–10 and grades 11–12. Like the other strands of the ELA Standards (Reading, Language, and Listening and Speaking), the Writing strand includes two levels of standards. The first level, the Common Core Readiness (CCR) Anchor Standards, identifies the basic knowledge and skills essential to becoming an effective writer (see Table 6.1). The same CCR Anchor Standards underlie the Writing standards for all grade levels, from kindergarten through grade 12.

TABLE 6.1 ● *Common Core Readiness (CCR) Anchor Standards for Writing, Grades 9–12**

Text Types and Purposes**
1. Write arguments to support claims in an analysis of substantive topics or texts, using valid reasoning and relevant and sufficient evidence.
2. Write informative/explanatory texts to examine and convey complex ideas and information clearly and accurately through the effective selection, organization, and analysis of content.
3. Write narratives to develop real or imagined experiences or events using effective technique, well-chosen details, and well-structured event sequences.

(*continued*)

TABLE 6.1 ● *(continued)*

Text Types and Purposes**

Production and Distribution of Writing

4. Produce clear and coherent writing in which the development, organization, and style are appropriate to task, purpose, and audience.
5. Develop and strengthen writing as needed by planning, revising, editing, rewriting, or trying a new approach.
6. Use technology, including the Internet, to produce and publish writing and to interact and collaborate with others.

Research to Build and Present Knowledge

7. Conduct short as well as more sustained research projects based on focus questions, demonstrating understanding of the subject under investigation.
8. Gather relevant information for multiple print and digital sources, assess the credibility and accuracy of each source, and integrate the information while avoiding plagiarism.
9. Draw evidence from literary or informational texts to support analysis, reflection, and research.

Range of Writing

10. Write routinely over extended time frames (time for research, reflection, and revision) and shorter time frames (a single sitting or a day or two) for a range of tasks, purposes, and audiences.

*These Anchor Standards apply to grades 6–12.
**These broad types of writing include many subgenres. See Appendix A (NGA & CCSSO, 2010b) for definitions of key writing types.
Source: NGA & CCSSO (2010).

The Anchor Standards provide a foundation for the second level of standards, which outlines specific grade-level expectations. In fact, the ELA Writing standards follow the same organization and numbering as the Anchor Standards (see Table 6.2). The developers of the CCSS describe the two levels of standards as "necessary complements—the former providing broad standards, the latter providing additional specificity—that together define the skills and understandings that all students must demonstrate" (NGA & CCSSO, 2010a, p. 41).

The 10 skills outlined in the Writing standards are organized into four clusters, or categories:

1. Text Types and Purposes
2. Production and Distribution of Writing
3. Research to Build and Present Knowledge
4. Range of Writing

As we will discuss throughout this chapter, these four clusters should represent the foci of writing instruction in the CCSS curriculum and classroom.

TABLE 6.2 ● *CCSS Writing Standards for Grades 9–12*

Grades 9–10 students:	Grades 11–12 students:
Text Types and Purposes	

1. Write arguments to support claims in an analysis of substantive topics or texts, using valid reasoning and relevant and sufficient evidence.

   a. Introduce precise claim(s), distinguish the claim(s) from alternate or opposing claims, and create an organization that establishes clear relationships among claim(s), counterclaims, reasons, and evidence.

   b. Develop claim(s) and counterclaims fairly, supplying evidence for each while pointing out the strengths and limitations of both in a manner that anticipates the audience's knowledge level and concerns.

   c. Use words, phrases, and clauses to link the major sections of the text, create cohesion, and clarify the relationships between claim(s) and reasons, between reasons and evidence, and between claim(s) and counterclaims.

   d. Establish and maintain a formal style and objective tone while attending to the norms and conventions of the discipline in which they are writing.

   e. Provide a concluding statement or section that follows from and supports the argument presented.

2. Write informative/explanatory texts to examine and convey complex ideas, concepts, and information clearly and accurately through the effective selection, organization, and analysis of content.

   a. Introduce a topic; organize complex ideas, concepts, and information to make important connections and distinctions; include formatting (e.g., headings), graphics (e.g., figures, tables), and multimedia when useful to aiding comprehension.

1. Write arguments to support claims in an analysis of substantive topics or texts, using valid reasoning and relevant and sufficient evidence.

   a. Introduce precise, knowledgeable claim(s), establish the significance of the claim(s), distinguish the claim(s) from alternate or opposing claims, and create an organization that logically sequences claim(s), counterclaims, reasons, and evidence.

   b. Develop claim(s) and counterclaims fairly and thoroughly, supplying the most relevant evidence for each while pointing out the strengths and limitations of both in a manner that anticipates the audience's knowledge level, concerns, values, and possible biases.

   c. Use words, phrases, and clauses as well as varied syntax to link the major sections of the text, create cohesion, and clarify the relationships between claim(s) and reasons, between reasons and evidence, and between claim(s) and counterclaims.

   d. Establish and maintain a formal style and objective tone while attending to the norms and conventions of the discipline in which they are writing.

   e. Provide a concluding statement or section that follows from and supports the argument presented.

2. Write informative/explanatory texts to examine and convey complex ideas, concepts, and information clearly and accurately through the effective selection, organization, and analysis of content.

   a. Introduce a topic; organize complex ideas, concepts, and information so that each new element builds on that which precedes it to create a unified whole; include formatting (e.g., headings), graphics (e.g., figures, tables), and multimedia when useful to aiding comprehension.

(continued)

TABLE 6.2 • *(continued)*

Grades 9–10 students:	Grades 11–12 students:
Text Types and Purposes	

Grades 9–10 students:

b. Develop the topic with well-chosen, relevant, and sufficient facts, extended definitions, concrete details, quotations, or other information and examples appropriate to the audience's knowledge of the topic.

c. Use appropriate and varied transitions to link the major sections of the text, create cohesion, and clarify the relationships among complex ideas and concepts.

d. Use precise language and domain-specific vocabulary to manage the complexity of the topic.

e. Establish and maintain a formal style and objective tone while attending to the norms and conventions of the discipline in which they are writing.

f. Provide a concluding statement or section that follows from and supports the information or explanation presented (e.g., articulating implications or the significance of the topic).

3. Write narratives to develop real or imagined experiences or events using effective technique, well-chosen details, and well-structured event sequences.

a. Engage and orient the reader by setting out a problem, situation, or observation, establishing one or multiple point(s) of view, and introducing a narrator and/or characters; create a smooth progression of experiences or events.

b. Use narrative techniques, such as dialogue, pacing, description, reflection, and multiple plot lines, to develop experiences, events, and/or characters.

c. Use a variety of techniques to sequence events so that they build on one another to create a coherent whole.

d. Use precise words and phrases, telling details, and sensory language to convey a vivid picture of the experiences, events, setting, and/or characters.

Grades 11–12 students:

b. Develop the topic thoroughly by selecting the most significant and relevant facts, extended definitions, concrete details, quotations, or other information and examples appropriate to the audience's knowledge of the topic.

c. Use appropriate and varied transitions and syntax to link the major sections of the text, create cohesion, and clarify the relationships among complex ideas and concepts.

d. Use precise language, domain-specific vocabulary, and techniques such as metaphor, simile, and analogy to manage the complexity of the topic.

e. Establish and maintain a formal style and objective tone while attending to the norms and conventions of the discipline in which they are writing.

f. Provide a concluding statement or section that follows from and supports the information or explanation presented (e.g., articulating implications or the significance of the topic).

3. Write narratives to develop real or imagined experiences or events using effective technique, well-chosen details, and well-structured event sequences.

a. Engage and orient the reader by setting out a problem, situation, or observation and its significance, establishing one or multiple point(s) of view, and introducing a narrator and/or characters; create a smooth progression of experiences or events.

b. Use narrative techniques, such as dialogue, pacing, description, reflection, and multiple plot lines, to develop experiences, events, and/or characters.

c. Use a variety of techniques to sequence events so that they build on one another to create a coherent whole and build toward a particular tone and outcome (e.g., a sense of mystery, suspense, growth, or resolution).

(continued)

TABLE 6.2 • *(continued)*

Grades 9–10 students:	Grades 11–12 students:
Text Types and Purposes	

e. Provide a conclusion that follows from and reflects on what is experienced, observed, or resolved over the course of the narrative.	d. Use precise words and phrases, telling details, and sensory language to convey a vivid picture of the experiences, events, setting, and/or characters.
	e. Provide a conclusion that follows from and reflects on what is experienced, observed, or resolved over the course of the narrative.

Production and Distribution of Writing

4. Produce clear and coherent writing in which the development, organization, and style are appropriate to task, purpose, and audience. (Grade-specific expectations for writing types are defined in standards 1–3 above.)	4. Produce clear and coherent writing in which the development, organization, and style are appropriate to task, purpose, and audience. (Grade-specific expectations for writing types are defined in standards 1–3 above.)
5. Develop and strengthen writing as needed by planning, revising, editing, rewriting, or trying a new approach, focusing on addressing what is most significant for a specific purpose and audience. (Editing for conventions should demonstrate command of Language standards 1–3 up to and including grades 9–10.)*	5. Develop and strengthen writing as needed by planning, revising, editing, rewriting, or trying a new approach, focusing on addressing what is most significant for a specific purpose and audience. (Editing for conventions should demonstrate command of Language standards 1–3 up to and including grades 11–12.)*
6. Use technology, including the Internet, to produce, publish, and update individual or shared writing products, taking advantage of technology's capacity to link to other information and to display information flexibly and dynamically.	6. Use technology, including the Internet, to produce, publish, and update individual or shared writing products in response to ongoing feedback, including new arguments or information.

Research to Build and Present Knowledge

7. Conduct short as well as more sustained research projects to answer a question (including a self-generated question) or solve a problem; narrow or broaden the inquiry when appropriate; synthesize multiple sources on the subject, demonstrating understanding of the subject under investigation.	7. Conduct short as well as more sustained research projects to answer a question (including a self-generated question) or solve a problem; narrow or broaden the inquiry when appropriate; synthesize multiple sources on the subject, demonstrating understanding of the subject under investigation.
8. Gather relevant information from multiple authoritative print and digital sources, using advanced searches effectively; assess the usefulness of each source in answering the research question; integrate information into the text selectively to maintain the flow of ideas, avoiding plagiarism and following a standard format for citation.	8. Gather relevant information from multiple authoritative print and digital sources, using advanced searches effectively; assess the strengths and limitations of each source in terms of the task, purpose, and audience; integrate information into the text selectively to maintain the flow of ideas, avoiding plagiarism and overreliance on any one source and following a standard format for citation.

(continued)

TABLE 6.2 ● *(continued)*

Grades 9–10 students:	Grades 11–12 students:
Text Types and Purposes	
9. Draw evidence from literary or informational texts to support analysis, reflection, and research.	9. Draw evidence from literary or informational texts to support analysis, reflection, and research.
a. Apply grades 9–10 Reading standards to literature (e.g., "Analyze how an author draws on and transforms source material in a specific work [e.g., how Shakespeare treats a theme or topic from Ovid or the Bible or how a later author draws on a play by Shakespeare]").**	a. Apply grades 11–12 Reading standards to literature (e.g., "Demonstrate knowledge of eighteenth-, nineteenth- and early-twentieth-century foundational works of American literature, including how two or more texts from the same period treat similar themes or topics").**
b. Apply grades 9–10 Reading standards to literary nonfiction (e.g., "Delineate and evaluate the argument and specific claims in a text, assessing whether the reasoning is valid and the evidence is relevant and sufficient; identify false statements and fallacious reasoning").**	b. Apply grades 11–12 Reading standards to literary nonfiction (e.g., "Delineate and evaluate the reasoning in seminal U.S. texts, including the application of constitutional principles and use of legal reasoning [e.g., in U.S. Supreme Court Case majority opinions and dissents] and the premises, purposes, and arguments in works of public advocacy [e.g., The Federalist, presidential addresses]").**
Range of Writing	
10. Write routinely over extended time frames (time for research, reflection, and revision) and shorter time frames (a single sitting or a day or two) for a range of tasks, purposes, and audiences.	10. Write routinely over extended time frames (time for research, reflection, and revision) and shorter time frames (a single sitting or a day or two) for a range of tasks, purposes, and audiences.

*The Language standards for grades 9–10 and 11–12 are provided on pp. 54–55 of the CCSS (NGA & CCSSO, 2010a).

**The Reading standards for grades 9–10 and 11–12 are provided on pp. 38 (literature) and 40 (informational text) of the CCSS (NGA & CCSSO, 2010a).
Source: NGA & CCSSO (2010).

Writing and the CCSS

The Focus on Text Types and Purposes

The first cluster of Writing standards, Text Types and Purposes, comprises three standards that state expectations for writing three different types of texts: arguments (Standard 1), informative/explanatory texts (Standard 2), and narratives (Standard 3). Each standard states the general purpose associated with the text type and then provides five or six subitems that identify the specific skills and knowledge needed to create a quality piece of writing (see Table 6.2). Subitems address points such as organization, supporting claims and facts, vocabulary and language use, style and tone, and techniques relevant to the specific type of text.

Before discussing expectations for writing these three types of texts, we should note several points about the terminology used in the Writing standards. First of all, the standards use the term *text types,* not *genres* or *modes* of writing. The latter terms are frequently used in the English language arts, whereas *text types* is applicable across the content areas. The use of *text types* is particularly appropriate for the CCSS because the interdisciplinary Standards for Literacy in History/Social Studies, Science, and Technical Subjects use nearly the same standards for writing as the ELA Standards (NGA & CCSSO, 2010a, pp. 63–65). (The exception is Standard 3 about narrative writing, which is less applicable to the content areas than to the English language arts; see the later section on Writing Narratives.) This selection of terminology is significant, because we know that when expectations for learning are articulated in common language across all of the content areas, students' achievement generally increases (Marzano, 2001; Beck, 2002; Marzano, 2004; Marzano, 2005).

A second point about the language used in the Writing standards is that the term *claim* is used to describe statements of opinion or inference, not *thesis*. Again, the latter term is associated with the English language arts, whereas *claim* is appropriate for use across the content areas. Teachers should understand that the word *claim* can be used interchangeably with *thesis* (commonly used in English and social studies classes), *hypothesis* (used in science), and *postulate* or *theorem* (used in mathematics).

Writing Arguments   Writing argumentative texts is not a new element in the writing curriculum. English language arts teachers have traditionally expected students to state claims (theses) in writing about literary works and to defend their interpretations or judgments (claims) by citing evidence from the text. However, the CCSS Writing standards place particular emphasis on writing arguments, a skill that is viewed as being essential for success in career and college (NGA & CCSSO, 2010b, p. 24).

In Appendix A of the CCSS, the term *argument* is defined as "a reasoned, logical way of demonstrating that the writer's position, belief, or conclusion is valid" (NGA & CCSSO, 2010b, p. 23). The purposes of argument include to change the reader's point of view, to rally the reader to take action, and to ask the reader to accept the explanation or viewpoint given of the topic at hand (p. 24). Examples of arguments include essays, as well as op-ed pieces from newspaper and magazines, speeches and other forms of rhetoric, and even electronic resources such as blogs.

In preparing an argument, the writer must assert a claim, locate and apply relevant evidence, and integrate reasoning to support his or her assertion. Moreover, when a writer is able to debate an issue by establishing a claim and explaining and supporting that claim with evidence and reasoning, he or she finds that readers are more willing to accept his or her position, belief, and conclusion. Neil Postman (1997), a cultural critic and media theorist, suggests that argumentation requires the application of high-level thinking skills. In creating claims and anticipating counterclaims, the writer must assess not only his or her own thinking but that of the audience.

Gerald Graff (2003, 2010), a noted scholar in writing pedagogy, suggests that "argument literacy" is fundamental to being well educated (NGA & CCSSO, 2010b, p. 24). He points out that a university is essentially an "argument culture" (p. 24) and that high school students should be prepared to engage in that culture. Many students are not adequately prepared, however, because argumentative writing isn't part of most high school curricula.

At the high school level, the expectations stated in the Writing Standard 1 go beyond merely being able to state an opinion. At this level, students are expected to be proficient in identifying and refuting alternate or opposing claims and in finding and applying source materials to support their arguments. When forming their argument and choosing their supporting material, students are also expected to anticipate their audience's knowledge and concerns. Finally, students are expected to attend to details of word choice, style, and tone in crafting an effective argument.

(See the later section Using the Written Samples, which reviews an argument written by a ninth-grade student and provided in Appendix C of the CCSS [NGA & CCSSO, 2010c].)

Writing Informative/Explanatory Texts   "Informational/explanatory writing conveys information accurately" (NGA & CCSSO, 2010b, p. 23) and serves several purposes: to increase the reader's knowledge about a topic, to help the reader understand a procedure or process, and to enhance the reader's comprehension of a concept. Examples of informational/ explanatory writing from academia include literary analyses, scientific and historical reports, and summaries, and examples from the workplace include instructions, manuals, memos, reports, applications, and résumés (p. 23). Other common examples include news articles in newspapers and magazines, nonfiction books, and electronic texts such as websites and informative blogs.

The developers of the CCSS distinguish between argumentative and informational/ explanatory types of texts. While both "provide information about causes, contexts, and consequences of processes, phenomena, states of affairs, objects, terminology, and so on" (NGA & CCSSO, 2010b, p. 23), they differ in purpose. An argument is intended to persuade the reader, whereas an informational/explanatory text is intended to make the reader understand. "In short, arguments are used for persuasion and explanations for clarification" (p. 23).

Informative/explanatory writing draws on the work of James Britton (1992) and colleagues (1975) in the Writing to Learn movement, which began in the 1980s. That movement was based on the notion that students' thinking and understanding can grow and become clearer through writing. Students who were able to write about what they know and understand were shown to have higher levels of comprehension. Students' ability to express personal knowledge through writing is strongly connected to the skills necessary for career and college readiness.

Informational/explanatory writing isn't limited to the reporting of facts. Rather, the student must develop a focus or controlling idea, locate supporting information from a range of sources, and incorporate relevant examples, facts, and details from those sources in his or her writing. The student is also expected to use a variety of writing techniques that are reminiscent of the verbs used in Bloom's (1956) taxonomy: *naming, defining, describing, comparing and contrasting,* and *representing.* If the student can apply these techniques in writing, he or she is a competent writer and able to demonstrate his or her understanding of content knowledge.

The CCSS Writing standards state expectations for high school students to have strong skills in writing informational/explanatory texts and to be able to use them to demonstrate what they know and understand in a wide variety of disciplines and domains. Standard 2 states specific expectations for organization and development, for formatting, for language use and vocabulary, and for style and tone.

Writing Narratives   In Appendix A of the CCSS, narrative writing is described as "convey[ing] experience, either real or imaginary, and us[ing] time as its deep structure" (NGA & CCSSO, 2010b, p. 23). Four general purposes are identified for narrative writing: to inform, to instruct, to persuade, and to entertain. Examples of narrative writing include fiction, science fiction, fantasy memoir, biography, and narrative nonfiction.

In the English language arts, students across the grades write narratives such as stories, memoirs, anecdotes, and biographies. As they develop skills in narrative writing, they add visual details, depict specific actions, create dialogue and interior monologue, and control the pace to suit the telling of the story. In the content areas, students may write narratives about individuals and events (history/social studies) and the procedures followed in an experiment or study (science). With practice, students develop increasingly sophisticated narrative strategies and learn how to apply them in different situations and for different purposes.

Writing Standard 3 states the expectations for narrative writing. High school students are expected to have a strong repertoire of narrative techniques (such as dialogue, pacing, multiple plot lines) and to be able to apply them in developing the story and engaging the reader. In addition, students should be able to use precise language and sensory details to capture the experience, event, setting, or person about which they are writing.

In Appendix A, the developers of the CCSS note that Standard 3 does not address all of the possible types of creative writing, including many types of poetry. "The Standards leave the inclusion and evaluation of other such forms to teacher discretion" (NGA & CCSSO, 2010b, p. 23). This exception is consistent with the statements in the introduction to the CCSS, in which the developers call for teachers and curriculum specialists to determine the instructional strategies and content best suited to support and develop the literacy skills articulated in the document (NGA & CCSSO, 2010a, pp. 4, 6).

Finally, in the interdisciplinary Standards for Literacy in History/Social Studies, Science, and Technical Subjects, Writing Standard 3 is noted as being "Not applicable as a separate requirement" (NGA & CCSSO, 2010a, p. 65). However, given the common use of narrative writing across the content areas, the developers of the CCSS provide this explanation:

> Students' narrative skills continue to grow in these grades. The Standards require that students be able to incorporate narrative elements effectively into arguments and informative/explanatory texts. In history/social studies, students must be able to incorporate narrative accounts into their analyses of individuals or events of historical import. In science and technical subjects, students must be able to write precise enough descriptions of the step-by-step procedures they use in their investigations or technical work that others can replicate them and (possibly) reach the same results. (p. 65)

Using the Writing Samples   Appendix C of the CCSS (NGA & CCSSO, 2010c) contains samples of students' writing that meet the expectations outlined in the Writing standards. Specifically, annotated samples are provided for the three types of texts (argument, informative/ explanatory text, and narrative) for students of specific grades (K–12). (Note, however, that for grades 9–12, samples are provided only for arguments and informative/explanatory texts, not narratives.) Teachers should view these samples as representative of the quality needed to meet the Writing standards for particular grades. Evaluating writing is a complex process, and teachers often have strong opinions about what constitutes a good piece of writing. These writing samples should be used to support teachers in making this determination.

In the introduction to Appendix C, the CCSS developers note that the samples represent a range of achievement with each grade, reflecting differences both in students' skills and in the conditions under which students worked (NGA & CCSSO, 2010c, p. 2). Some of the samples were written in class, whereas others were done as homework. Still others were written as on-demand assessments or as the products of sustained research projects. The student authors were from schools across the United States.

The first writing sample for grade 9 is an argument written as a class assignment, in which "students were asked to compare a book they read on their own to a movie about the same story and to prove which was better" (NGA & CCSSO, 2010c, p. 57). To complete this assignment, students were given six weeks to read the book and one-and-a-half weeks to write the argument; the writing was completed both in and out of class.

The sample argument is a traditional five-paragraph essay (approximately 1,500 words) with an introduction (one paragraph), body (three paragraphs), and conclusion (one paragraph). The student author uses the technique of comparison/contrast to discuss the supporting characters, irony, and themes in the book and movie versions of *The Boy in the Striped Pajamas,* by John Boyne (2006). The author presents his or her claim at the end of the introduction: in sum, that the movie is not as good as the book. Then the author supports the claim by providing evidence from the text and reasoning about the differences between the book and the movie. In the conclusion, the author restates the claim, summarizes the key points of the argument, and offers final thoughts about the value of the book.

The annotation that follows the writing sample identifies specific elements from the argument that meet specific expectations of Writing Standard 1. In the sample argument about *The Boy in the Striped Pajamas* (Boyne, 2007), the student author met these expectations for grade 9:

- **W.1.a:** Introduce precise claim(s), distinguish the claim(s) from alternate or opposing claims,
- **W.1.b:** Develop claim(s) and counterclaims fairly, supplying evidence for each while pointing out the strengths and limitations of both in a manner that anticipates the audience's knowledge level and concerns.
- **W.1.c:** Use words, phrases, and clauses to link the major sections of the text, create cohesion, and clarify the relationships between claim(s) and reasons, between reasons and evidence, and between claim(s) and counterclaims.
- **W.1.d:** Establish and maintain a formal style and objective tone.
- **W.1.f:** Provide a concluding statement or section that follows from and supports the argument presented (NGA & CCSSO, 2010a, p. 45).

The student author also met the following CCSS Language standards for grade 9:

- **L.1:** Demonstrate command of the conventions of standard English grammar and usage when writing or speaking.
- **L.2:** Demonstrate command of the conventions of standard English capitalization, punctuation, and spelling when writing (NGA & CCSSO, 2010a, p. 54).

Many of the skill expectations for conventions of standard English are integrated in other ELA strands, demonstrating the coherence of the CCSS. (See Chapter 5 for a discussion of the Language standards.)

As English language arts teachers, we should examine the samples of student writing in Appendix C for our respective grade levels and then discuss them with colleagues to explore how they represent the skills articulated in Writing standards. Having these professional discussions is the best way for us to determine areas in which our students are meeting the expectations of the standards and areas in which they are falling short. Once we clearly articulate what students can and cannot do, we can develop a focused curriculum and provide instruction that meets the rigorous expectations of the CCSS Writing standards.

The Focus on Process

The second cluster of the CCSS Writing standards, Production and Distribution of Writing, addresses the means by which students produce and share their writing. Standard 4 states the expectation for producing writing that is clear and coherent and that fits the parameters for development, organization, and style for the given task, purpose, and audience. (A cross-reference is provided to Standards 1–3, which outline the parameters for the three main types of texts.)

Standard 5 states the expectation that students follow a writing process "by planning, revising, editing, rewriting, or trying a new approach" (NGA & CCSSO, 2010a, p. 46). The developers of the CCSS do not advocate a particular writing process but clearly stipulate that one should be followed. Interestingly, CCR Anchor Standard 5 for Writing, when reviewed across the grade levels, is almost identical from kindergarten through grade 12. What this means is that students should continually develop and strengthen their writing skills by following a process that includes planning, revising, and editing. The expectations for the level of planning, revision, and editing become greater as students progress through the grades and achieve greater independence in applying these skills.

Standard 6 addresses the use of technology to produce and publish writing, whether individual or shared products. Students are expected to "[take] advantage of technology's capacity to link to other information and to display information flexibly and dynamically" (NGA & CCSSO, 2010a, p. 46). Anchor Standard 6 also stipulates the use of technology "to interact and collaborate with others" (p. 41). Standard 6 supports the concept of *media literacy,* which can be defined as "a series of communication competencies, including the ability to access, analyze, evaluate, and communicate information in a variety of forms, including print and non-print messages" (NAMLE, 2013). Although the CCSS do not address media literacy specifically, expectations for using technology are stated in both the Writing standards and the Listening and Speaking standards. Despite the prevalence of technology in today's world and many students' aptitude for using it, media literacy—like any type of literacy—must be learned.

The Focus on Research

In the Writing standards, the third cluster focuses on skills for conducting research and presenting information. As noted by the developers of the CCSS, "Because of the centrality of writing to most forms of inquiry, research standards are prominently included in [the Writing] strand, though skills important to research are infused throughout the document" (NGA & CCSSO, 2010a, p. 8).

Specifically, Standard 7 states expectations for students to complete both short- and long-term projects that are based on focused questions and that demonstrate understanding of the topic being explored. Standards 8 and 9 state expectations for students to use multiple forms of source materials, including print and digital sources (Standard 8) and literary and informational texts (Standard 9). Standard 8 also identifies skills for assessing the credibility of a source and integrating information from a source without committing plagiarism, and Standard 9 reiterates the importance of the reading–writing connection by expecting students to use and write about evidence from both literary and informational texts (NGA & CCSSO, 2010a, p. 8).

The standards in this cluster also reiterate the importance of students' skills in using technology. To demonstrate how technology and research can be combined in teaching writing, review the following WebQuest activity. The purpose of the activity is to build students' background knowledge as they prepare to read Harper Lee's (1960) novel *To Kill a Mockingbird,* which is commonly studied in grade 9 or 10.

Classroom Connection

Building Background for *To Kill a Mockingbird*

One of the challenges in teaching *To Kill a Mockingbird* (Lee, 1960) is that students don't have sufficient background knowledge of the Great Depression of the 1930s and life in the U.S. South before the Civil Rights Movement of the 1960s. Building students' background knowledge, or *schema,* is critical to improving their reading comprehension (as discussed in Chapter 3, Reading Comprehension). To build background for this novel, we can incorporate the skills addressed in CCSS Writing Standards 7, 8, and 9, as well as essential technology skills, in a WebQuest instructional activity. (Note that many of the Library of Congress resources mentioned in this activity provide links that identify applicable CCSS.)

Teachers who are not familiar with WebQuests are advised to visit the website WebQuest.Org (www.webquest.org), which provides resources for finding, building, and sharing WebQuests. Briefly, a WebQuest "is an inquiry-oriented lesson format in which most or all the information that learners work with comes from the web" (Dodge, 2007). The model was developed by Bernie Dodge at the San Diego State University Department of Educational Technology.

Great research begins with an interesting and engaging question. Here is a sample of a so-called essential question that can focus students' research:

> In the novel *To Kill a Mockingbird,* how does the author, Harper Lee, develop the themes of courage and cowardice using the historical context of the American South in the 1930s?

Using the WebQuest model, we can guide students through a variety of resources that provide them with key informational texts to supplement reading of the literary text. Here is a sample WebQuest about *To Kill a Mockingbird* designed for ninth-grade students.

Building Background for To Kill a Mockingbird: 1930s Time Capsule

INTRODUCTION: We are about to read Harper Lee's *To Kill a Mockingbird.* The historical context of the novel is rich and important for our close reading of the text. To build our knowledge about the time and place, or *setting,* of the novel, we are going to examine some historical documents and articles about the American South in the 1930s. As you examine the documents and related texts, consider what these artifacts tell us about American South in the 1930s.

TASK: You will be assigned to a group with three additional classmates. In your group, you will create a time capsule about the American South in the 1930s. Your time capsule should contain at least 10 artifacts. For each selected artifact, you must answer the following questions:

- What is the origin of this artifact?
- What does this artifact reveal about the American South in the 1930s?
- Why did your group select this artifact for your time capsule?

Once you and your classmates have identified which artifacts to include, use one of the following Web 2.0 tools to create your time capsule:

Glogster   www.glogster.com

LiveBinders   www.livebinders.com

Museum Box   http://museumbox.e2bn.org

PROCESS: As a group, review and complete the chart provided as you analyze and discuss the 10 artifacts that you selected (see Figure 6.1).

FIGURE 6.1 ● Chart for Recording Analysis of Artifacts

Title of Artifact	Summarize the information presented in the artifact.	What does the artifact reveal about the American South in the 1930s?	A question we have after reviewing the artifact is . . .	Should this artifact be included in our time capsule? (Why or why not?)

RESOURCES: Use the following websites to find artifacts about *To Kill a Mockingbird* and about life in the American South during the 1930s:

- **Shmoop** (www.shmoop.com/to-kill-a-mockingbird/resources.html)—This site has a variety of photos and video links to information about the novel and the 1962 movie based on it. It provides a wide variety of resources that you can examine for your group discussion.

- **Library of Congress, Farm Security Administration/Office of War Information** (http://memory.loc.gov/ammem/fsahtml/fahome.html)—This site displays a photo collection that features life in small-town America from 1935 to 1945, during the time of the Great Depression.

- **Library of Congress, Southern Mosaic: The John and Ruby Lomax 1939 Southern States Recording Trip** (www.loc.gov/teachers/classroommaterials/connections/ southern-mosaic/file.html)—This site documents the materials collected on a three-month trip throughout the southern United States, including sound recordings, field notes, and other materials.

- **Library of Congress, African-American Odyssey** (http://lcweb2.loc.gov/ammem/ aaohtml/)—This site includes materials that document the historical struggle of African Americans.

- **Library of Congress, Jim Crow in America** (www.loc.gov/teachers/ classroommaterials/primarysourcesets/civil-rights)—This site displays a range of primary source documents about the Jim Crow law, including the text of the law.

- **Chronicling America** (http://chroniclingamerica.loc.gov/lccn/sn83045433/1908-06-05/ ed-1/seq-12)—This site provides a 1908 newspaper containing an article about the Jim Crow law being upheld by the U.S. Supreme Court.

- **Encyclopedia.com: The 1930s** (www.encyclopedia.com/doc/1G2-3468301229 .html)—This site provides an overview of U.S. lifestyles and social trends in the 1930s.

- **American Studies at the University of Virginia: America in the 1930s** (http:// xroads.virginia.edu/%7E1930s/front.html)—This site includes an extensive collection of print documents about the era, including newspapers, advertisements, comics, and books.

EVALUATION: Your time capsule will be evaluated using the rubric provided (see Figure 6.2), which includes these four criteria:

1. Required elements
2. Relevance of artifacts
3. Grammar
4. Design and layout

CONCLUSION: As a group, post the link to your time capsule.

FIGURE 6.2 ● Rubric for Evaluating Time Capsule

Category	5	4	3	2	1
Required Elements	All required elements are included, as well as additional information.	All required elements are included.	One required element is missing.	Two or three required elements are missing.	More than three required elements are missing.
Relevance of Artifacts	All of the artifacts relate to the topic and develop the focus of the time capsule.	Most of the artifacts relate to the topic and develop the focus of the time capsule.	Some of the artifacts relate to the topic and develop the focus of the time capsule.	Few of the artifacts relate to the topic and develop the focus of the time capsule.	None of the artifacts relate to the topic and develop the focus of the time capsule.
Grammar	There are no grammatical errors.	There are one or two grammatical errors.	There are three or four grammatical errors.	There are four or five grammatical errors.	There are more than five grammatical errors.
Design and Layout	The time capsule is exceptionally designed and neat.	The time capsule is attractively designed and neat.	The time capsule is inconsistently designed somewhat messy.	The time capsule is poorly designed and messy, which makes it difficult to understand the content.	The time capsule is messy and unattractive, making it difficult to understand the content and focus.

Total score: _____ / 20

The Focus on Time Frames and Purposes

The final cluster in the Writing standards, Range of Writing, contains Standard 10: "Write routinely over extended time frames (time for research, reflection, and revision) and shorter time frames (a single sitting or a day or two) for a range of tasks, purposes, and audiences" (NGA & CCSSO, 2010a, p. 47). This focus on different times frames and purposes addresses the need to prepare students for college and career. In completing high school and moving on to college, in particular, students will be expected to write in a variety of settings, ranging from on-demand test situations to research papers completed across entire semesters. Likewise, in the workplace, individuals are expected to write both in daily correspondence and long-term projects. If students are able to meet these CCSS expectations, they will meet their goals for career and college readiness.

Writing in the CCSS Curriculum and Classroom

Creating a Culture of Writing

One of the gurus of writing instruction mentioned earlier in this chapter, Donald Murray, emphasizes the importance of students writing often. According to Murray (2003), students should be immersed in a culture of writing, in which writing is considered routine. The more opportunities students have to practice their writing skills, the better writers they become.

It's important to note, however, that little evidence supports the practice of writing just to write, which does not improve students' skills (Murray, 2003). Instead, deliberate and focused instructional strategies, such as Writing Workshop, should be used to offer students opportunities to develop and practice specific new skills. Writing Workshop is a particularly effective strategy because students are expected to produce a minimum number of pages per sitting; in doing so, they not only learn and practice new skills but also hone previously established skills. (For more information about Writing Workshop, see Fletcher and Portalupi [2001], *Writing Workshop: The Essential Guide.*)

The CCSS Writing Standards echo the importance of students writing often. The standards' emphasis on following a process and writing routinely both point to the expectation for students to write frequently. Indeed, the most effective path to developing writing skills is to provide substantial time for practice coupled with precisely scaffolded instruction.

Developing a Schoolwide Writing Plan

The CCSS apply to the development of literacy skills in all of the content areas, not only in the English language arts. The developers of the CCSS identify the integration of literacy skills across the content areas as one of their key design considerations:

> The Standards insist that instruction in reading, writing, speaking, listening, and language be a shared responsibility within the school. . . . The grades 6–12 standards are divided into two sections, one for ELA and the other for history/social studies, science, and technical subjects. This division reflects the unique, time-honored place of ELA teachers in developing students' literacy skills while at the same time recognizing that teachers in other areas must have a role in this development as well. (NGA & CCSSO, 2010a, p. 4)

This statement sends a clear message to schools: In terms of the writing curriculum, developing students' writing skills is no longer the sole responsibility of English language arts teachers. Writing is now viewed as the responsibility of all teachers, including those in the content areas.

Content area teachers may not have had significant training in writing instruction, so it's critical that they be included in selecting strategies for writing skill set development. Literacy is a necessary pedagogical tool for content teachers, just as it is for language arts teachers. Students with limited literacy skills won't be able to learn and enjoy the content that is being taught. A student who can't write about the content can't learn it, either.

Writing is a powerful skill for adolescent students to possess. To be able to articulate their thoughts in writing is not only about being college and career ready; it is also about becoming young men and women who have strong, articulate voices and can participate as adults in a democratic society.

Assignments for Developing Writing Skills

Argumentation and Critical Thinking

Writing Standard 1, which addresses writing arguments, states the expectation for students to "[use] valid reasoning and relevant and sufficient evidence" (NGA & CCSSO, 2010a, p. 45). At the high school level, students must employ critical-thinking skills to develop a claim and counterclaims and to anticipate the audience's knowledge and concerns. Applying these skills in crafting an effective argument is expected not only in the English language arts but in the content areas, as well.

Anna Spencer, a teacher at an international school, designed an assignment for grades 11 and 12 called "A Fuzzy Problem: Service at What Cost?" that has students consider a problem based on a real-life situation. In sum, the problem involves a fictitious student at New England Prep School, Veronica Vance, who within minutes of receiving a letter of acceptance to her number-one choice for college, Stanvard University, learns that she has too few hours of community service to graduate, based on the prep school's requirements. For instance, Veronica's advisor wonders how such a hard-working, successful student could have overlooked this requirement and is concerned that her oversight might reflect on him professionally. While he believes in the value of community service work, he isn't sure that students should be required to do this work in addition to their already heavy academic load. Veronica's father is from another country, and has been raised to believe that the way to provide for the poor is through effective government. In his home country, the common view is that the needy are best served by professionals, paid to put their best effort and experience into addressing social problems, rather than teenagers putting in time out of obligation. The head of the school feels that the community service policy is vital to the school's mission statement, and refuses to waive the requirement. She fears that if the administration is perceived as applying rules inconsistently, her ability to lead would be compromised and the school's reputation would be put at risk.

The case study provided with this assignment includes a detailed description of each person involved, including his or her view of Veronica's predicament, opinion of the value of performing community service, and personal concerns for the outcome (see the appendix to this chapter).

To complete this assignment, the student writer makes a claim from the point of view of one of the participants in the case. The student must support his or her claim given the evidence from the case study and acknowledge possible counterarguments. In preparing his or her argument, the student is asked to consider these four questions from the perspective of the participant:

1. How do you propose to solve the problem?
2. On what fundamental ideas do you base your solution?
3. What is the strongest argument against your point of view?
4. Who is likely to support you? Go against you?

Anna Spencer's "A Fuzzy Problem" assignment exemplifies a creative way to teach argumentative writing. It presents a problem to which students can relate; they are familiar with the participants' motivations and will likely have strong opinions about how the problem should be resolved. For adolescents, developing writing skills to present opinions and ideas is paramount to their ongoing development. Table 6.3 identifies the Writing standards that are met by this assignment.

Narrative Writing: Journals   Although the CCSS focus on writing arguments is distinctive, there is still a strong need for students to develop narrative writing skills. The following assignment, intended for students in grades 9–10, meets the CCSS for close reading and literary analysis (Reading Literature Standards 2 and 3), as well as the CCSS for narrative writing (Writing Standard 3). If the assignment is completed using Web 2.0 tools, it also meets Writing Standard 6, which addresses the use of technology to produce and publish writing.

TABLE 6.3 ● *Grades 11–12 Writing Standards Met by "A Fuzzy Problem" Assignment*

Writing standard	Element of assignment
W.1: Write arguments to support claims in an analysis of substantive topics or texts, using valid reasoning and relevant and sufficient evidence.	The student is presented with the problem about completion of required service hours by a high school student expecting to graduate in a few weeks.
W.1.a: Introduce precise, knowledgeable claim(s), establish the significance of the claim(s), distinguish the claim(s) from alternate or opposing claims, and create an organization that logically sequences claim(s), counterclaims, reasons, and evidence.	The student is presented with the case study materials and must closely examine the problem from a selected point of view. The student develops a claim and presents it from the point of view of one of the participants.
W.1.b: Develop claim(s) and counterclaims fairly and thoroughly, supplying the most relevant evidence for each while pointing out the strengths and limitations of both in a manner that anticipates the audience's knowledge level, concerns, values, and possible biases.	The student must closely read and analyze the information presented in the case study. The student uses the details provided in the case as evidence to support his or her claim.
W.1.c: Use words, phrases, and clauses as well as varied syntax to link the major sections of the text, create cohesion, and clarify the relationships between claim(s) and reasons, between reasons and evidence, and between claim(s) and counterclaims.	This element will be evaluated in the student's final draft.
W.1.d: Establish and maintain a formal style and objective tone while attending to the norms and conventions of the discipline in which they are writing.	This element will be evaluated in the student's final draft.
W.1.e: Provide a concluding statement or section that follows from and supports the argument presented.	This element will be evaluated in the student's final draft.

Source: NGA & CCSSO (2010).

Classroom Connection
Journal Writing Role-Play

Grade Level:
Grades 9–12

Time Needed:
This is a culminating activity to be done after reading a novel and will take several days to complete.

Learning Outcomes:
Students will identify the voice and perspective of a character and express that character's thoughts and feelings in writing.

Materials:
Each student should have the following materials:

- Copy of the novel
- Eight sheets of paper (or eight copies of the template)
- Pencil/Pen
- Colored pencils
- Clip art and/or photos from magazines or online (optional)
- Gluestick (optional)

Each student should also have access to a stapler.

Activities:
Writing in the voice of one of the characters in the novel, each student will create five journal entries. The journal entries should reflect the character's perspective and present thoughts and feelings not specifically described in the book.

Set-Up:
Each student should take eight sheets of paper and staple them together to create a 16-page "journal." The student should write page numbers on the bottoms of pages 3–15, as shown in Figure 6.3. (An alternative is to provide students with a template, in which the pages have already been numbered.)

Activities:

1. Ask students to write journal entries at five different points in the character's life. Have students date all of the journal entries. (They should make up dates based on the time in which the novel is set and details about what is happening in the story.)

2. Remind students that all of the journal entries must be written in complete sentences and follow standard English conventions. (Suggest that students write a rough draft of each entry and then proofread and edit/revise it before entering it as the final draft in the journal.)

FIGURE 6.3 ● Page-by-Page Layout for Journal

Front Cover Illustration No Page Number		Diary Entry Day 2 Starts Here 6	Diary Entry Day 2 Continues Here 7	Diary Entry Day 5 Starts Here 12	Diary Entry Day 5 Continues Here 13
This page will be blank No page Number	Illustration with Caption Will Go Here 3	Diary Entry Day 3 Starts Here 8	Diary Entry Day 3 Continues Here 9	Diary Entry Day 7 Starts Here 14	Diary Entry Day 7 Continues Here 15
Diary Entry Day 1 Starts Here 4	Diary Entry Day 1 Continues Here 5	Diary Entry Day 4 Starts Here 10	Diary Entry Day 4 Continues Here 11	Back Cover Illustration No Page Number	

3. Have students add illustrations to the front cover; pages 3, 8, and 13; and the back cover. Each illustration must include a one-sentence caption or explanation. (Suggest that students use colored pencils, rather than markers or crayons, so the colors don't bleed through to the other side of the paper. If students prefer, they can also use graphics from magazines, clip art, or websites and glue them into their journals.)

Helpful Hints:

Share these suggestions with students:

● Keep your journal in a plastic bag to keep it clean, neat, and unwrinkled.

● Write each journal entry in pencil so you can easily make revisions later.

● If you use a pen (blue or black ink), use white correction fluid to cover over mistakes. Do not cross out or write over text.

● If you type the entries on a computer, print them out and glue or tape them into the journal.

CCSS Standards:

This narrative writing assignment meets the following CCSS Reading and Writing standards for grades 9–10 (NGA & CCSSO):

Reading (Literature)

● **R.2:** Determine a theme or central idea of a text and analyze in detail its development over the course of the text, including how it emerges and is shaped and refined by specific details; provide an objective summary of the text.

- **R.3:** Analyze how complex characters (e.g., those with multiple or conflicting motivations) develop over the course of a text, interact with other characters, and advance the plot or develop the theme.

Writing

- **W.3:** Write narratives to develop real or imagined experiences or events using effective technique, well-chosen details, and well-structured event sequences.
- **W.9:** Draw evidence from literary or informational texts to support analysis, reflection, and research.

Adaptation Using Technology:

This project can be completed electronically on websites such as Storybird (www.storybird.com) and LiveBinders (www.livebinders.com).

Evaluation:

A rubric for evaluating this narrative writing assignment is provided in Figure 6.4. Both the journal entries and the illustrations are considered in determining an overall grade for the assignment.

FIGURE 6.4 ● Rubric for Evaluating Journal Assignment

Journal Evaluation Rubric

Journal Entries

Each journal entry will be evaluated on a 10-point scale according to the following range:

1	2	3	4	5	6	7	8	9	10

Poor	Requirements missing	Elaboration needed	Fair	Good	Very good	Excellent

Criteria for evaluation are as follows:

- contains required elements and was prepared according to directions
- provides an accurate portrayal and development of the character and his or her perspective
- includes generally high quality of content
- uses appropriate punctuation and correct spelling
- is written using complete sentences

Journal Entry 1

1	2	3	4	5	6	7	8	9	10

Journal Entry 2

1	2	3	4	5	6	7	8	9	10

Journal Entry 3

1	2	3	4	5	6	7	8	9	10

(continued)

FIGURE 6.4 ● (continued)

Journal Entry 4

| 1 | 2 | 3 | 4 | 5 | 6 | 7 | 8 | 9 | 10 |

Journal Entry 5

| 1 | 2 | 3 | 4 | 5 | 6 | 7 | 8 | 9 | 10 |

Illustrations

Each illustration will be evaluated on a 5-point scale according to the following range:

1	2	3	4	5
Poor/Lacks Effort	Messy	OK	Very good	Excellent

Criteria for evaluation are as follows:

- relates to the content of the journal
- connects with the character
- demonstrates creativity and reveals effort and neatness

Cover Page

| 1 | 2 | 3 | 4 | 5 |

Page 3

| 1 | 2 | 3 | 4 | 5 |

Page 8

| 1 | 2 | 3 | 4 | 5 |

Page 13

| 1 | 2 | 3 | 4 | 5 |

Back Cover

| 1 | 2 | 3 | 4 | 5 |

Overall Grade

| 1 | 2 | 3 | 4 | 5 |

Neatness, Creativity, Effort

| 1 | 2 | 3 | 4 | 5 |

Understanding of the Character, Perspective, and Actions of the Story

| 1 | 2 | 3 | 4 | 5 |

Additional Comments:

Narrative Writing: Poetry   Although Writing Standard 3 does not address narrative poetry, writing poems gives high school students an opportunity to experiment with written language. Providing a format or structure, such as haiku, is helpful to students who may be uncertain about how to approach writing a poem.

The following lesson on writing haiku is intended for students in grades 9–12 and was developed according to the balanced literacy model. It therefore meets not only the CCSS Writing standards (Standards 3 and 4) but also several Speaking and Listening standards (Standards 1 and 6). (See Chapter 7 for a discussion of the Speaking and Listening standards.)

Classroom Connection

Writing Haikus

Grade Level:

Grades 9–12

Time Needed:

This lesson takes approximately 45 minutes of class time, if students write their haikus as homework outside class. The lesson can be extended to allow in-class writing and sharing of poems.

Learning Outcomes:

After completing this activity, students will be able to define, identify, and write a haiku. In addition, they will learn to connect a piece of prose with a piece of their own poetry and gain experience in experimenting with language and orally presenting their work.

Materials Needed:

Each student will need the following materials:

- A copy of the short story "Seventeen Syllables," by Hisaye Yamamoto (1998)
- A copy of the handout "Practice Writing Haikus"
- Writing materials/computer

    Also make available to students models of haikus.

Set-Up:

Ask students to read the short story "Seventeen Syllables." Then introduce the concept of haiku to students, identifying the elements of the form and providing examples of poems.

Activities:

1. Distribute to students the handout "Practice Writing Haikus" (see Figure 6.5). Explain that each student will write a haiku. Review the directions and expectations of the assignment.

2. Complete the "Prewriting" step in class (see handout). Ask students to free-write about or sketch something important that has happened to them during the past week.

FIGURE 6.5 ● Handout for Lesson on Writing Haikus

Practice Writing Haikus

Prewriting

Please respond to the following prompt through free-writing or drawing:

> Describe something important that has happened to you during the past week.

What Is a Haiku?

A *haiku* is a Japanese form of poetry that uses a small number of words to create a large impact—usually, painting a vivid sensory image for the reader. A haiku follows this pattern of 3 lines and 17 syllables:

Line 1   5 syllables

Line 2   7 syllables

Line 3   5 syllables

Example of a Haiku

Read the following haiku and then review it to count the numbers of lines and syllables:

> For a lovely bowl
> Let us arrange these flowers
> Since there is no rice
> —Matsuo Bash, Japanese Haiku

Writing

Using your free-write or sketch as inspiration, write three haikus about the important event that has happened to you during the past week. Keep in mind that because you have a limited number of syllables to work with and must follow a specific pattern, you must be highly selective in choosing and arranging words. Use a thesaurus to find alternative forms of descriptive words that will help you create a vivid sensory image of the event.

Evaluation:

Your haikus will be evaluated based on these criteria:

- followed the specified line pattern
- followed the specified syllable pattern
- wrote three haikus, all focusing on the same event

3. Ask for a few student volunteers to share their responses with the rest of the class.

4. Assign the "Writing" component for homework, or have students write their haikus in class. Students should write three haikus about the event they identified.

5. When students submit their haikus, ask them to identify their favorite or best from among the three. Invite a few students to read their haikus to the rest of the class, and then discuss them.

6. Publish students' work by creating a class poetry magazine or bulletin board.

CCSS Standards:

This narrative poetry writing assignment meets the following expectations of Writing Standard 3 for grades 9–10 and 11–12:

Grades 9–10

- **W.3:** Write narratives to develop real or imagined experiences or events using effective technique, well-chosen details, and well-structured event sequences.

- **W.3.b:** Use narrative techniques, such as dialogue, pacing, description, reflection, and multiple plot lines, to develop experiences, events, and/or characters.

- **W.3.c:** Use a variety of techniques to sequence events so that they build on one another to create a coherent whole.

- **W.3.d:** Use precise words and phrases, telling details, and sensory language to convey a vivid picture of the experiences, events, setting, and/or characters.

Grades 11–12

- **W.3:** Write narratives to develop real or imagined experiences or events using effective technique, well-chosen details, and well-structured event sequences.

- **W.3.b:** Use narrative techniques, such as dialogue, pacing, description, reflection, and multiple plot lines, to develop experiences, events, and/or characters.

- **W.3.c:** Use a variety of techniques to sequence events so that they build on one another to create a coherent whole (e.g., a sentence of mystery, suspense, growth, or resolution).

- **W.3.d:** Use precise words and phrases, telling details, and sensory language to convey a vivid picture of the experiences, events, setting, and/or characters.

Evaluation:

Evaluate students' haikus based on these criteria:

- followed the specified line pattern
- followed the specified syllable pattern
- wrote three haikus, all focusing on the same event

REFERENCES

Atwell, N. (1998). *In the middle: New understanding about writing, reading, and learning.* Portsmouth, NH: Boynton/Cook.

Atwell, N. (2002). *Lessons that change writers.* Portsmouth, NH: Heinemann.

Beck., I. McKeown, M., & Kucan, L. (2002). *Bringing words to life: Robust vocabulary instruction.* New York, NY: The Guilford Press.

Bloom, B. (1956). *Taxonomy of educational objectives.* New York, NY: David McKay.

Britton, J. (1992). *Language and learning* (2nd ed.). Portsmouth, NH: Boynton/Cook.

Britton, J., Burgess, A., Martin, N., McLeod, A., & Rosen, R. (1975). *The development of writing abilities, 11–18.* London, UK: Macmillan Education for the Schools Council.

Calkins, L. (1994). *The art of teaching writing* (2nd ed.). Portsmouth, NH: Heinemann.

Dodge, B. (2007). What is a WebQuest? *WebQuest.org.* Retrieved from www.webquest.org.

Fletcher, R., & Portalupi, J. (2001). *Writing workshop: The essential guide.* Portsmouth, NH: Heinemann.

Flood, J., Lapp, D., Squire, J., & Jensen, J. (Eds.) (2003). *Handbook of research on teaching the English language arts* (2nd ed., pp. 721–737). Mahwah, NJ: Lawrence Erlbaum Publishers.

Gere, A. R., Christenbury, L., & Sassi, K. (2005). *Writing on demand: Best practices and strategies for success.* Portsmouth, NH: Heinemann.

Graff, G. (2003). *Clueless in academe: How schooling obscures the life of the mind.* New Haven, CT: Yale University Press.

Graff, G., & Birkenstein, C. (2010). *They say I say: The moves that matter in academic writing.* (2nd ed.). New York, NY: Norton.

Heller, R., & Greenleaf, C. (2007). *Literacy instruction in the content areas: Getting to the core of middle and high school improvement.* Washington, DC: Alliance for Excellent Education.

Murray, D. M. (2003). *A writer teaches writing* (2nd ed.). Belmont, CA: Cengage Learning.

Marzano, R. J. (2004). *Building background knowledge for academic achievement: Research on what works in schools.* Alexandria, VA: Association for Supervision and Curriculum Development.?

Marzano, R. J. (2005). *Building academic vocabulary teacher's manual.* Alexandria, VA: Association for Supervision and Curriculum Development.

Marzano, R. J., Pickering, D., & Pollock, J. E. (2001). *Classroom instruction that works: research-based strategies for increasing student achievement.* Alexandria, VA: Association for Supervision and Curriculum Development.

National Association for Media Literacy Education (NAMLE). (2013). Media literacy defined. *NAMLE.net.* Retrieved from http://namle.net/publications/media-literacy-definitions.

National Governors Association Center for Best Practices & Council of Chief State School Officers (NGA & CCSSO). (2010a). *Common Core State Standards: English language arts and literacy in history/social studies, science, and technical subjects.* Washington, DC: Authors. Retrieved from www.corestandards.org/assets/CCSSI_ELA%20Standards.pdf.

National Governors Association Center for Best Practices & Council of Chief State School Officers (NGA & CCSSO). (2010b). Appendix A: Research supporting key elements of the standards and glossary of key terms. *Common Core State Standards.* Washington, DC: Authors. Retrieved from www.corestandards.org/assets/Appendix_A.pdf.

National Governors Association Center for Best Practices & Council of Chief State School Officers (NGA & CCSSO). (2010c). Appendix C: Samples of student writing. *Common Core State Standards.* Washington, DC: Authors. Retrieved from www.corestandards.org/assets/Appendix_C.pdf.

National Institute for Literacy. (2007). *What content-area teachers should know about adolescent literacy.* Retrieved from http://www.nifl.gov/nifl/publications/adolescent_literacy07.pdf.

National Reading Panel (NRP). (2000). *Report of the National Reading Panel: Teaching children to read.* Washington, DC: National Institute of Child Health and Human Development.

National Writing Project & Nagin, C. (2006). *Because writing matters: Improving student writing in our own schools.* San Francisco, CA: Jossey-Bass.

Postman, N. (1997). *The end of education.* New York, NY: Knopf.

Romano, T. (1991). *Grammar and teaching writing.* Urbana. IL: National Council of Teachers of English.

LITERATURE CITED

Boyne, J. (2007). *The boy in the striped pajamas.* Oxford, UK: David Fickling Books.

Lee, H. (1960). *To kill a mockingbird.* New York, NY: Lippincott.

Yamamoto, H. (1998). Seventeen syllables. In *Seventeen syllables and other stories.* New Brunswick, NJ: Rutgers University Press.

Appendix

Source: Reprinted with permission from Deanna Gallagher.

A Fuzzy Problem: Service at What Cost?

COMMUNITY SERVICE REQUIREMENTS AT AN ELITE PRIVATE SCHOOL appear to unfairly penalize a college-bound Honor Student. What should be done?

The Problem

Veronica Vance was beside herself with excitement. It was April 1, 2009, and she had just received the e-mail she had been waiting for all week: a Congratulations and Welcome notification from Stanvard University, her number one college choice and a school she had set her heart on attending since she first visited it as a young girl. All the hard work, effort, and sacrifice of her past four years at New England Prep had finally paid off, and she couldn't wait to get a quiet moment to call her parents and tell them the terrific news. After all, they too had given up a great deal to make her dream possible, and they deserved to know the great news as soon as they awakened.

However, when Veronica walked toward her dorm room that afternoon, she was surprised by her guardian, Phil Hughes, standing at the door. *Does he know already?* she thought, but looking at his face, decided he must not be aware of her good fortune. "Hey, Phil!" she called out. "You'll never guess who I heard from today! I—"

"Veronica, I have something very serious to discuss with you. Whatever you have to say is going to have to wait. I received a call from Mrs. Smith at New England Prep. She's quite concerned about a situation that she's become aware of and wants to meet with us as soon as possible." Phil's face remained stern, and he seemed genuinely concerned about something; Veronica knew that this was no April Fool's joke. What could have happened?

She thought through the past few days at school. True, it had been a hectic week, with so many AP exams to study for and papers to write during the final stretch before graduation. The tension in school had escalated as many senior students received news, both good and bad, about their college applications; one day someone would be shouting out their acceptance in the hallway, and the next, another student might be found huddled in a corner, weeping over a rejection letter.

The fates of Veronica's two best friends provided evidence of how arbitrary the whole process seemed. On the one hand, Martyna Jones, her lab partner and trusted confidante of three years, had been accepted at every school she applied to; this surprised many people, but not Veronica, who knew her friend's inner qualities and character would lead her to succeed wherever she went, in spite of the fact that she often checked her own ambition in order to help others. On the other hand, her boyfriend Jim Michaels had just heard from his third choice college that the answer was negative, leading him to fear that the fourth and fifth schools he had applied to were going to have the same answer, and he would be left without a college for the next year. While Jim put on a brave face, joking that he was looking forward to joining the circus, Veronica knew he must be worried. She couldn't understand why he had not been accepted, either—his grades were terrific, his test scores outstanding, and his personality charmed smiles out of the sourest teachers' faces. He was a three-sport varsity athlete, too. What had happened to make schools decide against him? It did not seem fair.

Wait, Veronica thought. *What about me? What does Phil have to tell me? Was there a mistake? Am I not accepted at Stanvard after all?* She brought herself back to the present in time to tune into Phil's words: "It seems that when your files were being reviewed to prepare for graduation, it was discovered that you are missing one requirement, and if you don't fill it by April 15, you will not be granted a diploma by New England Prep. Why didn't you tell me you have never filled your community service requirement?"

"Community service requirement? What are you talking about?"

"The one that every single student who graduates must fulfill, that you must have known about—every other student seems to, and there's no one else who is missing the requirement. Every student has to fulfill 100 hours of community service-learning during their time as a student at New England Prep. According to Mrs. Smith, you've been given numerous opportunities to do service, and your records indicate you have only completed 25 hours."

Veronica's face showed her puzzlement. Then, with a sigh of relief, she turned to Phil. "Oh, I can explain why I missed all those times. They were scheduled on Saturday mornings, and you know I had cello lessons at the same time. They said I could make them up in the summer, but then I got accepted to the Youth Symphony, so I didn't have time then. I guess I just forgot about it. Mrs. Smith will understand if I explain it to her."

"Well, I wish it were so easy, Veronica. But evidently there are some very strict regulations regarding the rule, and in the past, students have actually not been allowed to graduate because they did not do the service. In any case, we'll learn more about what the school thinks tomorrow. For now, I need you to sit down and make a list of all the things you think you might need to talk to Mrs. Smith about to get her to consider your point of view. And I think you ought to call your parents and let them know what's going on."

Veronica looked at her cell phone. Mom and Dad would just be waking up, getting ready for their morning tea. She had planned to call them with her great news . . . now she had something else to tell them as well. She could barely hold back the tears as she excused herself and opened her room's door.

YOU ARE: Veronica Vance

Character Description: You've always been a hardworking student, someone who plays by the rules, who shows others it's possible to do it all. You have managed to balance taking the most demanding classes, playing an instrument well, and being a good friend to others—all while living in a foreign country, away from your closest childhood friends and, even more challenging for you, your family. Your father and mother have always supported you in whatever you have done; they encouraged you to dream big and made many sacrifices along the way to give you access to the best education available. You know that, even more than the money they've spent, your parents deeply miss having their oldest daughter at home and hope that all the time they have lost with you will one day make it possible for you to direct your destiny.

Most people assume that girls miss their mothers most. But it is your father, Mr. Vance, to whom you are truly close and after whom you have modeled yourself. He grew up in very rough times and, without any encouragement or means from his family, rose to the top of his profession. He has taught you that with hard work, organization, and respect for the rules, you can achieve whatever you want in life. Perhaps this is why you dread telling him about your mistake—and yes, even though you insisted to Phil that you would be able to fix things with Mrs. Smith, deep down you believe this situation is your fault and you are obliged to do something about it.

That said, you don't believe that Mrs. Smith would do something so drastic as taking away your diploma to teach you a lesson. True, she did her best to keep you aware of the situation last year, and she even suggested community service opportunities for you to pursue over the summer. On the other hand, she also encouraged you to join the Youth Symphony and often pointed to you as an example of a well-rounded student. Didn't she recommend that incoming freshmen talk to you about how to take advantage of the opportunities at New England Prep? It doesn't seem fair to you that she's now taking such a hard line. You believe she must have *some* flexibility—after all, does she really want you to lose your place at Stanvard?

And then there's Phil. He's been a great mentor and guardian for you over the past three years, and you've never had reason to doubt his support. But isn't it his job to help you stay on top of things? How could he have let this slip by and then acted as if it was entirely your fault for forgetting to fulfill the requirement? You hope he is able to help you come up with a solution—indeed, you expect him to help you figure something out. At the very least, he ought to be able to vouch for your character. After all, isn't community service supposed to help build character? Maybe Phil can help you show that your character needs less than 75 hours of building.

1. How do you propose to solve the problem?
2. On what fundamental ideas do you base your solution?
3. What is the strongest argument against your point of view?
4. Who is likely to support you? Go against you?

YOU ARE: Phil Hughes

Character Description: You have been a guardian and mentor to Veronica Vance for three and a half years. Throughout the time you have worked with her, Veronica has been a model student and all-around wonderful young woman. You have seen her take on more challenges than any other student you have worked with, and she has met her goals, even when you advised her that perhaps she was taking on too much at once. This is one of the reasons you were able to recommend her so highly to Stanvard University, your alma mater: you know she has what it takes to succeed there. In fact, you wrote a weaker letter of recommendation for Veronica's boyfriend, James Michaels, because he doesn't show that ability to push himself forward.

How could Veronica have overlooked such an important requirement for graduation? The call from Mrs. Smith was more than a shock—it was an embarrassment and threatens to reflect on your professional reputation as a guardian and mentor. While Mrs. Smith does not directly supervise you, she is the head of the school, and at the end of the day you know she will have a say in whether you are promoted, indeed, even retained by the school. You know she is a stickler for the rules—after all, most people in charge have to be—and you have to admit that if you were in her shoes, you might blame the guardian as much as the student for dropping the ball.

Of all things, how ironic that the fate of a star student might come down to a non-academic requirement. This is especially frustrating, considering all you have done to promote community service at New England Prep. While you didn't like the notion of it being a requirement—in your eyes, volunteer service should be just that, voluntary—you have supported the school's policy. You see the kids you supervise being stretched to the limit by all their academic activities and sympathize with their complaints that being forced to do good for others doesn't automatically make you a good person. But you've also seen a lot of the world outside New England Prep, and you know that the kids there will benefit from having to see how people less fortunate than themselves struggle from day to day just to survive.

In the end, you think that what kids learn from doing community service may be as important to their lives as any AP course they might take. Though what it is they're learning, you're not always sure. You've seen some students going through the motions to complete the service requirement, but their talk and actions show that they've learned very little about compassion or responsibility. In the end, you wonder whether the ability to serve others can be taught, or whether it is a true talent, like musicianship or mathematical ability. Students like Martyna Jones, with their amazing ability to give to others, are truly rare. In the end, you do think that Veronica has the responsibility to live up to school requirements. But you also sympathize with her and hope that she does not pay an unfair price for her mistake.

1. How do you propose to solve the problem?
2. On what fundamental ideas do you base your solution?
3. What is the strongest argument against your point of view?
4. Who is likely to support you? Go against you?

YOU ARE: Mr. Vance, Veronica's father

Character description: You had just sat down to lunch when Veronica called you early this afternoon. In your country it was a reasonable time to call, but you knew that for her, this was a very late call to be making. The way she sounded on the phone, you knew she had been crying, and you feared that something terrible had happened to her. When she told you the great news—that she had been accepted to Stanvard!—you felt like exploding with pride and joy. But it didn't make sense that she sounded so unhappy, and when you asked her why her voice trembled, she told you about her terrible predicament. "Please, Dad, do not think this is your fault. It is I who have failed you," she cried.

You wanted to reach out, comfort her and tell her everything would be all right. But you could not because she lives thousands of miles away in order to pursue her dream of the best possible education. Although you believe that an excellent education is the most important quality a person can obtain, and you have willingly supported her financially, there are times when you wonder whether you'll ever get over the loss of your daughter's companionship and presence in your life. You miss Veronica every single day, and you think anyone who provides care and education for her in your place should be doing the absolute best job possible.

That's what makes you so upset about this situation: clearly, *someone, some adult,* dropped the ball. Veronica has been raised to do everything by the book, to the best of her ability, and you are certain she would never knowingly ignore a graduation requirement. You're furious with her guardian, Phil, for not catching this problem before it surfaced. You also have strong feelings about the school's head, Mrs. Smith. After all, Veronica has been an exemplary student at New England Prep for three years, and you have made generous financial donations to school projects in addition to paying her tuition. The school's end of the bargain should be met, too. While they have made it possible for Veronica to gain entrance to her top-choice university, they now threaten to take her achievement away from her. And you.

Perhaps the most difficult point for you to understand is why on earth students at New England Prep are required to do community service in the first place. You see this rule as peculiarly American, and in this way, prejudicial against students who come from cultures that do not promote or value this strange notion of working for nothing to help others. In your country, you believe that the way to provide for the poor and needy is through effective government. You also think that people who are in need are best served by professionals, paid to put their best effort and experience into addressing social problems, rather than by teenagers putting in time out of obligation. In fact, the idea of Veronica "building character" by spending hours doing something other than learning and working on her future is ridiculous in your view. The school is going to learn your point of view soon enough, though. You are flying to the United States for a special meeting with Mrs. Smith.

1. How do you propose to solve the problem?
2. On what fundamental ideas do you base your solution?
3. What is the strongest argument against your point of view?
4. Who is likely to support you? Go against you?

YOU ARE: Martyna Jones, Veronica's best friend

Character description: What a week this has been. First, you received acceptance letters from Stanvard and Princemouth on the same day, when you thought neither school was going to give you a second look. Then, you found out that Veronica was accepted to Stanvard, too, and all the dream conversations you two have had over the past two years about rooming together in college seemed like a possibility. Things were going so well—then the bad news started to come in. First, your good friend James Michaels got rejected from another school, and just this afternoon, Veronica texted you with the unbelievable story of her not being allowed to graduate. And worst of all, this evening, you heard from the nursing home where you volunteer that your favorite elder client, Miss Sands, passed away in her sleep last night. You were planning to visit her tomorrow and finish reading her your story. Instead, you'll be getting ready to go to her funeral in two days. What a week.

You'd like to have some time to feel the sadness and honor Miss Sands' passing, thinking about what working with her meant to you, how she was the person who taught you what true giving means. But that will have to be set aside for now, because Veronica needs your support. She has asked you to attend a meeting with her to discuss the community service requirements. You know Veronica wants you to vouch for her character, to describe how Veronica has been there for you as a friend, how she is always ready to help out anyone who asks, how well she manages her time. It will be easy to say these things, because they are true. Veronica is your best friend for a reason: she's a terrific person, someone whom you wish you could be more like.

You hope, though, that you're not asked to give an opinion about whether the community service requirement is a fair rule for New England Prep to enforce on all of its students. Truthfully, you're not quite sure how you feel about this issue. On the one hand, it really doesn't seem fair that students should be forced to do volunteer work when they pay money to a private school for their education, not to learn other people's values. But on the other, you have seen how many students who began serving as reluctant volunteers are now committed, effective participants for causes and people they never would have known about were it not for the requirement. They don't regret it any more than they regret learning calculus or how to write a poem. And your own relationship with Miss Sands started out with a field trip to the nursing home that you almost skipped. How different would your life be if you hadn't met her?

You deeply believe that somehow, a solution to this situation can be reached that satisfies as many people as possible while meeting the spirit of the law. Phil Hughes, your guardian, has always told you that your two greatest gifts are your ability to see many sides to a situation and your compassion for others regardless of their ability to help you. You think both these traits are going to matter over the next few days.

1. How do you propose to solve the problem?
2. On what fundamental ideas do you base your solution?
3. What is the strongest argument against your point of view?
4. Who is likely to support you? Go against you?

YOU ARE: Mrs. Smith, Head of New England Prep

Character description: You are the leader of a highly regarded prep school, known for its traditions and values as much as for your students' college acceptance rate. You have been the school's head for nearly ten years, and have also taught history and served as the school's dean. Over the decades, you have dealt with many student disciplinary issues, but no situation has put you in a more difficult spot than Veronica Vance's community service requirement dilemma. You know she's a terrific student. You also know she has been accepted to a very prestigious university. Finally, you know her family has been not only supportive of the school's policies in the past, but financially generous to the school's scholarship fund for less wealthy students. The fact that Mr. Vance arranged to make an emergency trip to discuss the matter with you shows how seriously he regards the situation.

The facts are clear: Veronica did not fulfill a graduation requirement, and if she does not do so by April 15, the school's rule book stipulates that she cannot graduate. You provide multiple opportunities for students to meet this requirement, and you personally spoke to Veronica about completing community service last spring. Perhaps you did not make the rule crystal clear to her at that time, but it is well known by students, and Veronica has always been on top of all her studies and extracurricular commitments. It's not that you want to make an example of her, but neither can you make an exception for a student just because you personally like her and are aware of her parents' generosity. It's vital that you are seen as having the same standards for every student, regardless of their ability or financial background. If students came to perceive you as playing favorites, not only would your ability to lead be compromised, the school's reputation would be put at risk.

The entire issue of a community service requirement is at the heart of the problem. When you first began as head of New England Prep, you agreed to allow a group of parents and alumni to promote the idea of service-learning amongst the faculty and staff. They made a compelling case for requiring students to reach beyond the privileged campus atmosphere and into the lives of people less fortunate than themselves. It fit well with the school's motto: *Leadership for the benefit of all.* There was some disagreement over the real benefits of adding yet another requirement to the rigorous, time-consuming curriculum. But in the end, the trustees, faculty, staff, and students voted to amend the school's rule book and enact the requirement. And since then, you have seen the student body as a whole become more socially aware and more interested in public service. Just as importantly, New England Prep's standing in the community has improved—your students are no longer perceived as spoiled rich kids living in a bubble. Finally, the outreach of community service has resulted in very talented but financially needy students and their parents learning about the school, so your student body has become more socioeconomically diverse.

For these reasons and many more, you have enforced the rule in the recent past, even requiring students to repeat senior year in order to fulfill it. As difficult as this situation is, you see no other alternative but to hold Veronica to the standard everyone else must meet.

1. How do you propose to solve the problem?
2. On what fundamental ideas do you base your solution?
3. What is the strongest argument against your point of view?
4. Who is likely to support you? Go against you?

YOU ARE: Ivy Joyce, Admissions Representative, Stanvard University

Character description: You represent what *U.S. News and World Report* has ranked the top undergraduate institution in the nation for the past 15 years: Stanvard University. Acting as an emissary on behalf of your college, you have consented to attend this meeting at the request of both Mrs. Smith and Mr. Vance. You've had a great relationship with New England Prep, or NEP, over many decades. In fact, many parents choose NEP for their children because they claim that it serves as a "pipeline" to the best universities. And there is some truth to this rumor because admissions officers reviewing the files of students from NEP know that the grades students receive are not inflated, the recommendations written by guardians and teachers are honest, and the ethical standards of the school are incredibly high. You have never heard of parent donations influencing the school's policies in favor of the wealthy (a claim that, sadly, you cannot make for Stanvard University). You know Mrs. Smith to be a rigorous and fair-minded school head, and NEP alumni have gone on to make great contributions to your school.

When you accepted Veronica Vance for admission, you did so without reservation. Her grades were spectacular, her test scores stratospheric, her recommendations memorable. The director of her youth symphony wrote that "This young woman sets an example of discipline and passion for music that the entire orchestra emulates." Phil Hughes, a guardian known for his frank and understated recommendations, called her the strongest student in her graduating class. Veronica would clearly be at home at Stanvard, and her parents have the financial resources to not only pay for her education, but perhaps make the education of others possible through their generosity. This latter fact, of course, has no bearing on your position, even though Mr. Vance has indicated the desire to establish to a new scholarship program for needy students from his country.

You're fully aware, however, that for every Veronica you accept, there are 15 others who might take her place if it were available. The acceptance rate at Stanvard has remained at approximately 7% over the last two decades, and every year, you are forced to say no to students with amazing potential and a lifelong dream to attend your school. In fact, you've overheard that Jim Michaels, a student whom you considered accepting but ultimately did not because of his guardian's weak recommendation, plans to be at this meeting to support his girlfriend. (This selfless act seems to contradict one of his guardian's most damning statements: that Jim had never been known to do anything for anyone other than himself.)

Stanvard's position on community service may not be directly relevant to this case, but you do think it may come up in conversation, so you plan to briefly explain it to everyone at the meeting. Service to the community is an ideal and obligation of Stanvard and Ivy League colleges across the board—in fact, the organization Ivy Corps is entirely run by students and coordinates partnership efforts between schools. However, there is no undergraduate "requirement" for service in order to graduate. Your college believes that the voluntary aspect of service is what makes it such a powerful tool to change the lives of both servers and the served. Moreover, as adults, students have the right to direct their educational paths. That stated, you will support whatever policy NEP implements; it is not in your interest to interfere with the school's affairs. Furthermore, you must make clear that Stanvard's admissions policy does not allow for deferment of acceptance except in cases of serious illness or family tragedy. If Veronica is not able to attend in 2009–2010, she must reapply for the following year, go through the same rigorous process, and compete with 15,000 other applicants. You fear that Mr. Vance may change his mind about founding a scholarship program once he learns this news—but every time the rules are bent for privileged students, Stanvard's reputation is diminished.

1. How do you propose to solve the problem?
2. On what fundamental ideas do you base your solution?
3. What is the strongest argument against your point of view?
4. Who is likely to support you? Go against you?

YOU ARE: David Dirtdigger, Roving Reporter for the *New England Town Tattler*

Character description: A Mr. Jim Michaels contacted you a few days back, wishing to talk with you about a high-interest story taking place at his school, New England Prep. Evidently, a star student there may be denied the right to graduate because she has forgotten to fulfill what Jim described as an "academically irrelevant and controversial" requirement. You have chosen to pursue the story—in fact, you know it's a potential gold mine. Why?

The reasons are simple. Regardless of actual news value, scandals and gossip sell newspapers. Whenever your newspaper covers scandal and controversy taking place at an elite private school, your sales go through the roof. Your readership loves to gloat over the troubles of the rich and privileged—and according to them, that describes all students at private schools. And the fact that Stanvard University is involved makes the story that much juicier. After all, your story about their attempts to copyright words and phrases they deemed "their own" was the talk of the investigative news industry a couple of weeks ago. It made you some enemies at Stanvard—you'll never be allowed in their public relations office again—but it got you noticed.

Ironically, you are the product of a so-called "elite" education, and you know that the reality of what takes place at schools is much more complicated than what can be presented in a headline and article. However, your livelihood depends on finding the story, giving it legs, and getting it to run. You not only plan to interview everyone you can involved in this case, but your source Jim Michaels has agreed to wear a hidden microphone and record the proceedings of a closed-door meeting.

Your job is to interview everyone you can and get quotes from them about their position so that you are prepared to listen in on the closed meeting and hit the press with a story for the following morning!

Speaking and Listening

SEVERAL YEARS AGO, A STUDY REPORTED THE NUMBER of words that the average person speaks in a day. Remarkably, most of us utter about 16,000 words a day—women, a few more and men, a few less. Certainly, of all the forms of communication, verbal communication is still "the coin of the realm."

And so it's ironic that oral language has traditionally been the neglected or forgotten language art. Perhaps because oral language use is so prevalent, we've assumed that speaking and listening skills develop naturally. Generations of teachers have evaluated students on "classroom participation," recognizing the importance of oral language skills. Yet for the most part, little thought has been given to teaching the skills that underlie effective speaking and listening. We shouldn't be surprised then, that later in life, those students—now employees—experience tremendous angst when they face the prospect of leading a seminar or making a presentation. For many people, public speaking tops the list of their greatest fears.

Monkey Business/Fotolia

The twenty-first century, global economy will present plenty of opportunities for employees who can understand verbal instructions and respond to them appropriately; who can state a claim out loud and defend it in a coherent and orderly manner; and who can interact with colleagues and clients both in person and via technology, whether the telephone, a webinar, Skype, or another means of verbal communication that's still on the horizon. It's our responsibility, as teachers, to make sure our students are prepared to take advantage of these opportunities.

Key Observations about Teaching and Learning Speaking and Listening

THE NEGLECT OF SPEAKING AND LISTENING HAS BEEN reflected in many English language arts curricula and in many states' standards for oral language. Oral language skills have often been viewed as performance related—for instance, reading a text out loud or giving a speech or presentation. However, oral language involves much more than performance. It also involves thinking, knowledge, and skills, which means it requires training and practice. In sum, the goal of that training and practice is "to improve [students'] ability to talk or communicate more effectively" (Hong & Alex, 1995).

Discourse has always been a key element of teaching and learning (Fisher, Frey, & Rothenberg, 2008). However, in the classrooms of the past, teachers did most of the talking and students did most of the listening. When students were asked to speak, the activity often involved the oral recitation of facts that had been memorized. Over time, teachers realized that for students to become well educated, they had to speak more often and for various purposes. To develop students' discussion and conversation skills, teachers had to do less talking themselves, and provide more opportunities for students to engage in collaborative, small-group discussions.

Today, we know that for students to engage in academic discourse, they must have purposeful discussions with one another using academic language (Fisher et al., 2008). We also know that before students can engage in these kinds of discussions, they must be able to reason and reflect.

Scholars have long recognized the link between language and thought. Aldous Huxley (1958/2006) wrote, "Language permits its users to pay attention to things, persons and events, even when the things and persons are absent and the events are not taking place" (p. 109). Lev Vygotsky (1962/1986) suggested that thinking develops into language across several phases: from imaging to inner speech to oral speech. Following this process in reverse, then, suggests that "speech—talk—is the representation of thinking" (Fisher et al., 2008, p. 5).

Regrettably, this connection between language and thought was missing from previous generations of English language arts curricula and standards, in which logic and reasoning skills were usually placed in the domain of writing. However, today we realize that students must be able to critically assess and respond to the information they learn, rather than merely recite facts and details gleaned from written texts.

Finally, previous curricula and standards often approached technology as an add-on or afterthought, rather than a vital element worthy of integration. Integrating technology goes far beyond lessons in word processing and PowerPoint. To be successful in today's world, students must be sophisticated consumers and skilled users of a variety of digital media. By high school, students should have developed advanced skills in using and creating digital media to demonstrate their knowledge and understanding. In other words, they must be media literate.

Essentially, media literacy is the ability to demonstrate competency in various forms of communication. A media literate person is able to access, understand, and evaluate various forms of information, in addition to traditional print messages. They are able to respond using those same forms of communication. Like any other form of literacy, media literacy requires instruction. For example, in teaching our students to read, we encourage them to explore a wide variety of texts to develop skills in interpreting various written forms. In developing this ability, students learn to decipher, decode, and comprehend a range of written texts. Teaching media literacy is similar in that we want to provide students with a framework for use in accessing, analyzing, evaluating, and creating messages in a variety of forms—from print to video to digital. Identical skills are developed and applied in these two learning experiences: analysis, evaluation, and creation. As high school English teachers, we need to develop our own skills in technology-driven literacy so we can effectively integrate it into the curriculum.

Exploring the Speaking and Listening Standards

IN CONTRAST TO PREVIOUS SETS OF STANDARDS, the Common Core State Standards (CCSS) fully develop and articulate expectations for speaking and listening. In crafting the Speaking and Listening standards, the CCSS developers recognized the inherent importance of students' having well-developed speaking and listening skills. Students who can competently and effectively articulate their knowledge and beliefs orally will be well prepared for college and career.

The developers of the CCSS make this statement in the introduction to the Speaking and Listening standards for grades 6–12:

> To become college and career ready, students must have ample opportunities to take part in a variety of rich, structured conversations—as part of a whole class, in small groups, and with a partner—built around important content in various domains. They must be able to contribute appropriately to these conversations, to make comparisons and contrasts, and to analyze and synthesize a multitude of ideas in accordance with the standards of evidence appropriate to a particular discipline. Whatever their intended major or profession, high school graduates will depend heavily on their ability to listen attentively to others so that they are able to build on others' meritorious ideas while expressing their own clearly and persuasively. (NGA & CCSSO, 2010a, p. 48)

At the high school level, the CCSS English Language Arts (ELA) Standards outline expectations for two grade-level bands: grades 9–10 and grades 11–12. Like the other strands of the ELA Standards (Reading, Writing, and Language), the Speaking and Listening strand includes two levels of standards. The Common Core Readiness (CCR) Anchor Standards outline the basic knowledge and skills that underlie effective speaking and listening (see Table 7.1). The same set of Anchor Standards underlies the Speaking and Listening standards for all grade levels (K–12), demonstrating the coherence that runs throughout the CCSS.

TABLE 7.1 ● *Common Core Readiness (CCR) Anchor Standards for Speaking and Listening, Grades 9–12**

Comprehension and Collaboration

1. Prepare for and participate effectively in a range of conversations and collaborations with diverse partners, building on others' ideas and expressing their own clearly and persuasively.
2. Integrate and evaluate information presented in diverse media and formats, including visually, quantitatively, and orally.
3. Evaluate a speaker's point of view, reasoning, and use of evidence and rhetoric.

Presentation of Knowledge and Ideas

1. Present information, findings, and supporting evidence such that listeners can follow the line of reasoning and the organization, development, and style are appropriate to task, purpose, and audience.
2. Make strategic use of digital media and visual displays of data to express information and enhance understanding of presentations.
3. Adapt speech to a variety of contexts and communicative tasks, demonstrating command of formal English when indicated or appropriate.

*These Anchor Standards apply to grades 6–12.
Source: NGA & CCSSO (2010).

The Anchor Standards provide a foundation for the second level of standards, which state specific grade-level expectations. In fact, the ELA Speaking and Listening standards follow the same organization and numbering as the Anchor Standards (see Table 7.2). The two levels of standards were designed to "work in tandem to define college and career readiness expectations—the former providing broad standards, the latter providing additional specificity" (NGA & CCSSO, 2010a, p. 50).

The six skills outlined in the Speaking and Listening standards are organized into two clusters, or categories:

● Comprehension and Collaboration: Standards 1, 2, 3
● Presentation of Knowledge and Ideas: Standards 4, 5, and 6

A quick review of the standards reveals that they include but are not limited to skills for making presentations. As described by the developers of the CCSS:

> The Speaking and Listening standards require students to develop a range of broadly useful oral communication and interpersonal skills. Students must learn to work together, express and listen carefully to ideas, integrate information from oral, visual, quantitative, and media sources, evaluate what they hear, use media and visual displays strategically to help achieve communicative purposes, and adapt speech to context and task. (NGA & CCSSO, 20120a, p. 8)

In the first cluster, Comprehension and Collaboration, Standard 1 outlines a range of interpersonal communication skills: being prepared for discussions (1.a); collaborating with peers (1.b); facilitating conversations (1.c); and contemplating and responding to diverse perspectives (1.d). The need to listen is implied in all of these collaborative skills but

TABLE 7.2 ● *CCSS Writing Standards for Grades 9–12*

Grades 9–10 students:	Grades 11–12 students:
Comprehension and Collaboration	

1. Initiate and participate effectively in a range of collaborative discussions (one-on-one, in groups, and teacher-led) with diverse partners *on grades 9–10 topics, texts, and issues,* building on others' ideas and expressing their own clearly and persuasively.

   a. Come to discussions prepared, having read and researched material under study; explicitly draw on that preparation by referring to evidence from texts and other research on the topic or issue to stimulate a thoughtful, well-reasoned exchange of ideas.

   b. Work with peers to set rules for collegial discussions and decision-making (e.g., informal consensus, taking votes on key issues, presentation of alternate views), clear goals and deadlines, and individual roles as needed.

   c. Propel conversations by posing and responding to questions that relate the current discussion to broader themes or larger ideas; actively incorporate others into the discussion; and clarify, verify, or challenge ideas and conclusions.

   d. Respond thoughtfully to diverse perspectives, summarize points of agreement and disagreement, and, when warranted, qualify or justify their own views and understanding and make new connections in light of the evidence and reasoning presented.

2. Integrate multiple sources of information presented in diverse media or formats (e.g., visually, quantitatively, orally) evaluating the credibility and accuracy of each source.

3. Evaluate a speaker's point of view, reasoning, and use of evidence and rhetoric, identifying any fallacious reasoning or exaggerated or distorted evidence.

---

1. Initiate and participate effectively in a range of collaborative discussions (one-on- one, in groups, and teacher-led) with diverse partners *on grades 11–12 topics, texts, and issues,* building on others' ideas and expressing their own clearly and persuasively.

   a. Come to discussions prepared, having read and researched material under study; explicitly draw on that preparation by referring to evidence from texts and other research on the topic or issue to stimulate a thoughtful, well-reasoned exchange of ideas.

   b. Work with peers to promote civil, democratic discussions and decision-making, set clear goals and deadlines, and establish individual roles as needed.

   c. Propel conversations by posing and responding to questions that probe reasoning and evidence; ensure a hearing for a full range of positions on a topic or issue; clarify, verify, or challenge ideas and conclusions; and promote divergent and creative perspectives.

   d. Respond thoughtfully to diverse perspectives; synthesize comments, claims, and evidence made on all sides of an issue; resolve contradictions when possible; and determine what additional information or research is required to deepen the investigation or complete the task.

2. Integrate multiple sources of information presented in diverse formats and media (e.g., visually, quantitatively, orally) in order to make informed decisions and solve problems, evaluating the credibility and accuracy of each source and noting any discrepancies among the data.

3. Evaluate a speaker's point of view, reasoning, and use of evidence and rhetoric, assessing the stance, premises, links among ideas, word choice, points of emphasis, and tone used.

(continued)

TABLE 7.2 ● *(continued)*

Grades 9–10 students:	Grades 11–12 students:
Presentation of Knowledge and Ideas	
4. Present information, findings, and supporting evidence clearly, concisely, and logically such that listeners can follow the line of reasoning and the organization, development, substance, and style are appropriate to purpose, audience, and task.	4. Present information, findings, and supporting evidence, conveying a clear and distinct perspective, such that listeners can follow the line of reasoning, alternative or opposing perspectives are addressed, and the organization, development, substance, and style are appropriate to purpose, audience, and a range of formal and informal tasks.
5. Make strategic use of digital media (e.g., textual, graphical, audio, visual, and interactive elements) in presentations to enhance understanding of findings, reasoning, and evidence and to add interest.	5. Make strategic use of digital media (e.g., textual, graphical, audio, visual, and interactive elements) in presentations to enhance understanding of findings, reasoning, and evidence and to add interest.
6. Adapt speech to a variety of contexts and tasks, demonstrating command of formal English when indicated or appropriate.*	6. Adapt speech to a variety of contexts and tasks, demonstrating a command of formal English when indicated or appropriate.*

*The Language standards for grades 9–10 and 11–12 are provided on pp. 54–55 of the CCSS (NGA & CCSSO, 2010a).
Source: NGA & CCSSO (2010).

particularly the final skill. Recognizing and responding to others' points of view requires being an attentive listener. Standard 2 addresses integrating sources of information from a range of media and formats and evaluating the credibility and accuracy of sources, and Standard 3 addresses evaluating a speaker's perspective in terms of reasoning and supporting evidence.

In the second cluster, Presentation of Knowledge and Ideas, Standards 4 and 5 outline expectations for presentation skills, including presenting information in a clear, logical manner that's appropriate for the purpose, task, and audience and using digital media to enhance understanding and increase interest. Standard 6 applies specifically to speech—namely, the need to adapt speech to a given task or purpose and recognizing when it's expected or appropriate to use formal English.

The Focus on Integration

The expectations for skills and knowledge outlined in the Speaking and Listening strand of the ELA Standards are integrated with those of the other strands. As explained in the introduction to the CCSS, "Although the Standards are divided into Reading, Writing, Speaking and Listening, and Language strands for conceptual clarity, the processes of communication are closely connected" (NGA & CCSSO, 2010a, p. 4).

For instance, in the Reading standards, CCR Anchor Standard 7 states, "Integrate and evaluate content presented in diverse formats and media, including visually and quantitatively, as well as in words" (NGA & CCSSO, 2010a, p. 35). This standard is nearly identical to Speaking and Listening Anchor Standard 2 (p. 48). Several connections also run between the

Speaking and Listening standards and the Writing standards. Writing Anchor Standard 6 states expectations for students to interact and collaborate with others (p. 41), similar to Speaking and Listening Anchor Standard 1, and Writing Anchor Standard 8 states expectations for evaluating multiple sources from various media, similar to Speaking and Listening Standard 2.

The Focus on Technology

References to technology also run throughout the CCSS, but there is a special emphasis on using digital media in the Speaking and Listening standards. The developers of the CCSS describe the close connection between speaking and listening and technology and the needs for students to possess these skills as follows:

> New technologies have broadened and expanded the role that speaking and listening play in acquiring and sharing knowledge and have tightened their link to other forms of communication. The Internet has accelerated the speed at which connections between speaking, listening, reading, and writing can be made, requiring that students be ready to use these modalities nearly simultaneously. Technology itself is changing quickly, creating a new urgency for students to be adaptable in response to change. (NGA & CCSSO, 2010a, p. 8)

In the Speaking and Listening standards, Standard 5 states the expectation to "make strategic use of digital media (e.g., textual, graphical, audio, visual, and interactive elements) in presentations to enhance understanding of findings, reasoning, and evidence and to add interest" (p. 22). Technology is regarded as a valuable tool for enhancing students' ability to communicate effectively with others.

Standards 2 and 3, in particular, address skills related to media literacy. As noted earlier, media literacy comprises a set of skills for accessing, analyzing, evaluating, and producing a variety of forms of media (NAMLE, 2013). Applying these skills provides an understanding of how various media work (including the social and political influence they have) and allows using them for personal expression. Although the CCSS do not address media literacy specifically, the Listening and Speaking standards recognize the need for students to be critical consumers of information and adept users of technology.

As English language arts teachers, we need to seek out technological tools that will support students in developing the knowledge and skills outlined in the Speaking and Listening standards. Certainly, the number of opportunities to engage in speaking and listening is greatly expanded by the use of technology.

The Focus on Argumentation

Different types of oral presentations offer different opportunities for learning. Poetry recitations, for example, are valuable for helping students recognize how writers create aural effects by using literary elements such as alliteration, assonance, and onomatopoeia. Oral presentations of dramas enhance students' understanding of characterization and dialogue, as well as the playwright's commitment to time, place, and style. Even having a student read aloud from a textbook serves several purposes, both confirming that the entire class is familiar with the material being discussed and providing an example of making an informative/explanatory text audible.

However, like the CCSS Writing standards (which were discussed in Chapter 6), the Speaking and Listening standards place particular emphasis on students' developing skills in argumentation. Speaking and Listening Standard 1 states expectations for being persuasive (1); for clarifying, verifying, and challenging ideas (1.c); and for considering information against the evidence and reasoning presented (1.d). Standard 2 identifies the need to evaluate sources, and Standard 3 identifies the need to evaluate a speaker's viewpoint, reasoning, and use of evidence. Finally, Standard 4 addresses skills essential to delivering an effective oral argument: namely, presenting information and evidence so that listeners will be able to follow the argument. In sum, students are expected to make oral presentations that demonstrate their ability to develop and support a claim using reasoning and evidence and following a logical structure or sequence.

Speaking and Listening in the CCSS Curriculum and Classroom

IN APPENDIX A OF THE CCSS (NGA & CCSSO, 2010b), the developers clearly state the importance of oral language skills to the development of literacy:

> If literacy levels are to improve, the aims of the English language arts classroom, especially in the earliest grades, must include oral language in a purposeful, systematic way, in part because it helps students master the printed word. Besides having intrinsic value as modes of communication, listening and speaking are necessary prerequisites of reading and writing. (p. 26)

The developers of the CCSS go on to say that the development of oral language lays the foundation for the development of written language. In fact, children's oral language skills are strong predictors of their ability to learn how to read and write (p. 26). English language arts teachers of all grade levels should keep in mind these basic tenets of literacy and language learning.

Recognizing Effective Approaches to Instruction

English language arts teachers should also recognize which instructional approaches do and do not support the development of literacy and oral language skills. For instance, the teacher-directed lecture approach is not conducive to literacy and language learning, nor is the traditional ask-and-answer questioning approach, in which students provide short, often yes/no answers to teachers' questions.

Some teachers turn to these approaches when there doesn't seem to be enough time to hold a student-driven discussion. They reason that if they drive the discussion, they can cover more material in less time; in some cases, they ask the questions and provide the answers, as well. Using this approach does allow teachers to cover a large quantity of material in a short amount of time, but it provides limited opportunities to motivate, engage, and connect students to the material. For students to develop a genuine and lasting connection to material, they must be active participants in the learning process.

Engaging classroom discussion and speaking and listening experiences allow students to practice their valuable oral language skills. Students should be encouraged to speak in the classroom and to listen respectfully when others speak. To discourage or forbid students to speak or to create a classroom environment in which students are reluctant to speak sets up a barrier to learning.

Asking Effective Questions

Asking effective questions is one of the keys to fostering great classroom discussions. Encouraging students to develop and ask their own questions, in particular, leads to spirited discussions with engaged participants.

When students ask, answer, and discuss their own questions, they feel free to explore and represent their own ideas. Posing their own questions also gives students the opportunity to lead and direct the classroom discussion. Finally, having students create their own questions promotes the higher-level thinking expected across the CCSS.

Teaching students how to ask great questions is essential to the success of student-directed discussions. Here are some guidelines for students to consider as they develop their own questions:

1. Avoid questions that have yes/no or one-word answers.
2. Ask *how* and *why* questions, which prompt deeper thinking and often lead into meaningful discussion.
3. Avoid questions that reveal the answer or that are easy to answer.
4. Ask questions that matter to you.

By observing student-directed discussions and working with students to develop their own questions, we can gain valuable information about students' learning and understanding. More importantly, however, using this instructional approach gives all students the opportunity to be engaged in learning and to practice speaking and listening skills, regardless of ability level.

Strategies for Developing Speaking and Listening Skills

AS TEACHERS, WE SHOULD CONTINUALLY REEXAMINE AND REFLECT on the strategies and materials we use to help make our curriculum and instruction stronger and to help our students meet the expectations of the CCSS. The following strategies are recommended for strengthening instruction and helping students develop skills in speaking and listening.

CERCA

As noted earlier, the CCSS identify skills in creating and presenting an argument as fundamental to career and college readiness. The placement of argumentation in both the Writing standards and the Speaking and Listening standards is appropriate and requires us to create opportunities for students to develop these skills in both written and oral communication.

The CERCA (n.d.) model is a valuable framework that strongly supports the crafting of both written and oral arguments. In using this framework, the writer or speaker follows these steps:

1. **Claim:** Make a statement or assertion.
2. **Evidence:** Provide evidence using facts, statistics, and other sources.
3. **Reasoning:** Explain how and why the evidence that's presented proves the claim.
4. **Counterargument:** Address other points of view and contrary evidence.
5. **Audience-appropriate language:** Present the argument in the language and style appropriate for the purpose and audience.

Dramatic Activities

Dramatic activities provide excellent opportunities to develop students' speaking and listening skills, as well as other language arts skills. Dramatic activities also allow students to participate in a variety of roles, some more prominent than others. All of the roles, however, should engage students in oral language.

The following lesson meets a number of the CCSS for speaking and listening. Intended for students in grades 9–10, the lesson is based on the play *A Raisin in the Sun*, by Lorraine Hansberry (1958/2004). This lesson could easily be adapted for another play or to accommodate slightly older students.

Classroom Connection

Lights, Cameras, Action!

Grade Level:

Grades 9–10

Materials Needed:

Each student should have the following materials:

- A copy of the play, *A Raisin in the Sun* (Hansberry, 1958/2004)
- Handout: "Preparation Guide for Individual Group Members"
- Handout: "Self-Evaluation Form"
- Handout: "Peer Evaluation Form"

Each group should have a copy of the handout "Division of Tasks for the Group."

Setup:

Give students this overview of the activity:

Your task is to take one scene from the play *A Raisin in the Sun,* by Lorraine Hansberry, and perform it in front of the class. You may give a live performance of the scene, or you may perform the scene outside class, record it, and then submit the recording.

You will be allowed to form your own groups, although the number of people in each group will be based on the number of characters in the particular scene. Scenes will be assigned to groups first according to choice (if no other group wants that scene) and then based on need.

You don't have to memorize all of the lines in the scene, but you should try to. You *must* be familiar enough with the lines that you don't have to depend on notecards during the performance.

If you do need to look at the lines, you *may not* use your book. Instead, you should write the lines on individual notecards or on small pieces of paper. Doing so will prevent you from carrying around the book and having it get in the way of your performance. In addition, if you use notecards or pieces of paper, type the lines on the cards or papers so that you can easily see and read the words. You don't want to have to decipher your handwriting while on stage.

You must use props and costumes in your performance. If you need assistance, please ask me with enough advance notice. If you need any large props, such as a table and chairs, you must let me know well in advance. Also, if you would like any recording equipment, please let me know about that, as well.

In performing your scene, be as creative as you can while dramatizing the scene accurately. Follow the stage directions and recreate the play as Lorraine Hansberry wrote it.

When students form groups, remind them that the number of people allowed is based on the character requirements of the scene. Students can choose from these scenes:

Act I, Scene i	5 parts, pages 23–53	4 people in the group
Act I, Scene ii	6 parts, pages 54–75	6 (5) people in the group
Act II, Scene i	6 parts, pages 76–95	4 people in the group
Act II, Scene ii	7 parts, pages 96–109	4 people in the group
Act II, Scene iii	7 parts, pages 110–130	5 people in the group
Act III, Scene i	8 parts, pages 131–151	4 people in the group

For some scenes, there are more parts than people in a group. This means that some students will have to play more than one part. Make sure that both roles are minor characters in the play and that they don't appear in the scene at the same time.

Steps:

Give students these directions:

1. Select a group based on the designated number of people per scene. Also keep in mind that you want to work with people that you know are responsible, that you can get in touch with and meet outside class, and that you can work well with.
2. Select a scene and sign up.
3. Exchange phone numbers, e-mails, and addresses with members of your group so that you can keep in touch.
4. Look at your schedules and decide on the times and places you will meet outside class to practice.
5. Review the scene together, and select parts to perform.
6. Independently examine the character that you are playing. Record his/her appearance and manners. Record his/her thoughts and values during this scene in the play. Try to get a general feel for the character you are playing. What would the character wear? Gather clothes and props for your costume.

Have students look at the handout "Preparation Guide for Individual Group Members," where some of this information should be recorded (see Figure 7.1). Tell students that everyone must turn in his or her own "Preparation Guide."

7. Discuss the setting with your group members. Make a list of the props that need to be brought in for the performance, and assign who will be responsible for them.
8. Begin practicing, both independently and as a group.
9. Examine the stage directions, and make certain that you follow them correctly.

FIGURE 7.1 ● Student Handout: Preparation Guide for Individual Group Members

Lights, Camera, Action!
Preparation Guide for Individual Group Members

Name: _____

I am performing _____ (Name of Character)

in Act _____ Scene_____.

Directions: Use this guide while thinking about the character that you are portraying and planning your performance. Complete the following questions by writing complete sentences, and support your responses with references to the text.

1. Summarize the plot of the play, focusing on those scenes up to the scene that you are performing.

2. Summarize the scene that you are performing.

3. Describe the character's thoughts during this scene of the play.

4. What is this character's dream? How do you know?

5. Describe the character's actions during this scene of the play.

6. Select three significant quotes stated by this character. Cite the quote appropriately and then explain its importance.

7. Describe the character's appearance during this scene of the play. What will you wear? How will the costume reflect the character's personality, status, and demeanor?

8. Describe the setting of the scene that you are performing. What props does the character use and need to bring for this scene?

9. What are your goals in acting out this scene?

10. Do you have any other thoughts/plans?

10. Continue to practice, both independently and as a group.

11. Hold a dress rehearsal, in which you use the props and costumes and run through the entire scene using the stage directions.

12. Make sure that all of the written material is ready to turn in. Put someone in charge of bringing in the master copy of the "Division of Tasks for the Group." Individually, make sure that you complete the "Preparation Guide," the "Self-Evaluation Form," and the "Peer Evaluation Form." Enjoy and break a leg!

Make sure that each student has a copy of the "Preparation Guide" (see Figure 7.1), the "Self-Evaluation Form" (see Figure 7.2), and the "Peer Evaluation Form" (see Figure 7.3). Each group should have a copy of the "Division of Tasks" sheet (see Figure 7.4).

FIGURE 7.2 ● Student Handout: Self-Evaluation Form

Name: _____

I am performing _____ (Name of Character)

in Act _____ **Scene** _____.

How did I help my group prepare? These are the specific tasks that I had to complete to help my group prepare for the final performance. *(You might need to list only one task; you might need to list more. Use another sheet of paper if you were assigned more than three tasks.):*

1. _____   ❑ accomplished task well
   ❑ accomplished task somewhat
   ❑ didn't accomplish task

   My comments about this task:
   _____
   _____

2. _____   ❑ accomplished task well
   ❑ accomplished task somewhat
   ❑ didn't accomplish task

   My comments about this task:
   _____
   _____

3. _____   ❑ accomplished task well
   ❑ accomplished task somewhat
   ❑ didn't accomplish task

   My comments about this task:
   _____
   _____

(continued)

FIGURE 7.2 ● (continued)

How did I prepare for my own performance?

If I had a chance to do this project again I would (check one box for each task):

- Analyze the play, scene, and character:
  - ❑ spend more time on this task
  - ❑ spend less time on this task
  - ❑ spend just about the same amount of time on this task

- Familiarize myself with my lines:
  - ❑ spend more time on this task
  - ❑ spend less time on this task
  - ❑ spend just about the same amount of time on this task

- Familiarize myself with my blocking:
  - ❑ spend more time on this task
  - ❑ spend less time on this task
  - ❑ spend just about the same amount of time on this task

- Get comfortable with my props:
  - ❑ spend more time on this task
  - ❑ spend less time on this task
  - ❑ spend just about the same amount of time on this task

- Get comfortable with my costume:
  - ❑ spend more time on this task
  - ❑ spend less time on this task
  - ❑ spend just about the same amount of time on this task

The one thing I'm most proud of:

_____

The one thing I wish I could do again:

_____

FIGURE 7.3 ● Student Handout: Peer Evaluation Form

Lights, Camera, Action!
Peer Evaluation

Play/Author: Raisin in the Sun, by Lorraine Hansberry _____

Act: _____ **Scene:** _____

(continued)

FIGURE 7.2 ● *(continued)*

Student: _____ Evaluated by: _____

	Outstanding	Above Expectations	Met Expectations	Below Expectations
Preparation	This student came to all group meetings with the reading assignment and assigned task completed with evident care and effort.	This student came to group meetings with the reading assignment and assigned task completed.	This student came to some group meetings with the reading assignment and assigned task completed.	This student didn't complete the readings or assigned tasks before meetings.
Discussion	At all group meetings, this student's contributions led to better understanding of and deeper connections with the text for me and other members.	During most group meetings, this student's contributions led to better understanding of and deeper connections with the text for me and other members.	During some group meetings, this student's contributions led to better understanding of and deeper connections with the text for me and other members.	During most group meetings, this student did not actively participate.

FIGURE 7.4 ● Student Handout: Division of Tasks for the Group

Lights, Camera, Action!
Division of Tasks for the Group

Directions: When dividing up tasks, assign different members of the group to be in charge of the following: props, costumes, organizing meeting times and places, keeping all group members on task, recording the information for master copies, and other important tasks that arise during the planning of this performance.

For each of the following, write the group member's first and last names and specifically identify all of the tasks that he/she must complete in preparing for the final performance.

Group Member #1:

Tasks:

(continued)

FIGURE 7.4 ● (continued)

Group Member #2:

Tasks:

Group Member #3:

Tasks:

Group Member #4:

Tasks:

Group Member #5:

Tasks:

Group Member #6:

Tasks:

Common Core State Standards for Grades 9–10 (NGA & CCSSO [2010]):

Reading (Literature)

- **R.1:** Cite strong and thorough textual evidence to support analysis of what the text says explicitly as well as inferences drawn from the text.
- **R.2:** Determine a theme or central idea of a text and analyze in detail its development over the course of the text, including how it emerges and is shaped and refined by specific details; provide an objective summary of the text.

Speaking and Listening

- **SL.1:** Initiate and participate effectively in a range of collaborative discussions (one-on-one, in groups, and teacher-led) with diverse partners *on grades 9–10 topics, texts, and issues,* building on others' ideas and expressing their own clearly and persuasively.
- **SL.1.a:** Come to discussions prepared, having read and researched material under study; explicitly draw on that preparation by referring to evidence from texts and other research on the topic or issue to stimulate a thoughtful, well-reasoned exchange of ideas.
- **SL.1.b:** Work with peers to set rules for collegial discussions and decision-making (e.g., informal consensus, taking votes on key issues, presentation of alternate views), clear goals and deadlines, and individual roles as needed.

- **SL.1.c:** Propel conversations by posing and responding to questions that relate the current discussion to broader themes or larger ideas; actively incorporate others into the discussion; and clarify, verify, or challenge ideas and conclusions.
- **SL.1.d:** Respond thoughtfully to diverse perspectives, summarize points of agreement and disagreement, and, when warranted, qualify or justify their own views and understanding and make new connections in light of the evidence and reasoning presented.
- **SL.5:** Make strategic use of digital media (e.g., textual, graphical, audio, visual, and interactive elements) in presentations to enhance understanding of findings, reasoning, and evidence and to add interest.

Evaluation:

- Graded performance (see Figure 7.5)
- Self-evaluation (see Figure 7.2)
- Peer evaluation (see Figure 7.3)

Each student must submit his or her completed "Preparation Guide" on the day of the performance. Each group will turn in one completed copy of the "Division of Tasks."

FIGURE 7.5 ● Grade Sheet for Final Performance

Lights, Camera, Action!
Final Performance—Grade Sheet

Group Members	Requirements	Division of Tasks	Self-Evaluation	Peer Evaluation	Preparation Guide

Play/Author: Raisin in the Sun, by Lorraine Hansberry

Act: _____ **Scene:** _____ **Time of Live Performance/Video:** _____

Assessment Areas

Quality and Use of Props:
Props are used as described in the scene. Props enhance the performance and do not distract from it.

1   2   3   4   5   6   7   8   9   10

(continued)

FIGURE 7.5 ● (*continued*)

Quality and Use of Costumes:
Costumes reflect accurate characterization. Costumes enhance the performance and do not distract from it.

| 1 | 2 | 3 | 4 | 5 | 6 | 7 | 8 | 9 | 10 |

Movement on Stage:
Actors reveal familiarity with blocking and move smoothly on the stage.

| 1 | 2 | 3 | 4 | 5 | 6 | 7 | 8 | 9 | 10 |

Familiarity with Lines:
Actors make eye contact with the audience. Actors do not use their books. If actors use notecards, it does not distract from the performance.

| 1 | 2 | 3 | 4 | 5 | 6 | 7 | 8 | 9 | 10 |

Volume and Articulation:
Actors speak loudly enough and articulate clearly enough for the audience to hear and understand them.

| 1 | 2 | 3 | 4 | 5 | 6 | 7 | 8 | 9 | 10 |

Equal Division of Tasks:
All group members participate in the performance and are equally prepared.

| 1 | 2 | 3 | 4 | 5 | 6 | 7 | 8 | 9 | 10 |

Accuracy of Performance:
The performance accurately develops the action and mood, the characters, and the setting.

| 1 | 2 | 3 | 4 | 5 | 6 | 7 | 8 | 9 | 10 | 11 | 12 | 13 | 14 | 15 | 16 | 17 | 18 | 19 | 20 |

Quality of Overall Performance:
The performance shows that time and effort were put forth, reflects practice and preparation, and reveals the actors' enthusiasm.

| 1 | 2 | 3 | 4 | 5 | 6 | 7 | 8 | 9 | 10 | 11 | 12 | 13 | 14 | 15 | 16 | 17 | 18 | 19 | 20 |

Additional Comments:

Total: _____ / 100

Collaborative Conversations

The traditional instructional model of the teacher as "the sage on the stage" does very little to develop students' speaking and listening skills. Instead, we should create frequent opportunities for students to discuss texts and ideas in small, collaborative groups. Students can have these conversations with partners or in small groups of three to five. Whatever the size of the group, its discussion must have a curricular focus.

Also consider other ways that students can take greater responsibility for their learning. Supporting them as they develop skills in collaboration and presentation (as outlined in the Speaking and Listening standards) will help them gain both confidence and independence. Keep in mind this old saying: "The one who talks the most in class is probably the one who is learning the most."

Web 2.0 Resources

Many tools and strategies for developing students' speaking and listening skills are available on Web 2.0 sites. Here is a sampling of useful sites:

- **Audiboo.com:** Students can create "boos," which are simple audio recordings that are easy to e-mail and share.
- **Present.me:** This PowerPoint enhancement tool allows the student to video record his or her explanation of the slides and presentation. It can be fully integrated into a PowerPoint presentation.
- **Todaysmeet.com:** This is a simple backchannel where students can comment, question, and respond during large-group discussions. The discussion transcript can be saved as a Word document.
- **Vocaroo.com:** Students can create simple audio recordings and easily share them (similar to Audioboo.com).
- **Voki.com:** Students can create animated avatars that speak and use the site's other resources.
- **Voxopop.com:** Using this powerful tool, students can create recordings and permit others to listen and respond to those recordings.

REFERENCES

CERCA. (n.d.). ThinkCERCA.com. Retrieved from www.thinkcerca.com.

Fisher, D., Frey, N., & Rothenberg, C. (2008). Why talk is important in classrooms. In *Content-area conversations: How to plan discussion-based lessons for diverse language learners* (Chapter 1). Alexandria, VA: Association for Supervision and Curriculum Development. Retrieved from www.ascd.org/publications/books/108035/chapters/Why-Talk-Is-Important-in-Classrooms.aspx.

Hong, Z. & Alex, N. K. (1995). *Oral language development across the curriculum, K–12.* Digest no. 107, EDO-CS-95-10. Bloomington, IN: ERIC Clearinghouse on Reading, English and Communication. Retrieved from www.learn2study.org/teachers/oral_lang.htm.

Huxley, A. (2006). *Brave new world revisited.* New York, NY: Harper Perennial. (Original work published 1958)

National Association for Media Literacy Education (NAMLE). (2013). Media literacy defined. *NAMLE.net.* Retrieved from http://namle.net/publications/media-literacy-definitions.

National Governors Association Center for Best Practices & Council of Chief State School Officers (NGA & CCSSO). (2010a). *Common Core State Standards: English language arts and literacy in history/social studies, science, and technical subjects.* Washington, DC: Authors. Retrieved from www.corestandards.org/assets/CCSSI_ELA%20Standards.pdf.

National Governors Association Center for Best Practices & Council of Chief State School Officers (NGA & CCSSO). (2010b). Appendix A: Research supporting key elements of the standards and glossary of key terms. *Common Core State Standards.* Washington, DC: Authors. Retrieved from www.corestandards.org/assets/Appendix_A.pdf.

Vygotsky, L. S. (1986). *Thought and language* (rev. ed.), edited by A. Kozulin. Cambridge, MA: MIT Press. (Original work published 1962)

LITERATURE CITED

Hansberry, L. (2004). *A raisin in the sun.* New York, NY: Vintage Books. (Original work published 1958)

Curriculum Implications

AS I WRITE THIS CHAPTER, THE FULL CURRICULUM implications of the Common Core State Standards (CCSS) are being realized. Some school districts are just beginning to identify the knowledge and skills outlined in the CCSS and the resulting changes in curriculum and instructional that will be necessary for students to meet the standards. Other districts have already completed this evaluation and moved to the planning stage, creating literacy models and plans that fit the skills focus of the CCSS. Schools in these districts are well positioned to help their students meet the rigorous expectations of this new paradigm.

Like many educators, I'm relieved to see these changes taking place in literacy education. These changes provide opportunities for teachers to collaborate in sharing ideas and information and to instruct students in meaningful ways that support the development of literacy. Also, like many English and literacy teachers, I'm committed to understanding and

Monkey Business/Fotolia

implementing the curriculum and instruction that will best develop adolescents' literacy skills. When adolescents have mastered these skills, they are ready not only for college and career but also to serve as active participants in a democratic society.

Moving Beyond No Child Left Behind

THE TRANSITION TO A CCSS-BASED CURRICULUM INVOLVES SIGNIFICANT changes in several areas—perhaps chief among them, assessment. Two national consortia—the Partnership for Assessment of Readiness for College and Careers (PARCC) and the Smarter Balanced Assessment Consortium (Smarter Balanced)—have designed assessments to be administered at various times during the school year to gauge students' mastery of the skills and knowledge outlined in the CCSS. Implementation of these assessments is set for the school year 2014–2015 (ETS, 2012). (We will discuss these consortia later in the chapter.) Meanwhile, teachers are administering assessments that were created to meet the standards established by the No Child Left Behind (NCLB) Act of 2001.

Although each of the 50 states has its own system of assessment, most of the NCLB-based tests being used are largely misaligned in terms of evaluating students' literacy skills and providing useful information for informing instruction. For example, NCLB reading comprehensions tests usually consist of short passages of text followed by series of multiple-choice questions. These tests do not assess the literacy skills that English language art teachers consider as essential for college and career readiness, which are as follows:

1. to read a wide variety of complex and challenging texts while applying critical-thinking skills
2. to write essays, narratives, and researched-based texts

Both of these skills are hallmarks of the CCSS English Language Arts (ELA) standards and were written as a direct result of information gathered from national data during the NCLB era.

The current state-based tests are products of an unfortunate trend in which educational standards have continually been lowered. In response to this trend, teachers and schools have tended to match low-level testing with low-level instruction and curricula. To reinforce this trend even further, many states have responded to the NCLB requirement for annual testing (intended to demonstrate student progress) by simply lowering the demands of their own tests. In sum, we have witnessed diminished classroom expectations being further exacerbated by assessments that are largely composed of low-level, multiple-choice questions.

The result of this low-expectations/low-achievement cycle is demonstrated by data gathered throughout the 2000s by the National Assessment of Educational Progress (NAEP)—the only reliable, consistent measure of student performance in the United States. For high school students, in particular, the NAEP data reveal stagnation of student performance in reading (Buckley, 2013; NAEP, 2004, 2008, 2012). The NAEP data are definitive proof that, despite the optimism that accompanied NCLB, this attempt at educational reform failed.

Among the many criticisms leveled against NCLB is the demoralizing effect it has had on teachers. An article about the "side effects" of NCLB reported that because of the focus on high-stakes testing, teachers have felt compelled to teach to the test (Cawelti, 2006). As a result, they have often neglected the needs of individual students, bored students (and themselves) with repeated sessions of completing practice problems, and had limited time to "teach creatively." Similarly discouraging observations were reported from a survey of teachers from across the United States, conducted by the Center for Education Policy (CEP) (Rebora, 2006). Many teachers stated that curricula had become increasingly "prescriptive," telling them what and how to teach. Being unable to apply their skills and knowledge in the classroom left teachers feeling "stifled" and "squelched."

In contrast, the CCSS recognize teachers' professional integrity and expertise, and empower them to determine the best approaches for helping their students succeed. Perhaps the most important element in the CCSS document is the statement in the introduction that gives teachers and curriculum specialists the respect they deserve. In a section labeled "A focus on results rather than means," the CCSS developers write:

> By emphasizing required achievements, the Standards leave room for teachers, curriculum developers, and states to determine how those goals should be reached and what additional topics should be addressed. Thus, the Standards do not mandate such things as a particular writing process or the full range of metacognitive strategies that students may need to monitor and direct their thinking and learning. Teachers are thus free to provide students with whatever tools and knowledge their professional judgment and experience identify as most helpful for meeting the goals set out in the Standards. (NGA & CCSSO, 2010a, p. 4)

We are finally emerging from what I sometimes refer to as an era of "standards abuse" and, instead, are embracing a corpus of standards that's intended to provide a usable, generative framework for providing literacy instruction. I'm hopeful that the two assessment consortia (PARCC and Smarter Balanced) will provide the leadership, resources, and shared experiences to provide focus and direction in the implementation of the CCSS. While the CCSS are not a panacea for all of the challenges that confront English language arts teachers in today's classrooms, they do provide a means for us to reclaim our power and our responsibility for doing what we are meant to do: prepare our students for the demands of the twenty-first century.

Foundations of a CCSS Curriculum

WITHOUT A DOUBT, THE CALL FOR MORE RIGOROUS teaching and learning under the CCSS issues a challenge to schools and school leaders, teachers and curriculum specialists, and students and parents. As school districts prepare to transition to the CCSS, teachers and curriculum specialists must lead the effort. Indeed, the statement by the developers of the CCSS highlights the role of teachers and curriculum specialists as the caretakers of the implementation process.

Curriculum directors should focus on the following 10 points regarding the development of a CCSS-based curriculum for the English language arts. These points, while not exhaustive, highlight the most important aspects of the CCSS (NGA & CCSSO, 2010a, 2010b):

1. The more adolescents read, the greater their reading achievement. As discussed in previous chapters, students must be able to read a wide variety of complex texts to be prepared for career and college. To plan toward achieving that goal, teachers should consider how much their students currently read and explore ways to increase (in some cases, even double) that amount. Having students participate in Literature Circles, read independently after choosing books from a classroom library, and read complete works rather than excerpts or shorter works are all effective strategies for helping teachers and students meet this expectation.

2. Teachers need to employ strategies for reading comprehension that will help adolescents to hone their reading skills. Improving students' comprehension skills will make them better able to read independently and actively. Because comprehension strategies must be applied on an as-needed basis and require modification to meet individual needs, sufficient time must be allocated to teaching and learning of these skills.

3. Text complexity is determined by three equally important elements: quantitative dimensions, qualitative dimensions, and reader and task considerations. However, Lexile scores and other readability measures address only the quantitative dimensions of text complexity. In considering and selecting challenging texts, curriculum directors and teachers must address the qualitative and reader/task considerations, as well (such as motivation, setting, prior knowledge demands, dialect, and point of view).

4. Argumentation is an important focus of the CCSS Writing standards and is also addressed in the Speaking and Listening standards. All curricula should provide ample opportunities for students to state claims and support them using evidence and effective reasoning. Skills in crafting and presenting an argument are deemed essential to success in college and career.

5. Writing is a process, and like all processes, it requires adequate time for completion. Students must write frequently to sharpen their writing skills, and they should use digital media to develop their skills in various contexts (writing essays, research reports, blogs, and online discussion boards, for example).

6. The CCSS also note the importance of students' ability to respond to a text through writing. Writing about a text demonstrates both the student's level of reading comprehension and their ability to construct an effective argument.

7. Speaking and listening—the two aspects of oral language—are important literacy skills and have a synergetic relationship with reading, writing, and language learning. Students should be able to articulate their own thoughts and listen actively to others; in addition, they should be able to use multimedia to collaborate with others, to expand on their own understandings, and to effectively present their knowledge and ideas. Providing students with frequent opportunities to practice their speaking and listening skills is essential for career and college readiness.

8. The Reading Standards for Informational Text apply to all informational texts, both print and digital. Given this, it's important for curriculum directors to look beyond photocopies and print media and to encourage students to examine digital texts, as well. It's also important to recognize that informational texts are read across the content areas, not only in the English language arts. The CCSS encourage all teachers to help students develop strategies they can use in approaching informational texts. In addition, all teachers need to engage students in the close reading of challenging texts and to slow the pace of instruction to allow for the careful examination and discussion of ideas.

9. Teaching literature still belongs in the realm of the English language arts. Despite the CCSS emphasis on reading informational texts, literature is still an essential component of a strong language arts curriculum and provides a foundational experience in teaching English language content. Furthermore, the study of literature promotes higher-level comprehension skills, such as making inferences, understanding metaphors, and drawing deeper meanings from texts. These skills are largely accomplished when students read the linguistically complex texts that are inherent to the study of literature.

10. In creating assessments that are aligned with the CCSS, educators should look to the materials from the assessment consortia: PARCC and Smarter Balanced. (Again, both consortia are discussed later in this chapter.) The assessments developed by these consortia can be used

as cornerstones in the development of formative and summative assessments for all English language arts students. As teachers, department heads, and curriculum directors develop their own assessments and rubrics, they should ask themselves, "What does learning this skill look like?" Acquiring any kind of skill involves stops and starts, and there is always room for further development. Newly crafted assessments and rubrics should clearly reflect the generative nature of developing students' skills. Thus, in keeping with the spirit of the CCSS, rubrics and assessments should avoid deficit and punitive language.

CCSS-Aligned Curricula and Assessments

Balanced Literacy Model

The CCSS are founded on the balanced literacy model and supported by findings from large-scale assessments such as those conducted by the NAEP. In the English language arts classroom, the balanced literacy model promotes the expectation that students can read a wide variety of literature (plays, poems, short stories, novels, graphic novels) and informational texts (diaries, articles, manuals, blogs, wikis, web pages). At the high school level, the balanced literacy model offers strategies for supporting struggling and reluctant readers and for encouraging proficient and active readers. Through authentic learning activities, students learn literacy strategies that they can apply to a wide variety of complex texts. These experiences will ultimately prepare students for college and career.

An excellent example of an effective and usable literacy model is the one developed by the Berkeley County (South Carolina) Public Schools for grades 6–12 (under the direction of Laura Gardner). In many cases, models are long, bureaucratic documents that teachers find unwieldy and difficult to follow. That is not the case, however, with the Berkeley County literacy model (see Figure 8.1).

FIGURE 8.1 ● Sample Literacy Model

Foundations	Instructional Model	Gradual Release of Responsibility	Research
Vocabulary development Reading fluency Reading comprehension Written responses to text Application of reading and writing strategies through research	Direct instruction/ Modeling (focus lessons) Guided practice/ Collaborative learning (Literature Circles, etc.) Independent practice Assessment		*Making Middle Grades Work/High Schools That Work* *Ten Key Practices and Planning for Improved Student Achievement* *NCTE Principles of Adolescent Literacy Reform* *Oregon Reading First, the Florida Center for Reading Research, and the Alabama Reading Initiative*

Source: Reprinted with permission from Laura Garner.

In the Berkeley County model, the "Foundations" section identifies five essential skills: vocabulary development, reading fluency, reading comprehension, written responses to text, and application of reading/writing strategies through research. These skills are taught using the strategies listed in the "Instructional Model" section, such as guided practice and Literature Circles, and the "Gradual Release of Responsibility" promotes students' independence as they develop their literacy skills and content knowledge. Finally, the model identifies current research-based methodology in the teaching of English language arts, as outlined in the "Research" section.

The Berkeley County public schools' literacy model also provides a three-tiered instructional approach to meet the needs of students at different levels of ability (see Figure 8.2). Incorporating the Response to Intervention (RtI) model is intended to offer ongoing support for struggling readers. In this respect, the literacy model provides a structure for determining students' skill levels and providing differentiated instruction, as appropriate. Integration of the RtI model with the balanced literacy model provides a rich framework within which teachers can develop and deliver CCSS-based instruction.

Finally, to support teachers in implementing the literacy model, the Berkeley County Public Schools' document includes a chart of scaffolding techniques (see Figure 8.3). Daily techniques are provided to support students' reading and writing behaviors.

Comprehensive Literacy Plan

To successfully transition the curriculum to meet the expectations stated in the CCSS, another key element that must be in place is a comprehensive literacy plan. A *literacy plan* is essentially a "blueprint" designed to ensure the development of consistent literacy instruction,

FIGURE 8.2 ● Three-Tiered Approach to Instruction of Readers

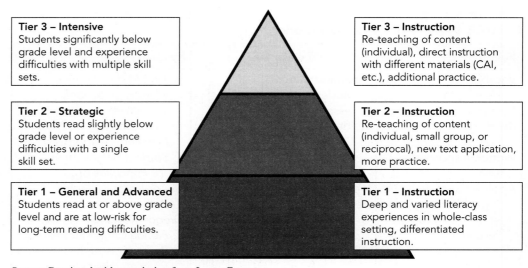

Tier 3 – Intensive
Students significantly below grade level and experience difficulties with multiple skill sets.

Tier 3 – Instruction
Re-teaching of content (individual), direct instruction with different materials (CAI, etc.), additional practice.

Tier 2 – Strategic
Students read slightly below grade level or experience difficulties with a single skill set.

Tier 2 – Instruction
Re-teaching of content (individual, small group, or reciprocal), new text application, more practice.

Tier 1 – General and Advanced
Students read at or above grade level and are at low-risk for long-term reading difficulties.

Tier 1 – Instruction
Deep and varied literacy experiences in whole-class setting, differentiated instruction.

Source: Reprinted with permission from Laura Garner.

FIGURE 8.3 ● Scaffolding Techniques for Supporting Reading and Writing Behaviors

Learning Behavior	Everyday Scaffolding Techniques			
	Before Reading	During Reading	After Reading	Writing
Student substitutes sight words from memory for decoded word on printed page.		Call attention to words with similar parts in reading.		Access decoding skills; address phonics through word parts.
Student reads aloud fluently but seems to understand little; cannot answer questions after reading.	Check reading level and adjust beginning text level accordingly.	Ask leading questions to encourage deeper investigation of concepts.	Craft post-reading activities that allow for specific student–teacher interaction.	Encourage reflective and double-entry journaling as a self-check of comprehension.
Student provides correct verbal responses to questions but cannot answer written questions.	Provide practice with analyzing questions to determine the information desired.		Model strategies for students to use during independent practice.	Record and then encourage student to script verbal responses until ready to make the leap to writing.
Student scores on MAP Reading show lower than expected growth.	Do self-check of questioning techniques to be sure student has access to thinking beyond knowledge level.	Compare student reading level with text level to ensure a match and appropriate challenge.	Provide practice with recognizing vocabulary of testing.	
Student has difficulty mastering content knowledge.	Ask students to contribute their own experiences that relate to the subject at hand.	Provide graphic organizers, chants, or mnemonic devices to ease memorization of key facts or procedures.	Model strategies for students to use during independent practice.	

assessment, and professional development across grade levels and includes elements such as the following:

- a statement of vision and core beliefs
- statements about expectations for student achievement and the standards on which those expectations are based
- descriptions of core content and expected learning outcomes for specific grade levels
- descriptions of recommended instructional strategies, schedules, and classroom environments
- resources for instructional support and teacher development

The comprehensive literacy plans of a number of states and school districts are available for review online (see the plan for the Milwaukee School District, for example). The state or district provides this plan to teachers and curriculum specialists to guide them in making important decisions about the curriculum.

The faculty at Achievement Academy Charter School in Albany, New York, created CCSS-based units in all of the content areas in line with the elements of a literacy plan. In designing each unit, the teachers incorporated the following elements to ensure consistency and coherence:

1. a strong essential question as the focus of the unit
2. a unit rationale that states the importance of studying the topic
3. a unit bibliography and list of materials
4. a set of unit goals that integrate the appropriate CCSS standards and state-based goals
5. a set of unit objectives that describe the specific behaviors, skills/knowledge, and products students are expected to demonstrate or produce
6. sets of procedures that ensure easy, effective implementation of the unit (including procedures for differentiated instruction and extension activities, completion of student work, and integration of technology)
7. an assessment plan that aligns with targeted standards and objectives and provides for multiple forms and applications of evaluation

These elements serve as the criteria for evaluating unit plans in the rubric shown in Figure 8.4, which was designed by the teachers at Achievement Academy. Using this rubric allows teachers to conduct a comprehensive evaluation and overview of the plans they develop for teaching and learning. Doing so ensures tremendous consistency in vertical alignment, since the teachers contributed to and then apply the same set of clearly articulated expectations. In addition, at Achievement Academy, giving teachers the opportunity to collaborate during the initial planning stages of the CCSS transition laid the groundwork for creating ongoing collaborative planning groups.

Assessment Systems

In 2010, two multistate consortia were awarded grants to develop comprehensive assessment systems that reflect the CCSS requirements for college and career readiness. Both the PARCC and Smarter Balanced consortia are committed to building new testing and instructional support systems for grades K–12 that align with the CCSS. Beginning in the 2014–2015 school year,

FIGURE 8.4 ● Rubric for Evaluating Unit Plans

Achievement Academy Charter School Unit Plan Rubric

Grade and Subject: _____

Unit Title and/or Number: _____

Target	Proficient	Developing
Unit Theme/Essential Question		
The Essential Question centers on a philosophical, moral, or thought-provoking theme that addresses the standards identified in the unit and requires students to think deeply about the concepts across units in a personal way.	The Essential Question centers on a topic that is either interesting or important to students and is written so they will understand it.	The Essential Question does not address either students' interests or concerns and/or is written in language they do not understand.
The Essential Question targets what students should learn in this unit and is broad enough to cover most of the topics within the unit.	The Essential Question is an important question for the unit. It is broad enough to include most of the topics within the unit.	The Essential Question is not a key question for the unit. It only covers a few topics within the unit.
Unit Rationale		
The rationale answers the question of "Why is it important to study this topic?" with a strong argument that relates the unit plan to the CCSS, by including the following: outcome goals for content knowledge and process skills, a description of the developmental suitability of the material, and the relationship between the unit plan and student/community concerns and interests. The response articulates how the knowledge and skills of the unit are applicable in other settings or disciplines (multidisciplinary connections).	The Unit Rationale includes a valid argument for the content, delivery, and focus of the unit. The rationale states the intended purpose of the unit and relates to students' past and future learning. It shows thought about the relevance of the content to students' lives and incorporates some multidisciplinary connections.	The rationale is vague in description of the unit's purpose and does not articulate how the unit relates to students' past and future learning. It also may show little or no connection to students' lives and/or lack multi-disciplinary connections.

(continued)

FIGURE 8.4 ● (continued)

Target	Proficient	Developing
Unit Bibliography and Materials List		
The bibliography and materials/ resource list include a range of instructional resources beyond a textbook/workbook. They show initiative in seeking teaching materials from sources beyond classroom/school boundaries. Ex. Books, journals, magazines, articles, Internet resources, etc.	The bibliography and materials/resource list includes a variety of instructional resources beyond a textbook/ workbook.	List of necessary resources and materials is missing or fails to designate specific materials needed by either the teacher or students. Appropriate technology resources (websites, software, etc.) are not included.
Unit Goals		
All standards identified in the unit are a focus of instruction and assessment throughout the Unit Plan.	The standards in the unit are implied throughout the Unit Plan, but some are not specifically shown as being part of instruction or assessment.	The Unit Plan does not address the standards in any meaningful way.
The duration of the unit is appropriate for the quantity and significance of the standards. Enough time is available to teach each standard adequately, and no standard receives unwarranted emphasis.	The standards selected are appropriate for the duration of the unit. There may be not quite enough time or slightly too much time to fit some standards in.	The Unit Plan has too many or too few standards than are appropriate for the length of the unit.
Unit Objectives		
The objectives describe specific behaviors, knowledge, and/or products that relate to standards and can be assessed and understood at a deep level. Objectives are appropriate for students' developmental and learning needs. Lesson objectives are aligned with Common Core and NYS standards (where necessary), and are	The objectives describe specific behaviors, knowledge, and/or products that meet standards and reflect understanding of relevant unit concepts. They are appropriate for students' developmental and learning needs. Objectives are aligned with Common Core, and are stated as learning outcomes, identifying student	The objectives describe vague behaviors, knowledge, and/or products that do not require understanding of unit concepts. They are not appropriate for students' developmental and learning needs or lesson objectives are not clearly aligned with Common Core, or NYS standards (for SS and Science).

(continued)

FIGURE 8.4 ● (*continued*)

Target	Proficient	Developing
clearly stated as learning outcomes, identifying student knowledge and performances. Objectives are specific and clearly build toward learning goals so that student learning is sequential.	knowledge and performances. Objectives are general and may not address incremental steps in the learning process. Many objectives are in the first three levels of the revised Bloom's taxonomy.	
Overall Procedures		
The Unit Plan has well thought-out, detailed instructions and procedures that make the unit easy to implement.	The Unit Plan has instructions and procedures that serve as an effective guide for implementation.	The Unit Plan lacks clarity and is not an effective guide for implementation.
There is a hook created for the unit that will provide an appealing entry point into the core of the unit.	There is a hook created for the unit.	There is no hook created for the unit or the hook may not be appealing for students.
Procedures: Differentiation/HOTS/Extension Activities		
Instructional strategies are varied and reflect knowledge of how children learn and develop. Learners will be actively engaged. Strategies address a variety of learning styles and include adjustments/modifications for learners with exceptional needs. Activities reflect several levels of Bloom's taxonomy.	Instructional strategies are varied and reflect knowledge of how children learn and develop. Strategies address learning styles and include adjustments/modifications for learners with exceptional needs. Activities reflect several levels of Bloom's taxonomy.	Instructional strategies are limited and repetitious OR are not sensitive to the developmental and learning needs of children. Adjustments for learning styles and/or learners with exceptional needs are not evident. Activities are at the lower levels of Bloom's taxonomy and do not provide sufficient challenge to actively engage all learners.
Procedures: Student Work		
The work the students complete in this unit is authentic, meaningful, and resembles the kinds of work people do in real life.	The work the students complete in this unit is meaningful and has elements that resemble the kinds of work people do in real life.	The work the students complete in this unit does not resemble authentic work in a discipline.

(*continued*)

FIGURE 8.4 ● (*continued*)

Target	Proficient	Developing
The student work for the unit takes diverse learners into consideration and provides well-defined and thoughtful accommodations.	The unit provides some accommodations to support a diversity of learners.	The unit does not provide any accommodations to support multiple types of learners.
Procedures: Technology Integration		
The technology in the Unit Plan deepens the students' understanding of important concepts, supports higher-order thinking skills, and develops students' lifelong skills. The technology enhances student learning, increases productivity, and promotes creativity. It also creatively supports and develops students' research, publishing, collaboration, and communication skills.	The technology in the Unit Plan helps the students understand concepts and develop skills. The technology enhances student learning, increases productivity, or promotes creativity. It also supports and develops students' research, publishing, collaboration, and communication skills.	The Unit Plan could be taught more effectively without the current use of technology as it is described in the Unit Plan. The Unit Plan does not take advantage of research, publishing, collaboration, or communication capabilities.
Various media and technology resources have been identified that will be used to enhance teaching/learning activities, such as interactive SMARTboard activities, use of the ELMO, graphic calculators, etc.	Some media and technology resources that will be used to enhance teaching and learning activities have been identified.	Very few media or technology resources have been identified in this unit.
Assessment Plan		
The assessment plan matches and addresses all of the targeted standards and objectives.	The assessment plan matches and addresses most of the targeted standards and objectives.	The assessment plan does not match or address the targeted standards and objectives.
Both formal and informal and peer- and self-assessments are used throughout the unit.	A variety of formative assessments are used throughout the unit.	Assessment in the unit is only done at the end of the unit and/or is only used for grading purposes.

(continued)

FIGURE 8.4 ● (continued)

Target	Proficient	Developing
The final product or performance assessment generally emphasizes content and higher-order thinking over design features of the project.	The final product or performance assessment appropriately emphasizes content over organization, structure, and graphic elements.	The final product or performance assessment emphasizes organization, structure, and graphic elements more than content and higher-order thinking.

Source: Developed by the instructional team of Achievement Academy Charter School under the direction of Principal O'Rita M. Swan M.Ed. Reprinted with permission.

these assessment systems will replace those currently in use by member states in the areas of English language arts and mathematics (ETS, 2012).

Both the PARCC and Smarter Balanced systems will measure student proficiency and individual growth. At each grade level, these systems will assess the extent to which a student is on track toward achieving the goal of high school graduation. This information can be used to improve teaching, learning, and curriculum decisions. It can also be used to assist in measuring teacher, principal, and school performance. And perhaps most importantly, this information can be used to assist students, parents, and counselors as they consider choices in course selection and college application.

PARCC and Smarter Balanced are collaborating to ensure comparability across the two systems of assessment. In addition, both consortia have joined technical and policy advisors to study cross-consortia comparability, and both have collaborated on a Technology Readiness Tool to help states identify gaps in infrastructure and plan for future needs.

Table 8.1 compares PARCC and Smarter Balanced along a number of qualities and also identifies which states belong to each consortium. Teachers and curriculum specialists should determine to which consortium their state belongs and consider the expectations of that assessment system in planning for curriculum and instruction. Updated information about the consortia, their progress, and their assessment prototypes can be found at their respective websites (see References).

Partnership for Assessment of Readiness for College and Careers (PARCC)

The PARCC assessments will be closely aligned with the CCSS and grounded in the key shifts that underlie the standards. PARCC's core commitments to the quality of assessment in the English language arts and literacy include the following:

- **Texts worth reading:** The assessments will use authentic texts, not artificially produced or commissioned passages.
- **Questions worth answering:** Sequences of questions will be asked that draw students into the text (as occurs in an excellent classroom), rather than sets of random questions that range in quality.
- **Custom items:** Instead of reusing existing assessment items, items will be developed that are customized to the CCSS.

TABLE 8.1 ● *Comparison of Assessment Consortia: PARCC and Smarter Balanced*

	PARCC	Smarter Balanced
Membership*	16 states	22 states
Governing States* (cast decision making votes on test design and policy)	Arizona, Arkansas, Colorado, the District of Columbia, Florida, Illinois, Louisiana, Maryland, Massachusetts, Mississippi, New Jersey, New Mexico, New York, Ohio, Rhode Island, Tennessee	California, Connecticut, Delaware, Hawaii, Idaho, Iowa, Maine, Michigan, Missouri, Montana, Nevada, New Hampshire, North Carolina, North Dakota, Oregon, South Carolina, South Dakota, Vermont, Washington, West Virginia, Wisconsin, Wyoming
Other State Involvement*	Participating states (consult on test design and policy but have no decision-making authority and must participate in pilot and field testing): Kentucky, Pennsylvania	Advisory states (consult on test design and policy but have no decision-making authority): Alabama, Pennsylvania
Procurement State (fiscal agent)	Florida	Washington
Project Management Partner	Achieve	WestEd
Higher-Ed Partnerships	More than 200 two- and four-year institutions (which typically receive 90% of all students across the PARCC Consortium states who enter college within two years of graduating from high school) will use the assessments as an indicator of readiness for credit-bearing, entry-level courses.	Some 175 public and 13 private systems/institutions of higher education have committed to participate in the consortium, help design the new assessments, and use the assessments as an indicator of readiness for credit-bearing, entry-level courses in lieu of existing placement tests. These participating institutions typically receive 74% of all students in Smarter Balanced Consortium states who begin college within two years of graduating from high school.
Award	$186 million total (assessment and supplemental grants), Race to the Top Assessment Program grants awarded September and October, 2010	$176 million total (assessment and supplemental grants), Race to the Top Assessment Program grants awarded September and October, 2010

*As of December 13, 2013 (U.S. Department of Education, 2013).

- **Fidelity to the standards:** PARCC evidences are rooted in the language of the CCSS, ensuring that expectations will be the same in both instructional and assessment settings (National PTA, 2012).

As noted, several key shifts underlie the design of the CCSS: namely, complexity, evidence, and knowledge. These three shifts are addressed in the PARCC assessments in these specific ways:

Shift 1. Complexity: Regular practice with complex text and its academic language.

1. PARCC builds a staircase of text complexity to ensure students are on track each year for college and career reading.
2. PARCC rewards careful, close reading rather than racing through passages.
3. PARCC systematically focuses on the words that matter most—not obscure vocabulary, but the academic language that pervades complex texts.

Shift 2. Evidence: Reading and writing grounded in evidence from text, literary and informational.

4. PARCC focuses on students rigorously citing evidence from texts throughout the assessment (including selected-response items).
5. PARCC includes questions with more than one right answer to allow students to generate a range of rich insights that are substantiated by evidence from text(s).
6. PARCC requires writing to sources rather than writing to decontextualized expository prompts.
7. PARCC also includes rigorous expectations for narrative writing, including accuracy and precision in writing in later grades.

Shift 3. Knowledge: Building knowledge through content rich nonfiction.

8. PARCC assesses not just ELA but a full range of reading and writing across the disciplines of science and social studies.
9. PARCC simulates research on the assessment, including the comparison and synthesis of ideas across a range of informational sources. (National PTA, 2012)

The PARCC assessment system has been developed differently from previous systems. To begin, the PARCC member states developed model content frameworks to provide guidance on key elements of high-quality instruction that align with the CCSS; those frameworks were then used to craft the assessments' design. The PARCC developers believe that following this unique development process means that, perhaps for the first time, assessments have been designed based on the same content that the CCSS expect of teachers and students (National PTA, 2012).

Smarter Balanced   Like PARCC, Smarter Balanced is committed to involving educators in the design and vetting of its assessment system. In fact, Smarter Balanced formed state-level teams of teachers to evaluate its assessments and professional learning resources. Representatives from higher education are also involved in the design of the assessment system, with the goal of having colleges and universities accept the findings of the assessments (Smarter Balanced, n.d.).

The developers of the Smarter Balanced assessment system describe it as being different from other assessments as follows:

> Smarter Balanced is guided by the belief that a balanced, high-quality assessment system—including formative, interim, and summative components—can improve teaching and learning by providing information and tools for teachers and schools to help students succeed. Timely and meaningful assessment information can offer specific information about areas of performance so that teachers can follow up with targeted instruction, students can better target their own efforts, and administrators and policymakers can more fully understand what students know and can do, in order to guide curriculum and professional development decisions. (Smarter Balanced, n.d.)

One of the major differences between Smarter Balanced and PARCC is that Smarter Balanced assessments will use computer adaptive testing (CAT) for both the mandatory summative assessments and optional interim assessments. This means that based on a student's responses, the Smarter Balanced system will automatically adjust the difficulty of the questions. Providing each student with a tailored set of questions will allow identifying exactly which skills he or she has mastered, and on a larger scale, this feature will allow determining more accurate scores for students at all levels of achievement. According to the Smarter Balanced developers, CAT assessments are usually shorter than paper-and-pencil assessments, because fewer questions are needed to determine the student's achievement level. Schools will therefore have the option of testing students' knowledge of specific topics on a frequent basis or the full range of skills and knowledge covered by the CCSS at scheduled intervals. Moreover, with CAT assessments, results will be received within weeks, not months (Smarter Balanced, n.d.).

Smarter Balanced is committed to assisting states as they implement the CCSS, providing support in these three ways:

1. by funding membership for governing states in the Council of Chief State School Officers' (CCSSO) Implementing the Common Core Standards (ICCS) collaborative
2. by participating in collaborative efforts with other professional organizations involved in the development and implementation of the CCSS
3. by developing a digital library of formative assessment practices and professional development resources that are aligned with the CCSS (Smarter Balanced, n.d.)

Useful Resources

In planning curricula, teachers and curriculum specialists should consider additional CCSS resources provided by other professional organizations. Examples of useful resources include the following:

- recommendations of the *Revised Publishers' Criteria for the Common Core State Standards in English Language Arts and Literacy, Grades 3–12* (Coleman & Pimentel, 2012) to ensure alignment
- information from the International Reading Association (IRA, n.d.) about how to address the learning needs of students in a CCSS-based classroom by clarifying research-based literacy concepts

- guidelines for creating text-dependent questions and conducting close reading lessons from Achieve the Core (n.d.), the American Society for Curriculum Development (ASCD; Boyles, 2012/2013), and other organizations

- information from CAST (2012) about the universal design for learning (UDL) framework to help meet the needs of diverse students

- ideas about planning for CCSS-based instructional units and lessons from teachers and other literacy leaders in the Tri-State Collaborative (Achieve, 2012)

- information from the assessment consortia (PARCC and Smarter Balanced) that may affect guidelines and mandates in individual states (PARCC, 2014; Smarter Balanced, n.d.)

REFERENCES

Achieve. (2012). *Tri-state quality review rubric for lessons and units: ELA/Literacy (grades 3–5) and ELA (grades 6–12),* version 4.1. *Achieve.* Retrieved from www.achieve.org/files/TriStateELA_LiteracyRubric1pageoverviewv4.1%20071712CC%20BY.pdf.

Achieve the Core. (n.d.). Text-dependent question resources. *AchieveTheCore.org.* Retrieved from www.achievethecore.org/page/710/text-dependent-question-resources.

Achieve the Core. (n.d.). Featured lessons: Close reading model lessons. *AchieveTheCore.org.* Retrieved from www.achievethecore.org/page/752/featured-lessons.

Boyles, N. (2012/2013). Closing in on close reading. *Educational Leadership, 70*(4), 36–41. Retrieved from www.ascd.org/publications/educational-leadership/dec12/vol70/num04/Closing-in-on-Close-Reading.aspx.

Buckley, J. (2013). *National Assessment of Educational Progress: 2012 Trends in academic progress.* National Center for Education Statistics. Retrieved from http://nces.ed.gov/whatsnew/commissioner/remarks2013/06_27_2013.asp.

CAST. (2012). About UDL. *National Center on Universal Design for Learning, at CAST.* Retrieved from www.udlcenter.org/aboutudl/whatisudl.

Cawelti, G. (2006). The side effects of NCLB. *Educational Leadership, 64*(3), 64–68. Retrieved from www.csun.edu/~krowlands/Content/SED610/NCLB/Side%20effects%20of%20nclb.pdf.

Coleman, D., & Pimentel, S. (2012). *Revised publishers' criteria for the Common Core State Standards in English language arts and literacy, grades 3–12.* Washington, DC: National Governors Association, Council of Chief State School Officers, Achieve, Council of Great City Schools, and National Association of State Boards of Education. Retrieved from www.corestandards.org/assets/Publishers_Criteria_for_3-12.pdf.

Educational Testing Service (ETS). (2012). *Coming together to raise student achievement: New assessments for the Common Core State Standards.* Center for K–12 Assessment and Performance Management at ETS. Retrieved from http://k12center.org/rsc/pdf/Coming_Together_April_2012_Final.pdf.

International Reading Association (IRA). (n.d.). ELA Common Core Standards: Overview. *Reading.org.* Retrieved from www.reading.org/Resources/ResourcesByTopic/CommonCore-resourcetype/CommonCore-rt-overview.aspx.

National Assessment of Educational Progress (NAEP). (2004). *NAEP 2004 Trends in academic progress.* National Center for Education Statistics. Retrieved from http://nces.ed.gov/pubsearch/pubsinfo.asp?pubid=2005464.

National Assessment of Educational Progress (NAEP). (2008). *The nation's report card: Long-term trends 2008.* National Center for Education Statistics. Retrieved from http://nces.ed.gov/pubsearch/pubsinfo.asp?pubid=2009479.

National Assessment of Educational Progress (NAEP). (2012). *The nation's report card: Trends in academic progress 2012.* National Center for Education Statistics. Retrieved from http://nces.ed.gov/pubsearch/pubsinfo.asp?pubid=2013456.

National Governors Association Center for Best Practices & Council of Chief State School Officers (NGA & CCSSO). (2010a). *Common Core State Standards: English language arts and literacy in history/social studies, science, and technical subjects.* Washington, DC: Authors. Retrieved from www.corestandards.org/assets/CCSSI_ELA%20Standards.pdf.

National Governors Association Center for Best Practices & Council of Chief State School Officers (NGA & CCSSO). (2010b). Appendix A: Research supporting key elements of the standards and glossary of key terms. *Common Core State Standards.* Washington, DC: Authors. Retrieved from www.corestandards.org/assets/Appendix_A.pdf.

National PTA. (2012). Advances in the PARCC ELA/Literacy assessment [PowerPoint]. Retrieved from www.PTA.org.

Partnership for Assessment of Readiness for College and Careers (PARCC). (2014). About PARCC. *PARCConline.org.* Retrieved from www.parcconline.org/about-parcc.

Rebora, A. (2006). NCLB's effects. *Education Week: Teacher.* Retrieved from www.edweek.org/tm/articles/2006/04/03/04nclb_trends.html.

Smarter Balanced Assessment Consortium. (n.d.) Frequently asked questions. *SmarterBalanced.org.* Retrieved from www.smarterbalanced.org/resources-events/faqs.

U.S. Department of Education. (2013). Race to the Top assessment program. *ED.gov.* Retrieved from www2.ed.gov/programs/racetothetop-assessment/awards.html.

Integrating the Language Arts/Literacy Standards in the Content Areas

ESSENTIAL QUESTIONS ARE THE CATALYSTS FOR LEARNING that matters in any curriculum, in any school. The three basic forms of essential questions—*Why? How?* and *What?*—serve specific purposes in planning and teaching a curriculum, unit, or lesson:

- The leading question—*Why?*—is at the heart of the course, unit, or lesson design. *Why?* questions guide curriculum design by determining the significance or relevance of a topic. They guide the "naming" element of curriculum design. At the unit and lesson levels, *Why?* questions advance critical inquiry and motivate discussion.

● The follow-up question—*How?*—prompts creation of a blueprint or roadmap. *How?* questions call for articulating procedures, processes, and benchmarks (such as the Common Core State Standards [CCSS]) to ensure deeper understanding. *How?* questions guide the "framing" element in curriculum design. They bring together the relevant experiences (shared and unshared) that help establish a way to learn at the course level and a context for learning at the unit and lesson levels.

● The *What?* question addresses needs, interests, and other concerns en route to delivering answers and taking actions. *What?* questions identify the expectations outlined in standards and invite creative ways of meeting them. At the curriculum level, *What?* questions guide the "gaming" element in design. At the course level, *What?* questions motivate teachers and students to engage in large-scale projects that present and share the outcomes of their inquiry. At the unit and lesson levels, *What?* questions guide the selection of texts and other materials that will help to achieve understanding (Rocco, personal correspondence).

These essential questions—*Why? How?* and *What?*—guided planning and instruction for a high school course called "Crimes Against Humanity (CAH): Paradoxes of Freedom." CAH is an integrated English–history course that was designed and taught by Warren Thomas Rocco at Global Citizenship Experience (GCE), a Chicago high school. Intended for students in grade 12, CAH involves the study of fictional literature in the crime genre, along with complementary texts, to explore social inequities that limit or enhance people's access to freedom at the local, national, and global levels. In addition to integrating English and history, the course also includes relevant science topics (forensics).

The essential questions for this course are as follows:

● Why is freedom unavailable to all?

● How are our paths to freedom influenced by society?

● What is my path to freedom? (GCE, 2012)

Crimes Against Humanity: Paradoxes of Freedom

GRADE LEVEL: Grade 12

CONTENT AREAS: English, Social Studies, Science

LESSON 1—SIICQ READING

Essential Questions (Naming Element):
- Why is crime fiction useful literature?
- How does crime fiction convey significant learning?
- What are some essential skills obtained through the study of crime fiction?

Overview: This lesson provides an opportunity to lead students through a variety of close reading exercises. The acronym SIICQ (pronounced "sick") stands for Summarize, Identify, Illustrate, Connect, and Question. This exercise should be used as part of a Literature Circle.

CCSS Focus Standards (Grades 11–12):

Production and Distribution of Writing

- **W.6:** Use technology, including the Internet, to produce, publish, and update individual or shared writing products in response to ongoing feedback, including new arguments or information (NGA & CCSSO [2010]).

Research to Build and Present Knowledge

- **W.7:** Conduct short as well as more sustained research projects to answer a question (including a self-generated question) or solve a problem; narrow or broaden the inquiry when appropriate; synthesize multiple sources on the subject, demonstrating understanding of the subject under investigation (NGA & CCSSO [2010]).

Suggested Materials:

- PC, laptop
- Selected text(s)
- Writing, drawing surface (paper or whiteboard)
- Writing, drawing instruments (pens, pencils, dry-erase markers)

Procedure: *Note:* Students will already have been introduced to the genre of crime fiction, elements of crime fiction, and a survey of pioneers of the genre.

1. Let students choose to read one of the following short novels or short stories in groups:
   The Great Impersonation, by E. Phillips Oppenheim (1920)
   The Red House Mystery, by A. A. Milne (1922)
   The Secret Adversary, by Agatha Christie (1922)
   "The Tell-Tale Heart," by Edgar Allan Poe (1843/1903)

   (All of these titles are available online for unrestricted viewing—see References.)

2. Assign jobs to individuals or small groups of individuals within each Literature Circle. Describe jobs for students as follows:

   - *Summarize:* Your job is to prepare a brief summary of this section of the reading. The other members of your group will be counting on you to give an account that conveys the main highlights of your reading assignment.
   - *Identify:* Select useful and perhaps thematic vocabulary words. Share the part of speech and definition for each new vocabulary, while copying the sentence from your text containing the vocabulary word. List the page and paragraph number so that students may locate contextual clues.
   - *Illustrate:* Your job is to draw anything about the story that you think is important to the events of the assignment. Again, these drawings may reflect certain thematic interests. Provide one drawing for every two paragraphs. Do any kind of drawing or picture you like. When your group meets, do not explain your drawing; let them guess. Then talk about it. Your drawings may include the following:

a character	a surprise
the setting	a prediction
a problem	anything else
an exciting part	

- *Connect:* Your job is to find connections between the selection your group is reading and the world outside. This means connecting the reading to your own life, to happenings at school or in the community, to similar events at other times and places, or to other people or problems that you are reminded of. You might also see connections between this work and other writings on the same topic or by the same author. Other things you can research include geography, weather, culture, or history of the selection's setting; information about the author and his or her life; information about the time period portrayed in the work; pictures, objects, or materials that resonate in the piece; the history and derivation of words or names used in the selection; and/or music that reflects the work or the time.
- *Question:* Your job is to develop questions that your group might want to discuss about this selection. Don't worry about the small details; your task is to help people talk over the big ideas in the reading and share their reactions. Usually, the best discussion questions come from your own thoughts, feelings, and concerns as you read.

Assessment: You may choose to assign components of SIICQ reading to individuals or let groups decide how to manage the workload. You may also collect paper-based assignments from students or use an application such as Google docs to organize students' contributions.

LESSON 2—INVESTIGATION OF THEMES

Essential Questions (Framing Element):

- Why is crime fiction an effective explainer of real-world phenomena?
- How are themes found in crime fiction validated in nonfiction texts?
- What are some nonfiction texts that enhance our understanding of crime fiction?

Overview: This lesson encourages students to expand their engagement in fiction by incorporating real-world context and complexity. Students select one of several large themes to explore in depth. (In the CAH course, appropriate themes include race, gender, culture, and power.) Each student applies this real-world context to one of the following assigned or selected crime fiction titles:

- *47th Street Black,* by Bayo Ojikutu (2003)
- *Batman: The Dark Knight Returns,* by Frank Miller (1986)
- *Crime and Punishment,* by Fyodor Dostoyevsky (1866/1914)
- *Hardball,* by Sara Paretsky (2009)
- *Our Man in Havana,* by Graham Greene (1958)
- *The Big Sleep,* by Raymond Chandler (1939)
- *The Children of Men,* by P. D. James (1992)
- *The Da Vinci Code,* by Dan Brown (2003)
- *The Godfather,* by Mario Puzo (1969)

CCSS Focus Standards (Grades 11–12) (NGA & CCSSO [2010]):

Text Types and Purposes

- **W.1:** Write arguments to support claims in an analysis of substantive topics or texts, using valid reasoning and relevant and sufficient evidence.

- **W.1.a:** Introduce precise, knowledgeable claim(s), establish the significance of the claim(s), distinguish the claim(s) from alternate or opposing claims, and create an organization that logically sequences claim(s), counterclaims, reasons, and evidence.

- **W.1.b:** Develop claim(s) and counterclaims fairly and thoroughly, supplying the most relevant evidence for each while pointing out the strengths and limitations of both in a manner that anticipates the audience's knowledge level, concerns, values, and possible biases.

- **W.1.c:** Use words, phrases, and clauses as well as varied syntax to link the major sections of the text, create cohesion, and clarify the relationships between claim(s) and reasons, between reasons and evidence, and between claim(s) and counterclaims.

- **W.1.d:** Establish and maintain a formal style and objective tone while attending to the norms and conventions of the discipline in which they are writing.

- **W.1.e:** Provide a concluding statement or section that follows from and supports the argument presented (NGA & CCSSO [2010]).

Production and Distribution of Writing

- **W.6:** Use technology, including the Internet, to produce, publish, and update individual or shared writing products in response to ongoing feedback, including new arguments or information (NGA & CCSSO [2010]).

Research to Build and Present Knowledge

- **W.7:** Conduct short as well as more sustained research projects to answer a question (including a self-generated question) or solve a problem; narrow or broaden the inquiry when appropriate; synthesize multiple sources on the subject, demonstrating understanding of the subject under investigation (NGA & CCSSO [2010]).

Suggested Materials:

- PC, laptop
- Selected text(s)
- Selected newspapers or magazines (print or online)
- Writing, drawing surface (paper or whiteboard)
- Writing, drawing instruments (pens, pencils, dry-erase markers)

Procedure: *Note:* As a primer for the investigation of themes found in crime fiction and in the world, students can participate in Harvard University's Project Implicit (Harvard, 2011). This project presents a range of tests that students can take to measure social preference and cognition. (In Rocco's CAH course, the class focused on tests that challenged their thinking about race, gender, culture, and power.) I recommend that teachers consult with appropriate administrators, counselors, and so on before having their students participate in this project. Project Implicit is a fascinating initiative, in which students can consider and discuss socialization in a safe, structured, mature manner. Teachers should bear in mind, however, that these results and conversations can sometimes be unsettling to students, parents, and teachers.

1. **Set up a workstation:** Ask students to start a research workstation in a venue such as Google docs, where they should create an outline as follows:

    I. State your theme.

        A. I am studying . . . (*insert theme here*).

        B. This is important to understand because . . . (insert reason for inquiry here).

        C. Transform your thematic interest into a guiding question (*see starters below*):
            1. Why . . . ?
            2. How . . . ?
            3. What . . . ?

2. **First response:** Have each student choose an article from a teacher-designated Trusted Sources bank as a case study. (Perhaps explain how you vet these sources.) Reliable, online destinations include the following:

    The Economist
    The New York Times
    The Wall Street Journal
    National Public Radio (NPR) (online)
    GOOD magazine

    Ask each student to respond in brief to this question: *How does this article satisfy my guiding question?* The student should find three supporting sources to substantiate his or her preliminary answer:
    - The first source should *confirm* the answer. The source may present a same or similar version of the case study. (Students will develop the habit of validating source integrity and reinforcing early impressions.)
    - The second source should *complement* the answer. The source may present a new wrinkle that broadens the student's impression from earlier sources. (Students will develop the habit of building layers within extended inquiries.)
    - The third source should *complicate* the answer. The source should cause the student to doubt his or her earlier impressions. (Students will develop the habit of evaluating issues from multiple, even contesting perspectives.)

3. **Second response:** Ask students to revisit their preliminary responses and involve their new learning to fashion more informed answers, or committals. (See the "confirm" question above).

LESSON 3—360° FICTION

Essential Questions (Gaming Element):
- Why is crime fiction an effective explainer of real-world phenomena?
- How are themes found in crime fiction validated in nonfiction texts?
- What are some nonfiction texts that enhance our understanding of crime fiction?

Overview: After examining and experimenting with Bob Thurber's 150-word story-building guide, "Anatomy of a MicroFiction" (Thurber, n.d.), students continue developing skills in microfiction with a creative writing activity designed by Rocco. That activity, called "360° Fiction," harnesses students' interest in select authors and texts and encourages them to construct their own imitative but original 180-word stories. Students' writing will represent a fusion of styles between established and emerging writers.

CCSS Focus Standards (Grades 11–12):

Text Types and Purposes

- **W.3:** Write narratives to develop real or imagined experiences or events using effective technique, well-chosen details, and well-structured event sequences.

- **W.3.a:** Engage and orient the reader by setting out a problem, situation, or observation and its significance, establishing one or multiple point(s) of view, and introducing a narrator and/or characters; create a smooth progression of experiences or events.

- **W.3.b:** Use narrative techniques, such as dialogue, pacing, description, reflection, and multiple plot lines, to develop experiences, events, and/or characters.

- **W.3.c:** Use a variety of techniques to sequence events so that they build on one another to create a coherent whole and build toward a particular tone and outcome (e.g., a sense of mystery, suspense, growth, or resolution).

- **W.3.d:** Use precise words and phrases, telling details, and sensory language to convey a vivid picture of the experiences, events, setting, and/or characters.

- **W.3.e:** Provide a conclusion that follows from and reflects on what is experienced, observed, or resolved over the course of the narrative.

Production and Distribution of Writing

- **W.4:** Produce clear and coherent writing in which the development, organization, and style are appropriate to task, purpose, and audience.

- **W.5:** Develop and strengthen writing as needed by planning, revising, editing, rewriting, or trying a new approach, focusing on addressing what is most significant for a specific purpose and audience.

- **W.6:** Use technology, including the Internet, to produce, publish, and update individual or shared writing products in response to ongoing feedback, including new arguments or information.

Suggested Materials:

- PC, laptop
- Selected text(s)
- Writing, drawing surface (paper or whiteboard)
- Writing, drawing instruments (pens, pencils, dry-erase markers)

Procedure:

1. Ask each student to peruse a crime fiction novel of choice for passages of interest. Each student should extract and record a lively 180-word excerpt (intact). Students may use ellipses (. . .) and creative punctuation to shorten a slightly long selection, but they cannot change the wording. When using ellipses, students should ensure that the excerpt remains coherent and that the author's intent isn't overly compromised.

2. Have each student explain to the class or group what drew him or her to capture a certain passage from the text of choice.

3. Have each student forge a connection that unites the writer's work and his or her own by completing the following statement: *My work connects to the selected writer's work because . . .*

4. Have each student "publish" an original 180-word microfiction.

Be prepared to model each step of the lesson for the class, taking time to think aloud and express the reason for each decision. Figure 9.1 shows a written model by Rocco based on the text "The Purloined Letter," by Edgar Allan Poe (1844/1903).

FIGURE 9.1 ● Sample Microfiction Created by the Teacher

> **Step 1:** *I extract and record a 180-word excerpt* from "The Purloined Letter" by Edgar Allan Poe:
>
> > *At Paris, just after dark one gusty evening in the autumn of 18—, in company with my friend C. Auguste Dupin, in his little back library . . . mentally discussing certain topics which had formed matter for conversation between us at an earlier period of the evening; I mean the affair of the Rue Morgue, and the mystery attending the murder of Marie Roget. I looked upon it, therefore, as . . . a coincidence, when the door of our apartment was thrown open and admitted our old acquaintance, Monsieur G—, the Prefect of the Parisian police.*
> >
> > *We gave him a hearty welcome; for there was nearly half as much of the entertaining as of the contemptible about the man, and we had not seen him for several years. We had been sitting in the dark, and Dupin now arose for the purpose of lighting a lamp, but sat down again, without doing so, upon G.'s saying that he had called to consult us, or rather to ask the opinion of my friend, about some official business which had occasioned a great deal of trouble.*
>
> The above excerpt, according to MS Word, is exactly 180 words. Note that I was able to achieve the prescribed 180-word count through subtle cuts and manipulation of punctuation in Poe's text. I've underlined the portions of the original text, below, that I chose to remove. Of course, it's no simple thing to determine 'the important parts' worth saving in a piece of classic fiction—but that is our job here (. . . and gosh, is it fun!).
>
> > *At Paris, just after dark one gusty evening in the autumn of 18—, <u>I was enjoying the twofold luxury of meditation and a meerschaum,</u> in company with my friend C. Auguste Dupin, in his little back library, <u>or book-closet, au troisieme. No. 33, Rue Dunot, Faubourg St. Germain. For one hour at least we had maintained a</u>*

FIGURE 9.1 ● *(continued)*

> *profound silence; while each, to any casual observer, might have seemed intently and exclusively occupied with the curling eddies of smoke that oppressed the atmosphere of the chamber. For myself, however, I was* mentally discussing certain topics which had formed matter for conversation between us at an earlier period of the evening; I mean the affair of the Rue Morgue, and the mystery attending the murder of Marie Roget. I looked upon it, therefore, as <u>something of</u> a coincidence, when the door of our apartment was thrown open and admitted our old acquaintance, Monsieur G—, the Prefect of the Parisian police.
>
> We gave him a hearty welcome; for there was nearly half as much of the entertaining as of the contemptible about the man, and we had not seen him for several years. We had been sitting in the dark, and Dupin now arose for the purpose of lighting a lamp, but sat down again, without doing so, upon G.'s saying that he had called to consult us, or rather to ask the opinion of my friend, about some official business which had occasioned a great deal of trouble.

Step 2: *I chose this excerpt because* it represents Edgar Allan Poe's unique approach to establishing tone. Poe's elevated, complicated prose involves a style that is diabolically comforting. Or put another way, we know that Poe is setting us up for something awful, but we are more than happy to oblige his tactics.

Step 3: *My work below connects to the selected writer's work because* I have attempted to use clever, antiquated, and sometimes foreign language to create both an elaborate opening and a prelude to murder.
Now for my own Edgar Allan Poe-inspired, 180-word microfiction!

Step 4: An original work, titled "The Dinner Guest" by Warren Thomas Rocco

> Six dear friends spent a fortnight retreat in the heart of Catalunya, whereby on the eve of our departure from the brilliant accommodations of Castillo d'_____, a magnificent feast was prepared, thus reviving an annual experiment for the tenth year in succession. And fortunate we were on this occasion to have possessed the fair company of Mr. B_____, procured from his occupations at a remote stead in L' Hospitalet de Llobregat. Our rendezvous with B_____, a hastily arranged and executed affair, could only be recalled and thus assigned character by those variegated persons in attendance.
>
> The ruse, then—the *raison d' etre* of our sojourn—required the drawer of a deed to attend to the concerns of this B_____until his lively effect at the castell were no longer plain. The dining arrangements were prepared with some craft and elaboration while others remained at leisure in separate quarters. Save for the excitable Mr. B_____, of course, who provided a reluctant hand in the kitchen despite a prior engagement prohibiting him from enjoying this first and final sup at the villa.

Notice how I've replicated Poe's distinct, heightened prose? It's an amateurish effort, no doubt, but I hope that you'll allow that we can perceive in small measure the master's hand in this affair.

LESSON 4—SOUNDTRACK STORIES

Essential Question:

- How is music a form of human expression?

Overview: In this lesson, students learn to use music as an inspiration for writing their own fiction. First, they "deconstruct" the music by focusing on the instruments and sounds, trying to forget previous associations with familiar tunes. Then, they craft detailed narratives with well-structured event sequences by doing what Rocco calls "picking up the notes that songs leave behind."

CCSS Focus Standards:

Text Types and Purposes

- **W.3:** Write narratives to develop real or imagined experiences or events using effective technique, well-chosen details, and well-structured event sequences.
- **W.3.a:** Engage and orient the reader by setting out a problem, situation, or observation and its significance, establishing one or multiple point(s) of view, and introducing a narrator and/or characters; create a smooth progression of experiences or events.
- **W.3.b:** Use narrative techniques, such as dialogue, pacing, description, reflection, and multiple plot lines, to develop experiences, events, and/or characters.
- **W.3.c:** Use a variety of techniques to sequence events so that they build on one another to create a coherent whole and build toward a particular tone and outcome (e.g., a sense of mystery, suspense, growth, or resolution).
- **W.3.d:** Use precise words and phrases, telling details, and sensory language to convey a vivid picture of the experiences, events, setting, and/or characters.
- **W.3.e:** Provide a conclusion that follows from and reflects on what is experienced, observed, or resolved over the course of the narrative.

Production and Distribution of Writing

- **W.4:** Produce clear and coherent writing in which the development, organization, and style are appropriate to task, purpose, and audience.
- **W.5:** Develop and strengthen writing as needed by planning, revising, editing, rewriting, or trying a new approach, focusing on addressing what is most significant for a specific purpose and audience.
- **W.6:** Use technology, including the Internet, to produce, publish, and update individual or shared writing products in response to ongoing feedback, including new arguments or information.

Suggested Materials:

- iPod/mp3 player with speaker
- Benny Goodman's version of "Sing, Sing, Sing (with a Swing)"

- "Why So Serious?" from *The Dark Knight* soundtrack
- Writing, drawing surface (paper or whiteboard)
- Writing, drawing instruments (pens, pencils, dry-erase markers)

Procedure:

1. Provide a personal account of your relationship with a favorite piece of music. Use this opportunity to illustrate how to find a story in a song that may be different from what the lyricist intended. Ideally, this sharing will encourage students to express passion for their favorite music, regardless of its genre. Hopefully, it will also inspire students to identify the intended story of a song and to consider other possible stories that were likely not intended by the artist(s).

   To offer an example, Rocco told the following story to his class before beginning this exercise:

   > As a boy, I fell in love with trains while listening to old Johnny Cash records. I remember that distinctive "boom-chick-a-boom" percussion that ignited so many of Mr. Cash's songs and transported me to a fantasy world of relentless fun ("All aboard, for the Wild West!"). It wasn't until I was an adolescent that I stopped humming along in attempted-bass-baritone and considered Johnny Cash's words and message, as well. The point is that I found inspiration in music, and I uncovered stories in music long before I considered a song in full.
   >
   > Take also The Who's "My Generation," which, for me, was first and foremost a story about a mischievous child dodging punishment. Listen to John Entwistle's optimistic, rope-a-dope bass solo and tell me otherwise! Or try not to imagine something good coming out of a traffic jam when Chicago bluesman Hound Dog Taylor pulls something bright and fuzzy from a poorly made electric guitar.

2. Listen to Benny Goodman's version of "Sing, Sing, Sing (With a Swing)," and ask students to try to determine what they hear—literally. The class should work together to answer the following questions. Remind students to support their claims by referring to specific sounds they hear.
   - What instruments are being played? If you don't know, can you guess?
   - Are the sounds natural, or are they synthetic (computer generated)?
   - What is the effect of one instrument in isolation?
   - What is the effect of the instruments working together?
   - What ideas are being communicated?

3. Come up with a few possible story-starters, based on students' answers to the questions. Work together with the students to suggest prompts. Consider this advice from Rocco:

   > Don't worry if your students don't get it at first. They'll warm to it. You may have to suggest some story-starters: "A beast rises from an oily grave . . ." usually works for most Soundgarden songs.

4. Have students write a soundtrack story together, recording their thoughts on the whiteboard as they are presented. Rocco shares this story:

> I remember a student who heard the first few notes of Benny Goodman's version of "Sing, Sing, Sing (With a Swing)" and exclaimed, "I just dropped a basket full of dirty clothes down the basement stairs!" Moments later, another student offered, "A million cockroaches swarmed and took the laundry away!" And yet another student began singing the all-too-familiar "There's a place in France . . . " when he heard Mr. Goodman's clarinet perform a mystic dance. Everyone laughed, and the band played on. Minutes passed until the student who began our story concluded, "This basement contains a portal to France. It's a time travel portal and the cockroaches are responsible for dressing Revolutionaries." *Je jure que c'est vrai!* I swear this is true!

5. Repeat step 2 but listen to the track "Why So Serious?" from *The Dark Knight*. Ask students to try to determine what they hear. They should forget what they may know about the film and focus only on what they can hear. This time, have each student answer the questions in writing.

   Here's a sample response from one of Rocco's advanced students:

> Why so serious? The instruments being played sound like a guitar that is distorted. It seems to mimic the sounds of a city (the loud incoherence of car engines running, people going about, and natural sounds). I hear the sound of flying insects buzzing by my ears and then going away. In the background, I hear scissors cutting something open. Now it sounds like violins; classical instruments mix in with synthetic sounds. In isolation, the individual sounds produce a frightening chill, a lot like the sound of train wheels against the rails in the winter and clocks ticking, counting down to something evoking panic. I hear engines revving and the sound of a blade turning quickly. In a moment, I heard the type of sound someone gets when they almost got knocked out and are filled of adrenaline. It kind of sounds tribal when I hear the sound of drums calling for war. I hear the sounds I would hear from a mechanic's shop, like a dent being made in a car door. Each sound challenges and compliments the sounds. United, the music sounds adventurous and desperate—like warfare.

6. Ask each student to create his or her own story-starter and write a soundtrack story based on "Why So Serious." The student quoted in step 5 came up with this story-starter:

> Erin dropped the spoon into the running garbage disposal and watched the sparks fly . . .

7. *Optional:* Consider showing your students "The Sound of Anarchy" (Zimmer, 2010), a clip in which Hans Zimmer, *The Dark Knight* composer, chronicles his unorthodox method of growing sounds and stories. Zimmer is full of creative ideas, and his work is inspirational.

8. *Optional:* Repeat steps 1–5 using other songs. Try various instrumental pieces, or see what happens when students suggest their own favorite music. As Rocco told his students:

> Now it's your turn! What emerges from a Boredoms, Konono N°1, or Sigur Rós song? Unless you understand screamed-Japanese, Lingala, or Vonlenska then you'll just have to imagine—same as the folks from Looney Tunes. They made a living out of wrapping timeless cartoons around classical music masterpieces.

Rocco also offers this advice to teachers:

> Understand that some of your students will attempt a story about someone's *thoughts*. Of course, you, dear instructor, know that that is *boring*. Unless the story takes place in John Malkovich's head, a good story usually requires *action!* Know that some of your students will heed your advice and write a story about *dancing*. They'll write, "I'm at a club and *this* song's playing in the background!" You'll inform them that using music as music isn't very original, but writing original stories *while dancing* would be something *quite special*. Then you'll slowly back away . . .

Reprinted with permission from Warren Thomas Rocco.

Warren Thomas Rocco also developed the following lesson for a course at Global Citizenship Experience (GCE) called "Vitalogies: Stories for Life." This integrated English–history course, offered to tenth-graders at GCE, challenges students to evaluate and convert real-life experiences into fictional "stories for life" that reveal people's vital connections (GCE, 2012).

The essential questions for this course are as follows:

- Why do stories matter?
- How do stories connect us?
- What is *my* story?

Vitalogies: Stories for Life

GRADE LEVEL: Grade 10

CONTENT AREAS: English, History/Science (classic elements, architecture)

LESSON 1—"ARCHAIKUTECTURE: BUILDING HAIKU THROUGH YOU" (*Note:* ARChaikuTECTURE is pronounced "ahr-khahy-koo-tek-cher.")

Essential Question:
- How does literature reflect or refract real-life stories?

Overview: This lesson combines appreciation of architecture, knowledge of the classic elements (water, earth, fire, and air), and creative writing of haiku. The strict structure of Japanese haiku (the smallest literary form) is traditionally used to express the poet's impression of an everyday natural occurrence. In this lesson, haiku is used to express the relationship between a humanmade structure and two or more classical elements. Architecture can be observed in person, in the students' own city or town, or through online "tours."

Here is some background from Rocco:

> I live in Chicago, where hard truths and lofty visions collide. Since its inception, the city has wrestled with the elements: Chicago was born on a swamp (water), raised on a sinking foundation (earth), burned to the ground (fire), and blasted for its "windy"-ness (air). But Chicago is also where the first skyscraper was built and where some of the most innovative and spectacular tall buildings in the world reside.

It is out of respect for this enduring relationship between natural and human-engineered structures that I developed ARChaikuTECTURE, an expression of learning that combines the timelessness of elements (water, earth, fire, and air) with the bold economy of haiku. But how does someone (like me), who's not especially schooled in the elements or particularly knowledgeable about efficient design, begin to explore these promising connections?

I found answers to this question and more on Ken Ward's Astrology Pages [Ward, 2012—see References].

Now I realize that mentioning, never mind promoting the investigation of an astrology site will be too much for some to bear ("He had me kinda interested until he dropped that *pseudoscience*!"). But fear not, enlightened one: Mr. Ward's site provides a creative context and a useful language for investigating the chemical and the ethereal.

Consider these insights:

- "Fire tends to go upwards, and can raise things into the clouds and beyond. . . . [It] goes high above the earth, is consuming, clinging and captivating and creates the new and removes the old. . . . Fire is raw energy."

- "Air is light, it pervades everything on earth. . . . [It] links everything to everything else. . . . [It's] associated with words and language . . . [and the] interrelationships between people and things."

Now where, oh where have I seen these ideas together before?

Perhaps in Chicago's iconic John Hancock Center, a structure with a wide base and a tapered, X-braced façade that suggests a flame rising through crosscurrents of air bringing heat back to the heavens.

After writing haikus about buildings, students reimagine the same element combinations as personal characteristics and write first-person haikus about themselves.

CCSS Focus Standards (Grades 9–10) (NGA & CCSSO [2010]):

Text Types and Purposes
- **W.3:** Write narratives to develop real or imagined experiences or events using effective technique, well-chosen details, and well-structured event sequences.
- **W.3.a:** Engage and orient the reader by setting out a problem, situation, or observation, establishing one or multiple point(s) of view, and introducing a narrator and/or characters; create a smooth progression of experiences or events.
- **W.3.b:** Use narrative techniques, such as dialogue, pacing, description, reflection, and multiple plot lines, to develop experiences, events, and/or characters.
- **W.3.c:** Use a variety of techniques to sequence events so that they build on one another to create a coherent whole.
- **W.3.d:** Use precise words and phrases, telling details, and sensory language to convey a vivid picture of the experiences, events, setting, and/or characters.

- **W.3.e:** Provide a conclusion that follows from and reflects on what is experienced, observed, or resolved over the course of the narrative.

Production and Distribution of Writing

- **W.6:** Use technology, including the Internet, to produce, publish, and update individual or shared writing products, taking advantage of technology's capacity to link to other information and to display information flexibly and dynamically.

Research to Build and Present Knowledge

- **W.8:** Gather relevant information from multiple authoritative print and digital sources, using advanced searches effectively; assess the usefulness of each source in answering the research question; integrate information into the text selectively to maintain the flow of ideas, avoiding plagiarism and following a standard format for citation.
- **W.9:** Draw evidence from literary or informational texts to support analysis, reflection, and research.

Suggested Materials:

- PC, laptop
- Photographs/brochures of interesting buildings
- Writing, drawing surface (paper or whiteboard)
- Writing, drawing instruments (pens, pencils, dry-erase markers)

Procedure:

1. Review the four classic elements with the class, if necessary.
2. View buildings online or in photographs. If possible, arrange a walking tour of your city or town to view interesting buildings in person. Ask students, working individually or in small groups, to assign combinations of elements to a building.

    Rocco describes how his class approached this step:

    My class researched, organized a walking tour, and presented on some of Chicago's finest architectural destinations. Here are just a few of the buildings we visited, along with the informed, mixed-elements designations adopted by my students:

    - Old Water Tower—water and fire (www.chicagoarchitecture.info/Building/374/Old-Water-Tower.php)
    - Tribune Tower—earth and air (www.chicagoarchitecture.info/Building/376/Tribune-Tower.php)
    - Aqua—water and air (www.chicagoarchitecture.info/Building/913/Aqua.php)
    - Willis Tower—fire and earth (www.chicagoarchitecture.info/Building/375/The-Willis-Tower.php)

3. Ask each student to select one building and its element combination and then write an architecturally and elementally inspired haiku based on that building. Here's an example of a haiku that one of Rocco's students wrote about the John Hancock Center and its fire/air combination:

A flame rises high,	(5 syllables)
Disappearing into space.	(7 syllables)
It is sunset now.	(5 syllables)

4. As a class, research how the four classical elements have been used throughout history to describe personality characteristics. Compare how different traditions have assigned different characteristics to each element. One of Rocco's favorite websites for this step is an astrology–numerology site that attempts to translate elements as personality traits or temperaments (McClain, 2013).

5. Ask each student to examine his or her "building" haiku and then rewrite it to express something about himself or herself. Consider the fire/air combination that inspired the previous student example about the John Hancock Center. When asked to convey his or her nature through haiku in the first person, that student wrote this haiku:

My spirit ascends,	(5 syllables)
Gathering power with height.	(7 syllables)
Wake up! It is sunrise.	(5 syllables)

Reprinted with permission from Warren Thomas Rocco.

Creativity and the CCSS

THESE SAMPLE LESSONS FROM ROCCO'S COURSES at the Global Citizen Experience clearly demonstrate that taking a creative approach to integrating English and history and basing teaching and learning on essential questions not only achieves but exceeds the expectations stated in the CCSS. Rocco piques his students' curiosity and channels their creativity into meaningful activities. His students will not just be ready for college and career; they will be prepared to excel.

REFERENCES

Global Citizen Experience (GCE). (2012). *GCE 2012–13 curriculum guide.* Retrieved from www .globalcitizenshipexperience.com/wp-content/uploads/2011/02/GCE-2012-12-Curr-Guide_6-4-12.pdf.

Harvard University. (2012). About us. Project Implicit. Retrieved from https://implicit.harvard.edu/implicit/.

McClain, M. (2013). The four elements in astrology. *Astrology-Numerology.com.* Retrieved from http: //astrology-numerology.com/astrology.html#elements.

Thurber, B. (n.d.). *Anatomy of a microfiction.* Retrieved from http://home.comcast.net/~bob-thurber /anatomy.htm.

Ward, K. J. (2012). Ken Ward's astrology pages. *Trans4Mind.com.* Retrieved from www.trans4mind.com /personal_development/astrology/LearningAstrology/triplicities.htm.

Zimmer, H. (2010). The sound of anarchy: Making of *The Dark Knight. YouTube.com.* Retrieved from www.youtube.com/watch?v=r-L1RCtgtoE&feature=related.

LITERATURE CITED

Brown, D. (2003). *The Da Vinci code.* New York, NY: Doubleday.

Chandler, R. (1939). *The big sleep.* New York, NY: Knopf.

Christie, A. (1922). *The secret adversary.* London, UK: Bodley Head. Retrieved from www.gutenberg.org
/ebooks/1155.

Dostoyevsky, F. (1914). *Crime and punishment* (C. Garnett, trans.). London, UK: Heinemann. Retrieved from
www.gutenberg.org/files/2554/2554-h/2554-h.htm. (Original work published 1866)

Greene, G. (1958). *Our man in Havana.* London, UK: Heinemann.

James, P. D. (1992). *The children of men.* London, UK: Faber & Faber.

Miller, F. (1986). *Batman: The dark knight returns.* New York, NY: DC Comics.

Milne, A. A. (1922). *The red house mystery.* London, UK: Methuen. Retrieved from www.gutenberg.org
/ebooks/1872.

Ojikutu, B. (2003). *47th Street black.* New York, NY: Three Rivers Press.

Oppenheim, E. P. (1920). *The great impersonation.* London, UK: A. L. Burt. Retrieved from www.gutenberg
.org/ebooks/5815.

Paretsky, S. (2009). *Hardball.* New York, NY: G. P. Putnam's Sons.

Poe, E. A. (1903). The purloined letter. In *The works of Edgar Allan Poe* (vol. II). Raven Edition. New York,
NY: F. P. Collier and Son. Retrieved from www.gutenberg.org/files/2148/2148-h/2148-h.htm#link2H_4_0.
(Original work published 1844)

Poe, E. A. (1903). The tell-tale heart. In *The works of Edgar Allan Poe* (vol. II). Raven Edition. New York,
NY: F. P. Collier and Son. Retrieved from www.gutenberg.org/files/2148/2148-h/2148-h.htm#link2H_4_0.
(Original work published 1843)

Puzo, M. (1969). *The godfather.* New York, NY: G. P. Putnam's Sons.

Index

Credits

Introduction Chapter: Pearson Education; **p. 5 (numbered list), p. 6 (quotation), p. 8 (Table I.1), p. 11 (Figure I.1 Anchor Standards), p. 16 (quotation), p. 18 (first quotation), p. 25 (all quotations), p. 27–28 (all quotations and bulleted list), p. 29 (Table 2.1), p. 29–30 (quotation), p. 31 (ELA Standards), p. 34–36 (ELA Standards), p. 51 (quotation), p. 65 (ELA Standards), p. 40 (Table 3.1), p. 41–42 (Table 3.2), p. 42–43 (Table 3.3), p. 84 (Figure 4.1), p. 88 (Figure 4.4), p. 95–96 (quotation), p. 96–97 (Table 5.1), p. 113–114 (Table 6.1), p. 115–118 (table 6.2), p. 127 (quotation), p. 128 (quotation), p. 130 (Table 6.3), p. 132–133 (Standards), p. 149 (quotation), p. 150 (Table 7.1 and quotation), p. 152 (Table 7.2 and quotation), p. 153 (all quotations), p. 154 (quotation), p. 162 (ELA Standards), p. 162–163 (Speaking and Listening Standards), p. 169 (quotation), p. 187 (Focus Standards), p. 189 (Focus Standards), p. 191 (Focus Standards):** © Copyright 2010. National Governors Association Center for Best Practices and Council of Chief State School Officers. All rights reserved. **p. 182 (quotation and bulleted list),** Smarter Balanced.